D0758033

Global Strategy

STRATEGIC MANAGEMENT SERIES

EDITORS
Michael A. Hitt, R. Duane Ireland, and Robert E. Hoskisson

Global Strategy

Creating and Sustaining Advantage across Borders

Andrew Inkpen

Kannan Ramaswamy

OXFORD
UNIVERSITY PRESS

2006

OXFORD
UNIVERSITY PRESS

Oxford University Press, Inc., publishes works that further
Oxford University's objective of excellence
in research, scholarship, and education.

Oxford   New York
Auckland   Cape Town   Dar es Salaam   Hong Kong   Karachi
Kuala Lumpur   Madrid   Melbourne   Mexico City   Nairobi
New Delhi   Shanghai   Taipei   Toronto

With offices in
Argentina   Austria   Brazil   Chile   Czech Republic   France   Greece
Guatemala   Hungary   Italy   Japan   Poland   Portugal   Singapore
South Korea   Switzerland   Thailand   Turkey   Ukraine   Vietnam

Copyright © 2006 by Oxford University Press, Inc.

Published by Oxford University Press, Inc.
198 Madison Avenue, New York, New York 10016

www.oup.com

Oxford is a registered trademark of Oxford University Press

All rights reserved. No part of this publication may be reproduced,
stored in a retrieval system, or transmitted, in any form or by any means,
electronic, mechanical, photocopying, recording, or otherwise,
without the prior permission of Oxford University Press.

Library of Congress Cataloging-in-Publication Data
Inkpen, Andrew C.
Global strategy : creating and sustaining advantage across borders / Andrew Inkpen and
Kannan Ramaswamy.
   p.   cm.—(Strategic management series)
Includes bibliographical references and index.
ISBN-13: 978-0-19-516720-7
ISBN 0-19-516720-1
1. Strategic planning.   2. Strategic alliances (Business)   3. International business
enterprises—Management.   I. Ramaswamy, Kannan.   II. Title.   III. Strategic management series
(Oxford University Press)
HD30.28.I53 2006
658.4'012—dc22   2005004318

9 8 7 6 5 4 3 2 1

Printed in the United States of America
on acid-free paper

Preface

This book was motivated by our joint interest in the area of strategy and globalization. Both of us have been teaching and conducting research in the strategy and international business area for about 15 years. Along the way we have observed that much of what is written about strategic management treats international and global strategy issues almost as an afterthought. In our view, linking strategic management and globalization requires some new thinking, such as how to compete in emerging markets, how to evaluate new approaches to value-chain thinking using offshoring, and how to integrate international corporate governance practices with corporate objectives. We decided that a book devoted to strategy and globalization could be useful both for students of strategy and for practicing managers confronting international business challenges.

In the book we examine the issues considered central to the study of strategic management in a global context. As global integration between companies and countries continues to march forward, managers and strategy researchers will have to find new ways to deal with globalization. The various topics examined in this book are intended to provide some guidance as to how to deal with the realities of globalization and strategic management. While we have anchored a substantial part of our thinking in contemporary theory, we have also attempted to go beyond the received wisdom to examine some of the practical realities that have yet to receive theoretical scrutiny. Thus, in many cases we blend the theoretical insights that form the mainstay for students of strategy with the practical relevance that international managers should find valuable. In walking that middle ground, we have had to make some tough choices. The book that resulted from this stream of thinking is one that is neither a conventional textbook on strategy nor a compendium of current theoretical perspectives but rather a mélange that, we hope, will capture the attention of academic and practitioner communities alike. We believe that the case studies offer significant insights into many of the issues that both international strategy researchers and practitioners are currently grappling with.

Many people helped make this project happen. Mike Hitt, Bob Hoskisson, and Duane Ireland invited us to write the book and provided useful feedback throughout the process. We would like to thank the research associates who assisted in the case study research, including Simon Algar, Jennifer L. Barrett, Chris Hormann, Vipon Kumar, Meredith Martin, and T. Hawk Sunshine. We would also like to thank faculty colleagues Ed Barrett, Michael Moffett, Anant Sundaram, and John Zerio, who helped us clarify some of the thinking that we present in this book. Outside colleagues who provided assistance in shaping our thinking include Wang Pien, Mary Crossan, Li Kou Qing, and Paul Beamish. Andrew Inkpen is grateful to Nanyang Technological University, where he spent a sabbatical year and wrote much of this book. We also thank the many companies, and their managers, who opened their doors to us for various research projects that we conducted. Without firsthand access to managers actually involved in global strategic management we would not have been able to credibly discuss the various topics. These companies include General Motors, Ericsson, Honeywell, and the Suzhou Industrial Park. Finally, Manish Gulati provided valuable help in editing the various chapters.

Contents

Global Strategy

Introduction

The impact of global competition is being felt in every industry. Firms and countries long used to dominance in their respective international markets must reckon with aggressive and innovative competitors from all corners of the globe. For example, the United States, long the world's largest exporter of agricultural products, now finds itself facing strengthening competition from countries such as Russia, Brazil, and Mexico. The steel industry over the past 150 years has seen a series of competitive jolts that have upset the established order of business. At the turn of the previous century, radical new technologies and fast-growing markets allowed the U.S. steel industry to surge ahead in size and productivity. After World War II, though, Japanese firms and then Korean firms became powerful low-cost competitors, decimating the U.S. steel industry. In 2004, a U.S. company called International Steel Group, Inc., agreed to a $4.5 billion buyout bid from a Dutch company that would create the world's largest steel company. International Steel Group was created by the financier Wilbur Ross, who purchased the bankrupt assets of U.S. steel companies including LTV, Bethlehem Steel, and Acme Steel. The Dutch company was controlled by Lakshmi Mittal, an Indian-born billionaire based in London. Mittal built up a global steel company by investing in countries such as Poland, Romania, Czech Republic, Algeria, South Africa, Mexico, and the United States (his company Ispat purchased the former Inland Steel plant in Illinois).

For many companies, the deployment of value-chain activities is increasingly being done on a global scale. An article in the *Economist* described how Brillian, an American company, is developing a new television. Brillian has a research and development (R&D) contract with Wipro, an Indian technology company based in Bangalore. Wipro was sourcing the television components from companies in America, Japan, Taiwan, and South Korea. Once the television was developed and ready for manufacturing, production would go to one of the contract manufacturing firms, such as Solectron or Flextronics; production might be in any one of a number of countries, such as Mexico, Taiwan, China, or Malaysia. The television would be marketed to consumers mainly in the United States who would pay with a credit card administered from a non-U.S. country. "After-sales service might be provided by a polite young Indian call-centre agent, trained in stress management and taught how to aspirate her Ps in the American way."[1] The *Economist* argues that while a few years ago cases like this would have seemed unique and at the cutting edge of globalization, they are becoming commonplace in many industries, especially for the development and manufacturing parts of the value chain (less so, for now, for the administrative, clerical, and managerial activities).

In industry after industry, the balance of power is shifting from region to region and country to country. In the current millennium, the emergence of China and India as powerful economies is one of the most significant events. In 2003, U.S. imports from China were more than $150 billion. A single company, Wal-Mart, imported $15 billion in goods from China in its 2004 fiscal year; about $7.5 billion of the imports were directly imported by Wal-Mart and the other $7.5 billion came indirectly through suppliers. Wal-Mart did not just buy goods from China—Wal-Mart also employed more than 20,000 people in China in 39 stores. Although few Chinese companies have yet established themselves as dominant players in any industry, Chinese companies are making headway outside their domestic market. Haier, the Chinese appliance company, opened a $40 million plant in South Carolina in 2000 and is now producing about 200,000 18– and 21–cubic foot refrigerators for sale in the highly competitive U.S. market. (Interestingly, among U.S. states, South Carolina has the second most foreign direct investment per capita.) Indian companies are making huge inroads in various information technology sectors and, in the process, generating much controversy over the shift of jobs from the developed economies. What many people often forget is that with development comes a thirst (and the discretionary income) for new products and services. U.S. services exports to India have tripled in the past decade and actually exceed imports of services from India.

Does Globalization Matter to Strategy Creation?

Does globalization matter to strategy creation? We would answer emphatically *yes*. There are various things that we know about globalization and international competition. First, multinational enterprises (MNEs) compete in much more complicated competitive environments than do domestic firms.

This complexity is the result of a variety of social, economic, and cultural factors. These factors mean that the various parts of MNEs must be internally differentiated to respond to the environmental differences that exist in different businesses and geographic markets. Second, globalization involves the integration of corporate activities across borders. The degree of integration required is driven by the global state of the industry. Third, globalization of an industry can be said to be increasing when transactions between buyers and seller become progressively less dependent on geographic distance. Fourth, global companies must understand customers from the perspective of both domestic and international standards and must have the ability to learn in multiple locations far from the home base.

This book deals with globalization and how firms compete in a global environment. We examine the issues considered central to the study of strategic management in a global context, such as the nature of global advantage, strategic alliances, competing in emerging markets, international corporate governance, global knowledge management, and ethical issues in international business. Unlike their domestic counterparts, firms competing across borders must deal with differences in political, legal, financial, cultural, governance, and macroeconomic contexts. These contextual differences shape competition in international strategy and make the study of international strategy more than just a simple extension of classic strategic analysis. Much has been written about the relevance of global/regional/domestic strategies to counter competition from overseas and as a means to enter foreign markets. However, our goal is different and broader. We seek to inform students and managers of global business about a diverse set of important strategic issues.

Overview of the Book

In this book, we will discuss some of the critical strategic issues that impact global competition and strategy. The book is organized around a set of strategic management themes that impact the global strategist. Each chapter focuses on a different strategic issue, such as approaches to competitive advantage, managing global knowledge resources, and international corporate governance. We focus on strategy issues that arise because the firm is international. While there is obviously some overlap between domestic strategic management and global strategic management, it is our contention that the differences between domestic and global strategy warrant specific attention.

In each chapter we integrate academic research with some practical examples and case studies. In doing so we have tried to convey a sense of how these strategic areas are impacted by globalization. Chapter 1 focuses on the meaning and importance of globalization and global strategy. We address the question "Why does it matter whether an industry is considered global or not?" and argue that, indeed, it matters a great deal. Specifically, the global characteristics of an industry have important implications for how managers think about strategy, organization structure, governance, human relations issues, marketing and finance decisions, and so on. We offer three case examples to illustrate how industries operate across borders and connect buyers and sellers regardless of the large geographical distances between them. The three industry case studies—diamonds, sushi, and trash—are certainly not the most well-known or even the most global industries. In fact, at first glance these industries might be described as having few global characteristics. In reality, all three industries are globalizing at a rapid rate and exhibit key characteristics of global industries. In this chapter we also consider the fundamental question of why firms pursue global expansion. We examine the concept of distance and its impact on global strategy and discuss some of the key competitive issues that MNE managers will face in the coming years.

Chapter 2 examines the strategic approaches that firms adopt in competing globally. Competing in global markets requires organizations to carefully consider an array of strategic options ranging from approaches that pursue localization at all costs to tight integration of markets and products across the globe. A fundamental premise is that any strategy seeking to address the global marketplace must leverage country-specific advantages. Organizations crafting global strategies must also make explicit choices about the location of value-chain activities in order to leverage location-specific advantages. To examine these issues the chapter uses the value-chain concept to examine MNE strategic choices. We consider the strategy of adapting value chains on a country-by-country basis and also the strategy of aggregating value activities in the home country so as to capture benefits through economies of scale and scope. The chapter also examines strategic decisions spanning aspects such as location choices, coordination mechanisms that help bridge the divide between headquarters and local subsidiaries, and the specific approach to technology and innovation.

Chapter 3 extends the discussion of strategic approaches by focusing on the organizational demands of global strategies, with an emphasis on MNE structural choices. The chapter begins with a case study to provide an example of the variety of organizational options available to MNEs. We then discuss the two typical patterns of MNE organizational choices that have been the subject of significant research over the past few decades. The choices correspond to the national responsiveness or localization imperative and the global integration or standardization imperative. The challenges associated with MNE organizational change from country centered to globally oriented is examined, followed by a discussion of the evolution of MNE organizations and the emergence of the transnational concept as an organizing model. The strategy and role of the MNE subsidiary are examined along with a discussion of the reasons the traditional country-based authority and power of subsidiaries is waning. The chapter concludes with some consideration of how the MNE of the future will manage the inevitability of increased organizational complexity.

Chapter 4 examines the nature of alliances with an emphasis on collaborative arrangements that create mutual benefits for the partners. Although once considered peripheral to competitive strategy, alliances have entered the mainstream and should be viewed as an integral and mandatory strategic tool for global strategy. Alliances are often essential for market entry in new geographic areas and can provide strategic flexibility for new businesses. The chapter analyzes the multiple reasons firms choose to use strategic alliances and considers various explanations for the rising trend in the number of alliances being formed each year. The discussion then shifts to the competitive risks and problems with alliances. In reality, there are several issues that are unavoidable when it comes to alliance management. We then consider some of the organizational approaches to maximizing partner mutual benefit. We argue that while some alliances may result in a zero-sum game of winners and losers, if alliances are to be an integral element of global strategy, firms should seek partners with whom they can achieve an effective working relationship by linking complementary assets. In the international arena, national culture adds an additional dimension to the challenge of partner selection and building successful alliances.

In chapter 5 the focus is on managing knowledge in the global organization. In the global economy, knowledge is moving around the world at a faster and faster rate. MNEs must develop their strategies by tapping into the repositories of knowledge that exist in all parts of the company. This chapter explores the nature of organizational knowledge and considers the transactional problem that results because knowledge is context dependent. In short, knowledge is difficult to capture, transfer, and make usable. Context dependence means that the more valuable the knowledge, the more difficult it is to replicate its application in other parts of the organization. Moreover, in the fast-moving global economy, innovation is critical for competitiveness. The chapter considers the knowledge source of innovation in the MNE. Firms must find and exploit valuable knowledge from inside and outside their organization in all the geographic markets in which the company operates. This means that all the units of the global firm should bear responsibility for finding and capturing new knowledge. In turn, headquarters must recognize that local knowledge bases within firms are real assets and knowledge transfer mechanisms must be built to ensure that local knowledge is not relegated to a peripheral role. Finally, the chapter discusses how MNEs can create knowledge-oriented cultures.

Chapter 6 continues the discussion of knowledge and shifts the focus to the global allocation of knowledge-based resources. This chapter argues that the current wave of globalization promises to change the way MNEs decide on the preferred location for their value-added functions and activities. While the cross-border migration of jobs with a strong service or knowledge component is quite consistent with the progress of globalization and the disaggregation of value chains, recent trends in the management of knowledge resources have important implications for the formulation and execution of global strategy. In particular, the controversial topic of offshoring gives rise to a new set of strategic issues. The chapter proposes that the decision to offshore functions with a large knowledge component should be a function of country-specific considerations. The considerations should center on the ability to leverage the unique location-specific characteristics to add superior value to the function and to the firm. The chapter also examines the type of knowledge functions that can be outsourced and the major decisions necessary to execute an outsourcing entry strategy.

Chapter 7 examines the nature of corporate governance with an emphasis on issues relevant to the MNE. The corporate governance practices of firms influence their strategies and competitiveness and, therefore, managers involved in global competition should view knowledge of international governance as an essential part of their strategy skills. The chapter reviews the corporate governance systems found in the United States, Japan, and Germany and also considers the nature of governance systems in emerging markets. An important theme in the chapter is that for international business managers, corporate governance will, in all probability, take on greater meaning as country practices evolve and more of the world's economic activity is conducted through markets and firms rather than states. When firms rather than states are involved in economic activity, all stakeholders will expect that value creation and transference are fair and that managers are held accountable for their strategic actions.

Chapter 8 argues that emerging markets represent the next big growth opportunity for the world's MNEs. After discussing the nature and characteristics of emerging markets, the chapter shifts to an examination of the barriers that must be overcome to succeed in emerging markets. We suggest that the barriers call for radically new thinking on defining and implementing corporate strategies. We also suggest that MNEs often make assumptions about emerging markets that are incorrect, leading to flawed strategies. For example, MNEs often assume that emerging-market consumers will prefer global brands over local brands, when the converse is often true. The chapter discusses the ownership structure and control issues associated with emerging-market partners and argues that these are likely to be quite unique. Given unique organizational and structural demands and a customer base with different expectations about the product price-performance ratio, MNEs must adopt new and innovative strategic thinking in order to succeed in emerging markets.

Chapter 9 focuses on the issues surrounding global strategy and the ethical dimensions of competing across borders. As globalization continues, managers will find that incorporating international ethical dimensions in their decision-making processes is unavoidable. It is not our intent to prescribe what we think global managers should do in international markets. Rather, we seek to inform readers about ethical issues and how they might be identified, analyzed, and linked to global strategy decisions. Creating strategy in the global arena inevitably means that MNEs will have to confront ethical issues. The question of "whose morals and whose ethical standards" confronts MNEs as soon as they cross a border. MNEs must deal with different laws in various countries and compete against firms from different countries and legal jurisdictions. We will consider the ethical concepts of relativism, objectivism, and pluralism and examine some of the means by which firms try to manage ethical challenges. We will also consider the advantages and disadvantages of formal corporate ethics programs.

In sum, this book was motivated by the premise that developing an understanding of global strategic management requires analytic tools different from those of purely domestic strategies. MNEs competing across borders operate in much more complicated competitive environments than do domestic firms. MNEs must deal with a host of challenging strategic issues and contexts such as emerging markets, offshoring, new market entries, and international knowledge transfer. These issues and contexts shape competition in international markets and ensure that global strategy analysis must incorporate both classic strategy theory and ideas shaped by the ongoing globalization efforts of many firms.

1

Globalization and Global Strategy

There are few industries, if any, untouched by global competitive forces. Behind the sushi served at trendy Japanese restaurants in New York, the secondhand clothing sold in Zambia, and the technical support call from Canada to a technician with a Canadian accent based in India are a profusion of buyers and sellers, coming together regardless of distance and borders. Hewlett-Packard's (HP) server, the ProLiant ML150, is an excellent example of globalization in action. The initial idea for the server came from HP's Singapore division. The concept for the server was approved at HP's Houston office. The concept design was done in Singapore, and the product was then transferred to an outside contractor in Taiwan who did the initial manufacturing development work with support from HP's Taiwan research center. Actual production of the server began in late 2003 and early 2004 in four plants in Singapore, Australia, China, and India.[1]

As another example, consider Mattel's new approach to developing and launching new toys. In the past, Mattel would usually introduce new toys sequentially: first in the United States and then, if they did well, in major international markets. Now Mattel tries to develop new products with global appeal. In October 2002, Mattel introduced Rapunzel Barbie in 59 countries simultaneously; this was the firm's biggest and most ambitious product launch ever. The introduction was accompanied by an ad campaign broadcast around the world in 35 different languages. Mattel's Barbie Web site, with its eight language options, featured Rapunzel stories and games, and an animated movie was broadcast on TV and released in video and DVD around the world.[2]

Four related factors support Mattel's ability to introduce products globally:

1. The globalization of fashion and pop culture
2. Advances in supply-chain management that allow Mattel to manage the logistics of manufacturing, shipping, and distribution on a global scale

3. The internationalization of media (especially television channels) used for advertising

4. The increasing global reach of retailers like Wal-Mart and Carrefour

In another case, Madonna's children's book *The English Roses* was simultaneously released in 2003 in 100 countries and in 30 languages (including Faroese, a language spoken by only 47,000 people in the Faroe Islands). This had never been done previously in book publishing. Innovations in digital file-sharing and printing technology and a unique collaborative arrangement between the publisher and printing firms made the multicontinent release possible. Similar global innovations can be seen in other industries such as cars, movies, shaving products, and clothing, which in turn drive the speed with which cultural images travel around the globe in all directions.

Despite the bursting of the dot-com bubble and the slowdown in world economies over the past few years, global integration between companies and countries continues to march inexorably forward. Yes, the threat of terrorism has had a chilling impact on travel and on investment in certain countries, such as Indonesia. Nevertheless, the vast majority of countries, and the world's industries, are becoming more globally integrated. Not long after the attacks on the World Trade Center, Federal Reserve Chairman Alan Greenspan said "globalization is an endeavor that can spread worldwide the values of freedom and civil contact—the antithesis of terrorism."

Consider table 1.1, which shows some indicators of globalization based on data from the past few years. This table provides evidence for the argument that most of the world's economies and people are becoming more globally integrated. As the Barbie and Madonna examples illustrate, globalization is happening for various reasons, including:

- Improved communication links
- Digitization that allows easy dissemination of information
- Convergence of consumer tastes
- Internationalization of the media
- The reach of the Internet
- Immigration
- The shift toward economic freedom (and, in some cases, political freedom) in countries like Brazil, China, India, and Indonesia
- Improved global management skills in the world's MNEs

The last of the above points is critical for this book, since we focus on the strategic management skills and knowledge necessary to compete in a global environment. In addition, the globalization determinants tend to reinforce each other. For instance, digitization and innovations in publishing allow books to

Table 1.1. Indicators of Global Integration

- Levels of foreign direct investment (FDI) in 2001, which fell more than 50 percent worldwide from $1.49 trillion to $735 billion, were still higher than any other year before 1999. And, when viewed as a share of global economic output, FDI flows in 2001 were nearly double their level in 1995. World flows of foreign direct investment increased from $200 billion in 1990 to $884 billion in 1999, and the ratio of world trade to gross domestic product (GDP) is generally rising in both high-income and developing countries.[a]
- By the end of 2001, the number of international tourist arrivals reached 597.5 million.[a]
- The International Telecommunication Union estimates that international telephone traffic grew more than 9 percent in 2001, reaching 120 billion minutes.
- The number of Internet users worldwide grew 22.5 percent, from 451 million in 2000 to 552.5 million in 2001 (and probably over 600 million by 2003).
- Of developing countries, 24 that increased their integration into the world economy during two decades ending in the late 1990s achieved higher growth in incomes, longer life expectancy, and better schooling. These countries, home to some 3 billion people, enjoyed an average 5 percent growth rate in income per capita in the 1990s compared to 2 percent in rich countries.[b]

---

[a]A. T. Kearney, *Foreign Policy Magazine Globalization Index*, 2003. See http://www.atkearney.com.
[b]World Bank Group, *Globalization, Growth and Poverty: Building an Inclusive World Economy* (2002). See http://econ.worldbank.org.

be printed in multiple locations at the same time, which permits retailers to coordinate their sales efforts, which supports global advertising efforts, which leads to economies of scale in marketing, which is enhanced by international television and entertainment firms, and so on. Internet-based systems that can link buyers and sellers have begun to impact the 400-year-old system of trade finance based on letters of credit. Consider UPS Capital, a subsidiary of United Parcel Service that was established in 1998. UPS Capital has utilized Internet-based technologies and some innovations in combining financial services with other traditional UPS services to enter a business long dominated by banks.

Indian immigrants to Silicon Valley have played a key role as programmers, consultants, entrepreneurs, and venture capitalists. In turn, many of these immigrants have become closely connected with the rising high-technology sector in India itself, which supports the Indian reforms in trade liberalization, financial services, and the growth of a well-educated and increasingly sophisticated middle class of consumers. In addition, India's economic transformation is leading to Indian-based MNEs that can compete as global competitors.

What Does Globalization Mean?

Globalization can be viewed at the country, industry, or firm level, which results in various definitions of globalization. Anthony Giddens, a sociologist, defines globalization as "the worldwide interconnection at the cultural, political and economic level resulting from the elimination of communication and trade barriers" and he states that "globalization is a process of convergence of cultural, political and economic aspects of life."[3] At the country level, Vijay Govindarajan and Anil Gupta define globalization as "growing economic interdependence among countries as reflected in increasing cross-border flows of three types of entities: goods and services, capital, and know-how."[4] As these and other authors point out, the amount of cross-border integration between countries, industries, and firms has reached unprecedented levels in recent years. Pankaj Ghemawat reviews the economic evidence about the international integration of markets. He found that although most measures of cross-border economic integration have increased significantly in the past few decades, the theoretical extreme of total market integration is still far away.[5] In response, Ghemawat proposes that we should be interested in semiglobalization, which spans the range of situations where both the barriers and the links to markets in different countries play a role in competition. Given that the many barriers to complete integration will undoubtedly exist for many years, it is certainly reasonable to view globalization as a process rather than an outcome.

Indeed, it is the lack of complete market integration that seems to bedevil analyses of globalization. Alan Rugman and Alain Verbeke have argued that sales of MNEs are unevenly distributed across the globe and mostly concentrated in just one geographic market, which means that products (and firms) are not really global in the sense of being equally attractive to consumers all around the world.[6] There is no question that distance still matters and that firms face a liability of foreignness when they enter new geographic markets. However, looking only at sales dispersion as a measure of globalization ignores the reality that, increasingly, MNEs must configure their value-chain activities on a worldwide basis or face competitive disadvantages.

Wal-Mart Stores, the largest retail chain firm in the United States and the world, for instance, has the majority of its sales in the United States. But its sales are rapidly growing in other regions, and many of its purchases are made from non-U.S.-based suppliers. In addition, Wal-Mart has many shareholders, employees, and competitors outside the United States and plans to expand into many new countries. Wal-Mart has recently entered Japan, one of the world's most difficult retail markets for new entrants, where high land prices, restrictions on store prices, a labyrinth of distribution channels, and extremely demanding customers (who often think low price must equal low quality) have been the bane of most foreign entrants. Wal-Mart's entry strategy incorporates several dimensions: a partnership with Seiyu, a Japanese supermarket chain, a five-year plan to reorganize Seiyu, closer relationships with suppliers, and extensive use of information technology to improve efficiency. With the Japanese entry, Wal-Mart as of 2004 was competing in nine countries, including huge retail markets such as in Germany, China, and Mexico.

So what can we conclude about globalization? First, let's consider what globalization does not mean. Globalization does not mean complete cross-border integration of countries and markets; that is an idealized state that is unlikely to exist for many years. But country integration is continuing and has reached levels never seen before. Second, globalization is not the production and distribution of products and services of a homogenous type and quality on a worldwide basis. At some level, value-chain activities must be local, which means that complete homogenization is impossible. Coca-Cola, often touted as a global product, cannot be produced and sold without local water, labels, marketing, and distribution channels. Moreover, in an era of mass customization, a combination of homogenization (e.g., the physical product Rapunzel Barbie) and heterogeneity (35 different languages used in advertising for Rapunzel Barbie) is an important element of a global strategy. Third, most of the largest MNEs still derive the majority of their sales from their home region and have a long way to go before they can be truly be considered to have global presence from a customer perspective. Fourth, globalization does not mean doing the same things everywhere, with firms becoming stateless and abandoning country images and culture.[7] Finally, globalization does not preclude the need for local responsiveness. Regional and local strategies have played, and will continue to play, a critical role in the strategies of MNEs.

That said, what are some of the things we know about globalization and international competition? First, MNEs compete in much more complicated competitive environments than do domestic firms. This complexity is the result of a variety of social, economic, and cultural factors. These factors mean that the various parts of MNEs must be internally differentiated to respond to the environmental differences that exist in different businesses and geographic markets. Second, globalization involves the integration of corporate activities across borders. The degree of integration required is driven by the global state of the industry. Third, globalization of an industry can be said to be increasing when transactions between buyers and seller become progressively less dependent on geographic distance.[8] Fourth, global companies must understand customers from the perspective of both domestic and international standards and must have the ability to learn in multiple locations far from the home base.[9] Finally, companies competing in the global arena will probably have several, or all, of the following "symptoms":

- Fewer total basic products
- More variants on these basic products

- A position in major emerging markets (not as a choice but a necessity)
- More worldwide products
- Foreign exchange risk as an important issue
- Significant interaction between managers from many countries
- More discussion about customers, competitors, technology, and suppliers with counterparts in other countries
- Multiple reporting relationships within and across the organization

What Is a Global Industry?

Like the definition of globalization itself, there are different opinions as to how to define a global industry. Why should we care whether an industry is considered global or not? We care because the characteristics of an industry have implications for how managers think about strategy, organization structure, governance, human resources issues, marketing and finance decisions, and so on. The more global the industry, the greater the need for coordination and integration of activities across country borders. Moreover, the decisions about where to perform the various value-creating activities will have to be made on a global basis, following which will be decisions about how to coordinate and integrate the various activities. The less global the industry, the less important it will be to think about where and how to manage a global network of activities.

In our view, the most useful approach in thinking about whether an industry is global or not is to identify some characteristics of global industries and then state a hypothesis: the more prevalent the characteristics in an industry, the more global the industry is. The characteristics that we believe capture the competitive dynamics of a global industry are shown in table 1.2. The automobile industry would be a good example of one that meets the definition of a global industry. The major competitors (DaimlerChrysler, Ford, General Motors [GM], Honda, Nissan, Toyota, and Volkswagen) all compete in the major world markets and manage their value chains from a global perspective. Cross-subsidization has allowed the major firms to enter China and suffer some early losses. The globalization at the original equipment manufacturer (OEM) level has forced the large component manufacturers such as Bosch, Delphi, and Denso to globalize their operations. Some of the smaller automobile companies, including Fiat, Peugeot-Citroen, and Renault, would have to be viewed as vulnerable, given the fact that they are not present in the United States and Canada, the world's largest market, and that they lack the scale to create a truly global network of activities.

There are many international industries that do not exhibit the characteristics of global industries. These industries, evolving into a global state, will have

Table 1.2.   Characteristics of Global Industries

- Industry products are sold internationally.
- Companies have the ability to serve international customers.
- Companies use coordinated (but not necessarily the same) approaches throughout the world.
- The same group of competitors is present in all major markets.
- Competition takes place on a global scale.
- Strategic positioning in one market fundamentally affects position in other markets.
- Cross-subsidization of markets by the major competitors is common.
- Headquarters are not country-specific.
- Headquarters management reflects the international makeup of the workforce.
- Value-chain activities are performed at optimal locations.
- Companies rely on inputs sourced from around the world.
- Companies combine advantages created in the domestic arena with others that result from doing business in many nations (e.g., economies of scale and transferable brand reputation).
- Leading companies create the same type of advantage in multiple markets (e.g., a firm with a differentiation advantage in country A has the same advantage in countries B, C, etc.).

---

characteristics such as those in table 1.3. In the less global industries, elements such as "same group of competitors are present in all the major markets" and "strategic positioning in one market fundamentally affects position in other markets" will be absent. For example, the cement industry is one that could be described as international but not global. Cement is used in every country, and the physical product changes little from country to country. There are four major firms competing internationally: CEMEX (Mexico), Heidelberg (Germany), Holcim (Switzerland), and Lafarge (France). Each of these firms has a strong local profit sanctuary in the home market and extensive international operations; for instance, in Mexico, CEMEX has a market share of about 50 percent in bulk cement (mainly sold in bags) and 60 percent in ready-mix concrete (the liquid form of cement used in construction). Although the cement MNEs are significant players in the cement industry, their market shares in other world markets are nowhere near that of, say, the large car companies or semiconductor firms. Collectively, the four big cement companies represent only about 25 percent of the global cement industry. All large markets have domestic cement industries and only the United States has a consistent production deficit that must be met by imports. Many large markets, such as China, India, and Brazil, have not been significantly penetrated by the major firms. Moreover, head-to-head competition is relatively rare in the industry. Most cement is shipped by road and the effective distribution radius is about 150–250 miles from cement plant to distribution. That said, the cement industry is rapidly evolving. Cement has

Table 1.3.   Characteristics of International, Nonglobal Industries

- Products are sold internationally.
- Companies serve primarily country or regional customers.
- Companies have subsidiaries with a high degree of autonomy in many countries.
- The same competitors are not necessarily present in all major markets.
- Competition takes place on a country-by-country basis, or possibly on a region-by-region basis.
- The strategic position of a company in one market has minimal effect on its position in other markets.
- Headquarters are highly country-specific.
- Headquarters management is largely dominated by home-country nationals.
- The majority of core value-chain activities are performed in the home country.

a unique characteristic that makes it highly suitable for globalization, and it is almost unique among internationally traded manufactured products in that, wherever it is produced, it is of a known consistent standard. As a result, any supplier can service any market provided the shipping cost is competitive. Recent innovations in shipping now allow cement to be shipped long distances from the plant to distribution terminals in distant markets, which effectively reduces the barrier of distance between producer and buyer.

Global Industries in Action

While most observers would agree that industries such as automobiles, commercial aircraft, oil and gas, consumer electronics, software, and investment banking are global, many other industries are becoming more global in structure and competition. We offer three industry case studies to illustrate how industries operate across borders and connect buyers and sellers regardless of the large geographical distances between them. The three industries in question—diamonds, sushi, and trash—are certainly not the most well known or even the most global. In fact, at first glance these industries might be described as having few global characteristics. On the contrary, all three have become very global over the past few years.

CASE STUDY: THE DIAMOND INDUSTRY

Diamonds were first mined in India thousands of years ago. Until diamond cutting was invented, though, likely in Venice sometime after 1330, diamonds were not considered especially valuable stones. Until the 18th century,

India was the only known source for diamonds. The gems were then discovered in Brazil and South Africa, which resulted in the beginning of a global industry. Today many countries have diamond mines, including Angola, Australia, Botswana, Canada, Russia, and Sierra Leone, and Botswana is the largest producer of diamonds by value in the world.

The De Beers Group is the world's largest diamond mining company, producing over 40 percent of the world's gem diamonds (by value) from its own mines in South Africa and in partnership with governments in Botswana, Namibia, and Tanzania. With this leverage, De Beers can artificially keep diamond prices stable by matching its supply to world demand. The company's London-based marketing arm, the Central Selling Organization (CSO), purchases the production of 13 mines owned or co-owned by De Beers in South Africa, Botswana, Namibia, and Tanzania.[10] The CSO also buys diamonds from Canada and Russia. De Beers's diamond-mining operations span every type of diamond mining, and its exploration activity extends across six continents. The De Beers Group's Diamond Trading Company, based in London, currently sorts, values, and sells about two-thirds of the world's annual supply of rough diamonds. Over the last 60 years, De Beers has actively advertised and promoted diamond jewelry around the world.

Until the 1990s, De Beers quietly controlled diamond supply and demand, but a series of global events resulted in the shaping of a very different industry. First, the collapse of the Soviet Union made it difficult for the CSO to control its agreement with Russia. Next, in 1996, Australia's Argyle diamond mine became the first mine to terminate its relationship with De Beers; instead, Argyle decided to market its own diamonds, which account for about one-third of total world output by volume and 5 percent of total world output by value. With the discovery of diamonds in Canada, De Beers was faced with another threat. De Beers has been able to control a sizable number of Canadian diamonds, but not 100 percent of them. In July 2003, the Diavik mine of Canada agreed to market its diamonds through Rio Tinto Diamonds NV in Antwerp, Belgium (Rio Tinto is now one of the partners in the joint venture that owns Diavik). These recent global competitive pressures have resulted in a new push by De Beers to differentiate the diamonds it markets. It has also led De Beers to try to settle a long-running price-fixing charge in the United States and thereby return to the U.S. market.

It is not just the diamond suppliers that have experienced global pressures. The rough stones produced from diamond mining must be cut and polished before they can be used in jewelry. The diamonds controlled by De Beers are shipped to the CSO, where they are combined and then separated into 14,000 categories, and divided by the company's 500 sorters into lots. Every five weeks De Beers distributes the lots to its 125 partners, setting the price of the diamonds in advance and determining the quality and quantity each partner receives. The price and quantity are nonnegotiable. The partners take the rough diamonds back to their factories, mainly in the cities of Antwerp, Tel Aviv, New York, Bombay, Johannesburg, and Smolensk, Russia, for cutting and polishing. The diamonds are then sold to wholesale and retail customers throughout the world.

Workers in the diamond-cutting industry cut and polish rough diamonds in such a way that they reflect maximum light. Fifty percent of the value and 80 percent of the volume of diamonds sold worldwide are cut and polished in India. India's diamond industry began in earnest in the 1960s and became successful mainly because of low costs. Until about 30 years ago, most of the world's annual output of diamonds were very small and considered useful only for industrial purposes such as drill bits. However, some entrepreneurial Indians in Mumbai began to cut and polish small stones to be used in jewelry. As they took advantage of low-cost labor and an influx of small diamonds from various sources, a new industry sector focused on inexpensive jewelry emerged.

Today, more than 500,000 diamond cutters work in India, mainly polishing the so-called rough, the lowest quality gemstones. As India has garnered more and more of the cutting activity, the older diamond-cutting centers of Tel Aviv and Antwerp have suffered substantial loss of market share. In the 1980s and 1990s, the Indian industry was forced to modernize and move away from its traditional sweatshop approach, mainly because of pressure from Israel's highly organized and efficient diamond-cutting industry and from new entrants from countries such as China, Malaysia, Sri Lanka, and Thailand. And in recent years, Indians have had a major impact on diamond polishing and trading outside India, especially in Antwerp. About half of the world's cut and polished diamonds are sold each year in Antwerp; the city, which has a trolley stop called Diamant, is home to about 1,500 retail and wholesale diamond companies and four diamond exchanges. One of the oldest exchanges, the Beurs voor Diamanthandel, was founded in 1904. Historically, the diamond business in Antwerp was dominated by Jewish merchants, going back to the 15th century, when Jews expelled from Spain and Portugal settled in what is now Belgium. But in the 1970s, large numbers of Indian traders, attracted by relatively easy immigration laws and the prospects for gaining a foothold in the diamond industry, migrated to Belgium. According to a *Wall Street Journal* article, Indians in Antwerp now control about 65 percent of the diamond revenues, and the Jewish share has dropped from almost 100 percent to about 25 percent.[11] Rosy Blue, a firm started in India in 1960, opened an Antwerp branch in 1973. Today, as a manufacturer of diamonds and finished diamond jewelry, Rosy Blue employs 25,000 people in nine countries and has sales of more than $1 billion.[12] One of the keys to the Indian firms' success has been access to low-cost cutting and polishing in India. In addition, many Indian traders have aggressively expanded their businesses to new markets in New York and California. In response, some of the Jewish diamond companies have moved their cutting and polishing operations out of Belgium to lower cost countries such as Thailand and China.

CASE STUDY: THE SUSHI INDUSTRY

The sushi industry is another business that has evolved globally over the past few years. Not long ago, sushi was a novelty item found in a few Japanese restaurants outside Japan. Today, though, sushi is found in neighborhood malls from Singapore to Sydney to Stockholm. At expensive Japanese restaurants in New York and London, the sushi on the menu may include tuna caught by fishermen from New England, Australia, Spain, or Croatia. The tuna has probably been shipped to Japan, processed, and then shipped back to the same country where it was originally landed. Theodore Bestor, a professor of anthropology at Harvard, has extensively studied the sushi industry. In a *Foreign Policy* article Bestor describes the industry as follows: "The tuna trade is a prime example of the globalization of a regional industry, with intense international competition and thorny environmental regulations; centuries-old practices combined with high technology; realignments of labor and capital in response to international regulation; shifting markets; and the diffusion of culinary culture as tastes for sushi, and bluefin tuna, spread worldwide."[13]

In Japan, tuna has been popular for many years and until a few decades ago the tuna industry for sushi had limited involvement by non-Japanese. New fishing laws in the 1970s, however, kept Japanese fishermen away from coastal waters, which meant that Japanese tuna buyers were forced to look for new suppliers. The bubble economy of the 1980s created a huge demand for expensive consumer products, including high-end sushi. When the bubble collapsed, the sushi industry would have collapsed, too, were it not for the globalization of the industry. A food that was once a quirky and somewhat strange (to non-Japanese tastes) product has become global in demand; in the United States there is the California Sushi Academy, where American students learn how to incorporate sushi into non-Japanese menus, in addition to specialty-food catalogs that sell home sushi-making sets.

To satisfy the huge demand for tuna, tuna farms have sprung up in Spain, Morocco, Tunisia, Croatia, Australia, and various other countries. In the United States and Canada, tuna has long been prized by sport fishermen as one of the most thrilling fish to catch. In the 1960s when tuna were caught as trophies, the fish would be brought ashore for the traditional photo and then the captain would pay someone a few dollars to dump it in the woods; if the boat captain was lucky, he might get 10 cents a pound from a pet food company. Today, buyers from Japan and the United States are prepared to pay more than $20 a pound for top-grade tuna. The tuna fishing industry is supported by Japanese capital and trading expertise, aquaculture expertise from various countries, herring from Holland to feed the tuna, local fishermen, and a global telecommunications network that links the fishermen, traders, processors, and customers.

Although the demand for sushi has globalized, sushi remains closely identified with Japanese culture and under Japanese control. The center for the global trade in tuna is Tsukiji, Tokyo's wholesale fish market, which does $6 billion in business a year (and bidding privileges can cost as much as a seat on the New York Stock Exchange). Bluefin tuna caught in New England are sold to Japanese buyers shortly after they are brought ashore. Special paper is sent from Japan to wrap the fish before it is packed in ice. Although half the tuna is unusable, and despite high shipping costs, whole tuna are sent to Japan because Japanese workers are much more skilled in cutting and trimming tuna than are American workers. At auction in Tsukiji, a tuna caught in the United States could sell for as much as $30,000. In sushi restaurants the world over, a Japanese, or Japanese-looking, sushi chef is critical to ensure that the product appears authentic (often the sushi chef outside Japan is Chinese, Korean, or Vietnamese).

CASE STUDY: THE TRASH INDUSTRY

The trash industry seems like the quintessential local industry: a homeowner puts trash in a bin and a local company picks it up and drops it off at nearby landfill, dump (or rubbish tip, as it is called in the United Kingdom), or recycling center. Trash is worth little (otherwise it would not be trash), which means it must be disposed of near where it is created. How could there possibly be any value in household trash that would bring international buyers and sellers together?

There is a lot of value in trash, though, and the reason is recycling. All household and industrial trash no longer gets dumped into a hole in the ground. According to data from the Commerce Department, in 2002 the

United States exported waste and scrap to China with an estimated value of $1.2 billion, up from $194 million five years earlier.[14] Total scrap exports from the United States totaled about $5.2 billion. After China, the biggest foreign purchasers of all kinds of U.S. scrap are Canada, the United Kingdom, Korea, and Mexico. In 2002, the United States exported more than 2 million metric tons of steel and iron to China. Trash was the third largest item by value imported into China, next only to aircraft and semiconductor products, according to the Beijing-based *Economy Monthly*. The increase in exports has pushed up the prices for U.S. scrap, especially in markets close to ports with container terminals. Scrap steel in particular has seen substantial price increases, and some countries have tried to limit scrap steel exports by creating export duties.

Over the past decade Japan has become a major exporter of scrap steel and paperboard used to make corrugated cardboard sold to China and other Asian countries. Entrepreneurs in Hong Kong import plastic from the United States and Europe, transform the plastic into pellets, and sell the pellets to manufacturers in China, that in turn produce products that are exported back to some of the same countries that produced the scrap.

Insights from the Three Global Industry Cases

Collectively these industries offer interesting insights into the burgeoning world of global competition. First, all three industries illustrate the bringing together of far-flung buyers and sellers in a network of local, regional, and global players. Second, the three industries are in a constant state of evolution, from the influx of Indian diamond traders, to the conservative Antwerp diamond industry, to the growing taste for high-end sushi in restaurants outside Japan, to the voracious demand for scrap in China. Third, the industries may be global in certain aspects but the firms (and industries) retain their cultural identities, although not without some pressure and need for adaptation. Indeed, cultural traditions can play a critical role in helping carve out a strategy, as the Indian diamond traders proved by building a network drawn from members of the Jain religion. In the tuna and sushi industry much of the value created is a direct function of the Japanese authenticity of the product. If the tuna were caught and processed in the United States by American workers, the price for the end product would surely drop. Fourth, the global shifts in these industries impact the local elements of the industry. The demand for scrap in China has driven up the price of scrap in the United States, while the Belgian diamond firms have been forced to look for lower cost manufacturing outside Belgium. Finally, local support firms and industries play a key role in global industries.

Why Do Firms Pursue Global Expansion?

We have examined industry globalization and will now consider the question of why firms expand globally. We define global expansion as the crossing of international borders to perform upstream and downstream value-chain activities. Govindarajan and Gupta identified five reasons or imperatives that drive global expansion.[15] They suggested that the presence of any one reason could help explain why a firm makes a strategic decision to cross borders. The imperatives, which are examined in greater detail below, are as follows:

- To seek revenue growth opportunities
- To compete against global competitors
- To support global customers
- To access global knowledge
- To achieve efficiency in managing value-chain activities

The most obvious global imperative involves the need to grow. It is a truism that all firms must grow. Those that do not grow will struggle to find new human assets and capital because a firm that is not growing will be an unattractive investment and will provide few opportunities for personal development for the firm's employees. In some industries, global growth opportunities will greatly exceed those that exist in domestic markets. For firms in small countries such as Switzerland, Belgium, or Singapore, globalization will be a much stronger imperative than in large economies such as the United States or Japan. Consequently, the percentage of firms in the smaller countries that are multinational will be much larger than in larger nations (as is the relationship between trade and gross national product [GNP]; in small economies such as Singapore the ratio is substantially greater than one).

In a global industry, not competing globally will lead to a significant competitive disadvantage. When global competitors exist, firms seeking a leadership position must compete on a global basis. For example, in the upstream oil industry (i.e., oil and gas exploration and production), the oil majors such as ExxonMobil, Shell, and British Petroleum (BP) compete globally and view the entire world as a potential source of petroleum resources. While there are many small regional players in the oil industry, these small firms cannot compete for a leadership role in major upstream development projects. Major upstream projects require enormous capital, knowledge, and ability to manage risks, which is one of the reasons the oil industry has seen so many mergers and acquisitions in recent years. The brewing industry is another example of an industry where the emergence of global competitors has precipitated a variety of global expansionary strategic actions. Many regional brewing companies have been swallowed up by larger MNE brewers. The U.S. brewer Miller, formerly a division of Philip Morris, was acquired by South African Brewers in 2002. Labatt Breweries of Canada was acquired by the Belgium-based company Interbrew in 1995. Interbrew concluded a complex merger agreement with Ambev of Brazil in 2004, displacing Anheuser-Busch as the world's largest brewer. In 2004, most of the world's major brewers, including Anheuser-Busch, Carlsberg, Heineken, Interbrew, SABMiller, and Scottish & Newcastle, were jockeying for position in China. In mid-2004, an interesting battle took place between Anheuser-Busch and SABMiller for control of Harbin Brewery Group, China's oldest brewer. According to some analysts, the winner of Harbin Brewery would be the loser because of the excessive price being paid, which illustrates that the rush to beat global competitors in new markets is fraught with peril.

Supporting global customers can be imperative when the global customers hold a significant amount of bargaining power. When Wal-Mart asks a supplier to supports its entry into a new international market, a refusal by that supplier could jeopardize an existing domestic business. When the Japanese automakers entered North America in the 1980s, they encouraged their Japanese-based suppliers to follow them. If the Japanese suppliers had refused to follow their customers to North America, they would have risked damaging the intricate network of implicit trade agreements that exist in Japan between suppliers and manufacturers.[16] In many cases, the Japanese suppliers were reluctant to enter North America but had no real choice in the matter. More than a decade later, Toyota, Nissan, and Honda are well entrenched as producers in international markets and their Japanese supply base has become globalized. Japanese suppliers such as Denso now have significant manufacturing operations outside Japan.

While a somewhat overused term, *knowledge-based competition* is a reality in many industries, which means that gaining access to knowledge beyond one's border is often a strategic necessity for survival. In all global industries there are centers of excellence or clusters of competitors,[17] such as the automobile industry in Detroit, high technology in Silicon Valley, cosmetics in Japan, and fashion in Paris. (In chapter 2 we discuss clusters in more detail.) Take cosmetics: Japanese women spend more per capita on cosmetics than women in any other country. To be a global leader in the cosmetics industry, a firm must compete in Japan, and probably Paris, too. By being in Japan and Paris, the cosmetics firm will be exposed to competition with leading firms and will have to deal with the world's most demanding customers. A cosmetics firm in Japan will also be exposed to state-of-the-art knowledge across all value-chain activities. As another example, in the 1990s the lines between telecommunications and computing blurred, prompting the major telecom equipment firms to establish offices in Silicon Valley. Similarly, in recent years Japanese automotive firms have been increasing their design and development operations in the United States because of a need to learn more about automotive consumer behavior in their largest market. In chapter 5 we examine global knowledge and how firms capture and manage their knowledge-based resources.

The final imperative is global expansion for efficiency reasons. There are two facets of global efficiency. One involves a per unit calculation: once a firm outgrows its home market in any value-chain activity, the logical course of action is to seek international markets in order to exploit scale advantages. For example, as the cost of developing commercially viable drugs continues to rise, pharmaceutical firms have no choice but to seek international markets to justify the huge R&D expenditures. The other facet of efficiency involves selecting a location outside the home market in order to perform a value-chain activity at a lower cost. In the opening paragraph we mentioned HP's development of a new server. This case illustrates how companies seek to optimize labor costs, tax burdens, technological expertise, logistics, and country-based incentives in order to be as cost-effective as possible. This means looking closely at the value chain and identifying the optimal location in which to perform the various value-chain activities.

Every firm will be faced with a different set of global imperatives. Some firms face none of the five imperatives. For example, Southwest Airlines, the very successful U.S. airline company, has no international flights and has invested no significant capital in international markets. Southwest continues to grow by entering new U.S. markets. That said, an examination of Southwest's value chain would show that the firm is tightly integrated into the global economy. Southwest's fuel purchases are connected to a global market and aircraft (themselves the product of a global industry) are sourced through a supply chain that is highly global. Within the airline industry, Southwest has influenced the strategies of many recent entrants, such as Ryan Air and easyJet (Europe), Air Arabia (United Arab Emirates), and Air Asia (Malaysia). In that sense, Southwest is setting the global standard for discount air travel, and even though the company does not actually fly internationally, its influence on the global airline industry has been significant. Thus, it could be argued that Southwest has established the global benchmark for strategic success as an airline.

Other firms face most, if not all, of the five imperatives. As we have indicated, the major automobile competitors compete in the major world markets and manage their value chains from a global perspective. It is inconceivable to think that an automobile company could achieve a leading position (let alone survive) by competing in only one country or region. There are automobile companies, such as Malaysia's Perusahaan Otomobil Nasional (manufacturer of the Proton Saga) or Russia's AvtoVaz (manufacturer of the Lada), that compete mainly in one country. However, these firms survive only because of tariffs or other forms of government intervention. If Malaysian car tariffs were dismantled, Proton Sagas would quickly disappear from Malaysian roads. The Proton Saga's manufacturing costs are far too high and quality far too low for the company to compete in a real competitive environment that consists of huge, globalized competitors ruthlessly pursuing competitive advantage.

Distance and Global Strategy

While Internet and telecommunications technologies allow individuals and firms to connect across long distances, distance continues to play a factor in global expansion decisions. It will always be easier to cross an immediate border than to enter a market many thousands of miles away. For example, Canada and the United States share the longest undefended border in the world and, not surprisingly, each has the other as its major trading partner. Thus, as Ghemawat argues, distance still matters.[18] Ghemawat identified four dimensions of distance: cultural, administrative, geographic, and economic. Cultural distance includes language, religious, cultural, and social differences. Administrative distance involves a country's institutions and the degree to which they are related to those of another country. For example, countries that were connected through colonial ties, such as Malaysia and the United Kingdom, will likely have a close relationship. Geographic distance involves both the miles between countries and the access to the infrastructure of trade, such as harbors and airports. Economic distance primarily involves the relative wealth or income of a country's consumers.

Understanding the distance between countries is crucial for global expansion decisions. Industries and firms will be affected by the distance dimensions in different ways. If a firm's expansion imperative involves the need to identify lower cost factor inputs, countries with significant economic distance will be the target. On the other hand, if the objective is growth in revenue, a high economic distance could mean that the local population has insufficient income to afford the product. If the distance is primarily cultural, successful global expansion will require the ability to adapt to local market differences by tailoring the products and services to local customers and dealing with local competitors.

An interesting example of distance involves international law firms. In recent years, MNEs have been putting pressure on law firms to extend their global reach.[19] With the increase in the number of cross-border mergers and acquisitions and new emphasis on corporate governance, the ability to provide trans-national legal advice has increased in importance. However, the globalization of the legal profession has not kept pace with the legal services requirements of MNE clients. With the two biggest markets for international law services in London and New York, the logical route to globalization would be through mergers between law firms from the two cities, perhaps also involving firms from other countries such as Germany and France. With a few exceptions, mergers between large international law firms have not happened. A key factor in stymieing such deals is corporate cultural distance. New York law firms are much more profitable than London firms, and partnership compensation is based on an "eat-what-you-kill" system, which means profits are shared by partners based on how much business each of them generates. In the London firms, profit is allocated based on partner seniority. When the large London law firm Clifford Chance merged with firms in the United States and Germany, one of the world's largest international law firms was created. Since the merger, the New York office of Clifford Chance has lost almost two dozen of its most productive partners, primarily because of the compensation system. Aside from Clifford Chance, no U.K. law firm has managed to establish a significant U.S. presence A few U.S. law firms have been pursuing international strategies because they believe an international presence is necessary to capitalize on areas such as cross-border mergers and acquisitions. Additionally, areas such as environment, shipping, aviation, antitrust, corporate governance, employment law, pensions, international arbitration, and intellectual property are demanding international legal expertise, suggesting that the legal profession will continue to globalize, albeit at a relatively slow pace befitting its cozy professional services culture.

Managers and MNEs in a Global World

As discussed in the previous section, firms globalize for a variety of strategic reasons. The extent of globalization efforts in the past few decades can be seen by looking at the increase in the number of MNEs. Clearly, MNEs are the engine that drives the global economy. According to a recent study, there were 7,258 MNEs in 1969 and more than 63,000 by 2000.[20] Table 1.4 shows some of the increases and decreases within the 500 largest companies. The table leads us to some interesting speculative questions:

- When will there be Chinese and Indian companies among the largest MNEs in the world?

Table 1.4.   The 500 Largest Multinational
Enterprises (MNEs) in the World

Country	1962	1999
United States	398	179
Japan	31	107
Germany	36	38
South Korea	0	12
Switzerland	6	11
Brazil	0	3
Great Britain	55	38
France	27	35
China (includes Hong Kong)	0	10
Italy	1	9

Note: Not all countries are shown.
Source: Medard Gabel and Henry Bruner, *Global, Inc.: An Atlas of the Multinational Corporation* (New York: The New Press, 2003).

- Will continued economic integration in Europe, along with the expansion of the European Union (EU) in 2004, lead to larger and more powerful European MNEs?
- Will MNEs from Africa and South America ever establish themselves in significant numbers as real global players?
- Will the percentage of the world's largest MNEs in the United States and other developed nations continue to decrease?
- Will the Japanese and South Korean experience of rapid economic development accompanied by the emergence of large MNEs be replicated in other emerging-market countries?

While these questions remain to be answered, there is no doubt that the list of largest MNEs and their countries of origin will continue to evolve. Some other speculative questions associated with MNEs and their role in the global economy are as follows:

- Is there a limit to the size of an MNE, or can companies like Wal-Mart relentlessly march forward toward unprecedented organizational size?
- Currently, the major technological drivers for globalization and the increase in the number of MNEs are communication and transportation. Will new technological drivers emerge in coming years?
- Will new international institutions emerge to regulate, monitor, and facilitate international trade and MNE activity (in addition to the

Global Agreement on Tariffs and Trade [GATT], the World Trade Organization [WTO], and others)?

- As the economic and social effects of globalization become better understood, how will the behavior of governments change in terms of their willingness to either open or close borders to international business?

A manager in today's global environment must be prepared to deal with myriad challenges and opportunities. The questions identified above incorporate issues and ideas that managers must be thinking and speculating about. Strategy is about growth and change, which means that managers must be constantly evaluating their assumptions and the conventional wisdom. In the global environment, the depth and breadth of environmental issues are substantially greater than in a single domestic market. We consider some of these issues in the next section.

The Global Environment and the Global Manager

The global environment is characterized by constantly shifting competitive forces and environmental pressures. The diamond, sushi, and trash industries examined earlier are constantly changing and evolving, as are all industries. One implication of this evolution is that historical industry structures are likely to be poor predictors of the future competitive environment. A key objective in this book is to examine the critical areas that influence global strategy formulation and implementation. In doing this we had to deal with the fact that the global environment is changing every day. If you ask managers "Is your competitive environment more complex today than it was a few years ago?" they will almost certainly say yes. Ask the same question a year from now and the answer will again be yes. The competitive world is getting more complex, and today's global manager must deal with issues such as those shown in table 1.5, each of which is growing more, rather than less, complex.

All of the issues in table 1.5 have international implications. Although examination of all of these issues in detail is beyond the scope of this book, we raise them to illustrate the nature of today's competitive environment. The world is complex, global strategy is complex, and the complexity therein will continue to increase. For example, consider China's recent economic development. One school of thought suggests that China poses a huge threat to developed nations because of its increasing manufacturing base. If China does all the manufacturing, what will happen to manufacturing in the developed

Table 1.5.   International Management Challenges and Issues

- China's emergence as the main manufacturer of the world
- India's emergence as an information technology (IT) power and potential emergence in many other industries
- Other emerging markets and their development
- The Asian tigers' transition to developed economies
- E-commerce
- Corporate governance
- Growing importance of trade blocs
- Intense global competition
- Mergers and acquisitions (in a down cycle, as of 2003) and alliances (in a steadily increasing mode for more than 20 years)
- Rapidly changing technology
- Focus on quality and customization
- Continued uncertainty (Japan, Indonesia, Venezuela)
- Threat of terrorism
- Growing green movement
- Changing demographics and an aging population
- Declining birthrates and immigration issues in Europe
- Need to respond quickly (e.g., shorter time cycle)

economies? An opposing line of thinking is that the more developed China becomes, the greater the market opportunities for sophisticated products that China cannot produce. In other words, the United States can buy Barbie dolls from China and then China can use the foreign currency to buy semiconductors and aircraft from the United States. Since semiconductors and aircraft create far more value added than toys, the United States should encourage a shift of low-end manufacturing to China. A related factor in assessing China's role in global economies involves India's competitiveness relative to Japan. Conventional wisdom is that India is no threat to China—look at the tiny amount of foreign direct investment (FDI) in India compared to China. Moreover, China's infrastructure (roads, power, ports, etc.) far surpasses that of India. However, in an article in *Foreign Policy*,[21] the authors argue that China's growth is largely because of foreign investment and not local innovation. They argue that India's homegrown entrepreneurs, such as Dhirubhai Ambani, the founder of the Reliance Group, compete against the best companies in the world, especially in software, giving the country a potential advantage over China in the global economy. No matter which country achieves the greatest global presence, the race is sure to be exciting and provide many business opportunities for both local entrepreneurs and MNEs.

Conclusion

As the cross-border flow of people, knowledge, ideas, products, services, and management practices accelerates, the notion of home-based advantage is becoming weaker. In many industries, geographic distance is becoming increasingly irrelevant to buyers and sellers. In other industries where distance still matters, such as cement, innovations in logistics or manufacturing or advertising, or some other part of the value chain, are causing a shift away from local or regionalized competition.

As a last thought on the nature of globalization, we offer a few thoughts from managers who are fighting global battles. From a senior manager in a large pharmaceutical and consumer products firm, "Globalization is the movement of people and ideas around the world." Carlos Ghosn of Renault has said "Globalization means that when you come to a new environment, you can be sure that nothing is guaranteed!"[22]

2

Strategic Choices in a Global Marketplace

As we discussed in chapter 1, globalization forces are impacting all industries. This chapter examines the strategic choices facing the global firm. Competing in global markets requires that organizations carefully consider a wide array of strategic options. These options can range from an approach that pursues localization at all costs to the other extreme of integration of markets and products across the globe. While these polarized approaches are idealized strategy options at best, the shades of gray that lie in between often help define an organization's strategy in world markets. In this chapter we explore strategic choices and the design of global strategy.

Much of the academic literature on strategic positioning has coalesced around three dominant positions for international strategy. One school of thought suggests that organizations should standardize their offerings across the world. This stance can help address the growing pressures of homogenization that are dampening the dissimilarities that historically have made each market unique. Thus, the aspirations of consumers in one part of the world are assumed to be no different from the aspirations of people in another part of the world. Driving economies of scale through a standardized array of product/service offerings can help build competitive advantage on a global scale. When asked, students typically volunteer "Coca-Cola" as the archetypal global product that is marketed and sold as a homogenized brand in just about every country. The reality is that most of the Coca-Cola value chain is very local, including production and bottling, sales, and distribution. Soft drinks, unlike beer and wine, cannot be shipped profitably across distant borders.

A second school of thought coalesces around the belief that organizations should view the global market as a collection of dissimilar markets, each with distinct needs. Thus, managers should be counseled to think and behave along "local" lines and to "localize" their operations. The major advantages of this approach are access to knowledge within the network of independent subsidiaries, access to deep pockets that the parent might possess, and other intangible sources of competitive advantage such as well-recognized brands. Organizations such as Fiat of Italy and Philips of the Netherlands are often held up as exemplars of the virtues of localization. When these organizations first established their manufacturing subsidiaries they typified the localization approach. They crafted strategy for their international markets as a collection of individually tailored, country-specific strategies with an overarching corporate umbrella that sought to leverage some resources across the geographic portfolio. However, both Fiat and Philips have struggled over the past decade as their respective core industries (automobiles and consumer electronics) have become increasingly global in scope. Companies like Toyota in automobiles and Samsung in electronics have adopted global strategies around brands, platforms, and technologies that have diminished the ability of locally oriented producers to create advantage (see the case study later in this chapter called "Competitive Choices in the Consumer Electronics Industry").

The third school of thought is a hybrid approach that has received significant attention in recent years. A number of scholars have articulated different variations on this theme, which seeks to capture the best elements of both the localization and the global integration approaches. Variously titled *transnational strategy* (Bartlett and Ghoshal), *administrative coordination* (Prahalad and Doz), and *cross-subsidization* (Hamel and Prahalad, 1985), this hybrid approach calls for balancing the pressures to localize with the demands for cross-border integration and scale economies.[1] The transnational approach (discussed in detail in chapter 3) seeks to resolve the inherent tensions between the pressures to integrate and standardize and the pressures to adapt and localize. In theory, the transnational firm would be good at both global integration and local responsiveness. In reality, these are conflicting pressures, and satisfying one often means compromising on the other. Moreover, these strategies introduce complex organizational challenges, which are the subject of chapter 3.

While each school of thought offers powerful arguments in defense of its own position, the commonalities across the three perspectives are useful in grasping the realities of creating strategy for the global marketplace.[2] Although they each offer different prescriptions, much of the thinking in the three streams is driven by the same factors: product characteristics, industry attributes, and location-specific advantages. In short, the choice of strategic approach will revolve around issues related to factors such as:

1. The nature of home-country-specific advantage and similar advantages that can be leveraged across the MNE's network of operations

2. The determinants of the dynamics of industry competition, such as concentration, rivalry, and strategic variety among competitors
3. Product characteristics such as the nature of technology involved, the relative power of branding, and physical features of the product and its use

Global Strategy and Country-Specific Advantage

Chapter 1 explored the concept of distance and concluded that distance still matters. That said, it is now much more feasible to move goods and services across long distances independent of geography, especially if those goods and services can be digitized. As a result, a wide range of organizations can access the global marketplace for inputs as well as for eventual sale of finished goods and services. Labor, once thought to be immobile, is also being harnessed across borders with the aid of liberalized trade regimes and advances in science and technology. Yet, despite these changes, much of the way in which an organization charts and plans its global strategy depends on the specifics of a given location. Although many scholars have proclaimed the "death of distance," location continues to play a significant role in the success of a strategy.

Any strategy that seeks to address the global marketplace must leverage country-specific advantages that help the organization maintain a sustainable lead over the competition. These country-specific advantages offer a *comparative* edge for firms that either are located in or originated in a specific country. Most often, these factors underlie efforts to build *competitive* advantage in the global arena.

Michael Porter focused on the relationship between a firm's ability to establish competitive superiority and its national identity.[3] He argued that country-specific advantage is a major reason a disproportionate number of firms in a given industry cluster in a particular country. For example, a large majority of companies in the computer software business tend to be from the United States. This can be traced to the inception of electronic computing in the United States, the evolution of a strong computer hardware industry, the availability of scientific talent, access to risk capital giving rise to an entrepreneurial class of inventors, and the growth in sophistication among buyer groups in the country.[4] Silicon Valley's strength as a cluster site is based on its social capital, created through collaborative partnerships that drive technological dynamism. Trust based on performance provides the foundation, which means that newcomers and outsiders can enter the network as long as they deliver on their promises. Silicon Valley also has some unique people networks created by immigrants. For example, Silicon Valley's immigrant engineers and entrepreneurs have helped establish transnational networks, especially between Taiwan, China, India, and the United States. These networks are a powerful source of global knowledge transfer into and out of Silicon Valley.[5]

Porter describes other clusters, such as Italian companies in the footwear business, Scandinavian companies in the specialized area of diabetology and insulin-related therapies, and Japanese companies in the manufacture of machine tools.[6] In each of these successful industries, global players have relied on the advantages provided by the location. Most of these firms are headquartered in the countries offering advantages of specific relevance to their industries. Alternatively, some global players establish a network of operations in the advantaged locations to tap into location-specific benefits.

Synthesizing disparate strands of literature from economics to geography, Porter proposed a "diamond" framework comprising four factors at the country level that drive locational advantage. These factors encompass (a) factor conditions, (b) demand conditions, (c) related and supporting industries, and (d) firm strategy, structure, and rivalry (see figure 2.1).

Factor Conditions

The factor-conditions dimension captures all the advantages related to specific aspects of inputs such as raw materials, labor availability and quality, and infrastructure that the location offers. Comparative advantage can originate both from the superior quality and/or the more attractive cost structures of the factor inputs. India, for example, has been recognized as offering a talent pool that is

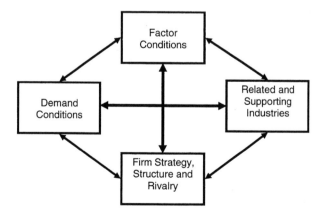

Figure 2.1.   Diamond framework. Source: Michael E. Porter, *The Competitive Advantage of Nations* (New York: Free Press, 1990).

highly qualified and willing to work in technically advanced jobs for a fraction of what it would cost to employ a similar workforce in most developed countries. Similarly, Saudi Arabia has a comparative advantage in the oil and gas business because it has the world's largest reserves of crude oil and natural gas while also having some of the lowest production costs. Thus, technology firms in India and oil industry firms in Saudi Arabia could build on the comparative advantage offered by their country location to develop a competitive edge in world markets.

Demand Conditions

The characteristics of the country market, such as the quality of local demand, sophistication of local buyers, and the prevalence of multinational buyers, have an important bearing on the dominance and growth of global markets. Home-demand conditions in fashion-conscious France, for example, present a challenging market environment that requires designers and retailers to create superior competitive positions to hold their own. The French consumer provides an early indication of sales potential for fashion lines premiered in this market context. Retail chains in fashion apparel often look to French consumers for clues to the product lines they should carry for the coming fashion season. Similarly, consumer electronics companies in Japan benefit from the high level of sophistication of the Japanese consumers, who have a penchant for miniaturization and technological complexity. As the level of buyer sophistication rises, these buyers demand a higher level of excellence that firms might not, in and of themselves, seek. The presence of multinational buyers helps globalize demand early since these buyers serve as visible early adopters in the global marketplace.

Related and Supporting Industries

The dominance of related and supporting industries provides another critical element that fortifies comparative advantage. Proximity to a world-class supplier base offers the buyer industries important technological and logistical advantages. Supplier clusters present readily available repositories of industry-specific knowledge and, hence, play a vital role in helping sustain the comparative advantage of a location in specific industries.[7] For example, U.S. automakers benefited from a vibrant steel industry following the Second World War. The geographic proximity to steel mills allowed the automakers to minimize their transaction costs and helped them benefit from technological advancements pioneered by the local steel makers at that time. Similarly, the strong position of the United Kingdom in manufacturing automobile engines is strengthened by the country's superiority in lubricants and engine oils. The strength of the French fashion industry can be traced, in part, to advantages historically conferred by an equally powerful textile industry focused on luxury textiles such as silks.

Firms, Structures, Strategies, and the Intensity of Rivalry

Local rivalry can winnow the field in many ways to ensure that the successful few organizations have the ability to build competitive advantage on a global scale. For example, Honda faces eight rivals on its home turf, all with global portfolios to match (although the last decade has seen the majority of Japanese automakers align themselves with non-Japanese firms: Nissan with Renault; Mazda with Ford; Isuzu, Subaru, and Suzuki with GM; Mitsubishi with DaimlerChrysler—leaving only Toyota and Honda without international partners). Similarly, LVMH, the world leader in luxury fashion retailing, faces stiff competition from several equally well-known design houses, such as Hermès, Chanel, Balmain, Yves Saint Laurent, and Cacharel. In coping with this intense rivalry, the leaders must be innovative in their offerings, their strategies, and their internal organizational arrangements.

Taken together, these four dimensions of Porter's diamond framework offer important insights into the roots of global competitive advantage. Although competition in most industries transcends national borders, many factors that explain sustainable advantage reside in the local uniqueness that an organization brings to the market. Often, advantages such as preferential access to superior local talent, local institutional infrastructures, and local knowledge relationships cannot easily be copied by distant global competitors, making local organizations ideal seeds for growing sustainable competitive advantage in the global arena. In some cases, the nationality of the firms confers a product advantage, such as watches made in Switzerland, wines from France, cameras from Japan, and hockey equipment from Canada. The following case study of the Belgian gourmet chocolate industry illustrates how local firms have been able to capitalize on location-specific advantages in creating a global strategy for their confections.

CASE STUDY: BELGIUM—LOCATION-SPECIFIC ADVANTAGE IN THE GLOBAL GOURMET CHOCOLATE INDUSTRY

Belgium, the part-Flemish, part-French nation with a population of just 10 million, leads the world in the production of gourmet chocolate. Although the Swiss dominate the overall chocolate industry, Belgium produces some of the finer varieties of the confection consumed worldwide. The path to dominance in this industry has been a lucky mix of history, culinary tradition, access to high-quality inputs, and the sheer genius of famous chocolatiers such as Pierre Marcolini, Christian Vanderkerken, and Claire Mancq, all familiar names to connoisseurs of gourmet chocolates.[8] The competitive advantage of many of Belgium's leading chocolate purveyors can be understood through an application of Porter's diamond.

Factor Conditions: History dealt a favorable hand in the form of the Belgian Congo, a former Belgian colony that proved to be an excellent source of cacao beans. In 1857, famed chocolatier Jean Neuhaus created the first pralines. By 1930 Frans Callebaut had produced a version of the chocolate called *couverture* that could be used to coat fruits and candies. These twin developments ensured that chocolate developed a cult following around the world. Chocolate has become an integral part of Belgian culture and tradition, akin to wine in France and caviar in Russia.

Related and Supporting Industries: Culinary arts and related education play a central role in the sustained dominance of Belgium's chocolatiers. The country has over 1,000 restaurants and four chocolate museums. A well-established network of culinary schools provides training and education to aspiring chocolatiers.

Demand Conditions: The demanding Belgian palate has ensured that only the best chocolatiers are patronized by the local population. The country consumes close to 20 pounds of chocolate per capita, among the highest in the world. With prices averaging $28 per pound, the locals seem to appreciate fine chocolates. For its relatively small population, Belgium has over 2,100 chocolate shops, an indicator of the depth of local demand. The proliferation of chocolatiers has meant that each chocolatier has to distinguish its offerings in meaningful ways to attract the patronage of a discriminating clientele. Many have developed narrow specialties emphasizing variations in ingredients, design, and brand. For example, Pierre Marcolini, often considered the Hermès of chocolate, has leveraged the exotic origins of the cacao beans by marking its products with a country-of-origin label such as Madagascar, Ecuador, or Venezuela. Riding on its reputation, Marcolini has established shops in many countries outside Belgium such as Japan, the United Kingdom, and France. Along similar lines, the powerhouse Witamer has been a chocolate purveyor of choice for well over a century; it specializes in bonbon varieties, handcrafting 85 variations with seasonal themes. These distinctive product-positioning approaches have ensured that the intense competitive rivalry has a remarkably positive impact on the skills development that has emerged among the gourmet chocolatiers.

Where Should Value-Chain Activities Be Located?

In crafting their global strategies, organizations must make explicit choices about locating value-chain activities to ensure that location-specific advantages are optimally leveraged. For example, a global fashion retailer might leverage design expertise in France; optimize low-cost production in countries such as China, Sri Lanka, or Bangladesh; and source its fabric inputs in India.[9] Each activity along the value chain has to be matched with locations that offer the best combination of comparative advantages that can be translated into competitive advantage in global markets. This does not automatically imply that all value-chain activities must be globally dispersed. However, it does suggest that organizations carefully analyze each value-building activity and the impact of location on cost and competitive advantages associated with that activity. Within this broad context of tapping location-specific advantages, organizations often have a wide range of strategic options that they can pursue (in the book's introduction we used the example of Brillian, the American company developing televisions, to illustrate a global value chain). Firms may decide to locate complete value chains in each country in which they do business, or disaggregate their value activities and operate in specific locations that offer comparative advantages. Thus, much of the traditional literature argues that the very essence of available strategic options is a choice between (a) *adaptation* of value chains on a country-by-country basis, and (b) *aggregation* of value activities in the home country so as to leverage benefits such as economies of scale and scope.

Aggregation Approaches

Within the context of the "standardize versus localize" debate, scholars have presented a bipolar world within which firms formulate and implement strategies to corner foreign markets. The aggregation view is exemplified by Ted Levitt, who synthesized the core arguments that favored standardization of products and services across the globe. Levitt observed, "Everywhere everything gets more and more like everything else as the world's preference structure is relentlessly homogenized."[10] This homogenization of consumer preferences, he argued, was the opening of the door that organizations around the world would be well advised to enter. Absent any salient local variations in need or consumer choice, it is possible for manufacturers to produce products in scale-efficient plants, distribute them around the global marketplace, and reap the benefits of scale-related cost benefits that would follow. This relentless pursuit of scale efficiency and cultural homogenization is the centerpiece of the aggregation strategy.

Levitt and others presented anecdotal evidence of convergence in consumer tastes across world markets. They believed that every so-called unique local-market niche does indeed have global equivalents, and it is possible to formulate strategies to serve common segments that are independent of geography, local tastes, and traditions. At its most general level, the argument for aggregation rests on the notion of the convergence of commonalities in aspirations of people everywhere. This convergence, Levitt wrote, originated in the advantages of the technological advances that created mass media. "It has proletarianized communication, transport, travel. It has made isolated places and impoverished peoples eager for modernity's allurements. Almost everyone everywhere wants all the things that they have heard about, seen, or experienced via the new technologies."[11]

A standardized approach may be feasible if there is a fortuitous mix of supporting elements beyond the assumed convergence of aspirations and desires among consumer populations. This mix would include:

1. Relatively low trade barriers
2. A favorable bulk-to-value (or weight-to-value) equation to ensure that logistics costs are not uneconomical
3. Product and services that are built on core technologies that demonstrate significant benefits associated with large-scale production
4. A customer population that demands very little if any customization

Thus, the interplay of industry characteristics at the global level and product/service characteristics at the organizational level are important determinants of the success potential for an aggregation strategy.

Industry characteristics that favor a standardization approach usually center on the beneficial relationships between economies of scale and economies of scope. Industries that exhibit higher levels of capital intensity usually reflect a higher incidence of scale economies than those that are less capital intensive. Along similar lines, mass manufacturing technologies lend themselves to leveraging economies-of-scale benefits compared to either batch or custom modes of production. Thus, global industries such as automobiles, fine chemicals, petrochemicals, and steel are very sensitive to volumes of throughput. Settings such as these usually have ideal characteristics for implementing aggregation strategies, provided the barriers to cross-border trade are absent or relatively insignificant.

An example that fits a standardization approach is the watch industry. (See the following case study, which describes how the watch industry has evolved over the past few centuries.) The geographic power base for the large players has shifted multiple times as technological and marketing innovations have provided companies with new opportunities to exploit worldwide demand for a product with the following attributes: a common global standard in timekeeping (i.e., 24 hours, 60 minutes, and 60 seconds), a high value-to-weight ratio, large scale economies in manufacturing, and relatively few trade barriers.

CASE STUDY: THE WATCH INDUSTRY

It's hard to imagine functioning in today's world without a watch. The total number of watches produced globally in 2002 was 1.245 billion units. Besides telling time, watches serve as status symbols and fashion accessories. Prices range from almost free to outrageous, making timepieces available, if not essential, to almost everyone in the world. But while the watch's main function of telling time has not changed over the past 500 years, the worldwide watch industry has. The center has shifted among three different continents, and while Switzerland, Japan, Hong Kong, and the United States are the industry leaders today, there is no guarantee they will remain on top tomorrow.[12]

The world's oldest known watches were made around 1500 in Germany. From Germany, the craft of watchmaking quickly spread into France and Switzerland. By the late 1500s, the French were leading the European watchmakers in design and innovation. Over the next century many French and German Protestant Huguenots, fleeing religious persecution, moved to England and Switzerland, taking their watchmaking expertise with them. The city of Geneva, where Protestants had driven out Catholic religious authorities in 1535, provided a haven for many of the refugees and evolved into the center for the high-end watch industry, which continues hundreds of years later (i.e., a cluster of producers, suppliers, supporting firms, educational institutes, and so on).

The Swiss established their first full-fledged, mechanized watch factory in 1839 and the process quickly allowed Swiss watchmakers to overtake their English counterparts. By mid-century, Swiss exports were estimated at about a half-million watches a year. By the end of the 19th century, American watchmakers had become serious competitors. But the Swiss industry embraced the American factory method of production and also began producing its own sophisticated machine tools. By the 1920s, watchmaking had become one of the most important and lucrative Swiss industries.

In 1967, the first quartz wristwatch was introduced and would radically disrupt the global watch industry. Unfortunately for various producers, including the American companies Timex and Bulova, the importance of quartz technology was not realized until some years later. Digital watches had gained in popularity so quickly that the trend caught many watchmakers by surprise. At Timex, *Fortune* magazine reported that "there was flat panic!"[13] In 1981, the company announced that it would reduce the percentage of mechanical watches it produced from 90 percent to 30 percent within a five-year period.

Japanese producers were the first to seize the opportunity in quartz watches. Two companies in particular became global giants: Seiko and Citizen. Seiko was founded in 1881 and in 1913 began exporting timepieces to China. Citizen was incorporated in 1930 and emerged as Seiko's main competitor in both Japan and the broader Asian market. By 1936, Japan's total watch and clock production had reached 3.54 million units annually and Seiko was marketing more than half of them. By 1965, Citizen and Seiko accounted for about 80 percent of total watch production in Japan. In the early 1960s, Seiko entered the U.S. market and soon was producing watches for five of the largest American watch companies; the company also entered the mid-range U.S. watch market directly in 1966, granting 23 distributors exclusive rights to market its Seiko watches in America. In 1960, exports accounted for about one-fifth of Seiko's total sales. By 1967, exports made up 45 percent of total sales and the United States had surpassed Asia as the company's major export market.[14]

In the late 1950s, Hong Kong firms began making inexpensive watch components. Into the 1990s, Hong Kong and Japan took turns as the top watch exporter in the world. Japan eclipsed Switzerland as the number one watch producer (by volume) in 1979 and the two jostled for the top position until 1983, when Hong Kong took the lead (though Japan retained a higher sales volume in monetary terms). Over the next decade, the watch industry became one of the top four industries in Hong Kong. In the mid-1990s more than 600 watchmakers belonged to the Hong Kong Watch Manufacturer's Association.

In 1960, Switzerland was exporting about $418 million in watches annually. However, by the end of the 1970s, the Swiss share of the world market (by volume) had plummeted from 43 percent to 15 percent, and the number of exports had been slashed in half.[15] In 1970, there were 1,620 Swiss watch companies employing 89,000 people. In 1985, the number of companies had shrunk to just 600, and the workforce had been slashed by two-thirds as well, to about 32,500 employees.[16] By the end of the 1980s, the Swiss watch industry was on its way to recovery, thanks in large part to the success of the Swatch brand. Swatch was a cheap, colorful plastic watch that represented a radical innovation for the Swiss industry. The Swatch style, shape, and size were unique for its price range. The Swatch was thinner than most of the traditional analog watches produced in Switzerland. SMH, the company that developed Swatch (now called Swatch Group), slimmed down the Swatch by cutting the watch movement's components to 51 (compared to as many as 150 in other watches on the market). In 1992, production costs for the Swatch were estimated at just seven Swiss francs per unit—largely as a result of the automated production process. The watch was shock-resistant and water-resistant (up to 100 feet below the surface). The company marketed the trendy synthetic watches to young consumers with the idea that as they grew older they would upgrade their watches to higher-end SMH brands like Omega, Blancpain, or Longines.

Localization or Standardization?

Localization approaches center on the potential for customizing offerings to address local market variations. Such variations range from differences in customer needs and tastes to dissimilarities in local technology. Typically, these local markets are lucrative enough for the firm to forgo the benefits of scale economies and still remain profitable on the basis of customized adaptation. These markets are often the product of distinct differences in local cultures and traditions; however, they can just as easily be created by protective local regulations. For example, much of the electrical distribution industry segment that targets power transmission within commercial and residential buildings is highly local. Most countries have local codes that are unique and, hence, defy any attempt to standardize. Thus, it is almost impossible for a standardized approach in the electrical distribution sector.

   In essence, industry-specific and market-specific characteristics determine the viability of standardized or localized approaches. Although these forces are likely to impact all firms within a specific industry or market context along similar lines, individual organizations may choose to respond differently to these competing pressures. Each approach to reconcile these contradictory forces (the desire for cost efficiency through economies of scale and the demands for customization) can be seen as a product of both industry and market factors, as well as the unique blend of internal competencies that a specific organization can bring to bear. For example, the global automotive industry reflects equally strong pressures to both localize and standardize (see figure 2.2). Manufacturers must rein in costs while at the same time managing the pressure from buyers to customize their offerings to suit local conditions. Environmental and safety regulations vary from country to country, as do road conditions, driving laws, climate, gasoline taxes, and other factors that impact automobile design. This means a range of smaller, aesthetically pleasing, and more fuel-efficient

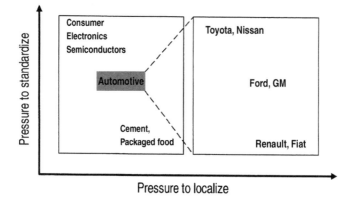

Figure 2.2. The conflicting pressures. Source: Based on C. K. Prahalad and Yves Doz, *The Multinational Mission: Balancing Local Demands and Global Vision* (New York: Free Press, 1987).

cars in parts of Western Europe; more powerful automobiles with automatic transmissions in markets such as the United States and Canada; and a more standardized bare-bones offering in emerging markets in Asia. Automakers have to reconcile these different demands with their own drive to maximize efficiency and productivity to keep margins comfortable, especially in the face of pricing pressures from competitors. Thus, some manufacturers, such as Fiat, have responded with a small range of cars customized to local markets, typically in Eastern European countries where the company historically enjoyed privileged access when many of those countries had centrally planned economies. Fiat learned to navigate the complex system of central planning and governmental subsidies in return for assured markets that were fairly small but unique. (Unfortunately for Fiat, the fall of communist governments and the opening of Eastern European markets have eroded Fiat's advantages in these markets.) Nissan, Toyota, and Honda, on the other hand, emerged as volume players that focused on reaping efficiency gains by leveraging scale economies in significant areas of their value chains, such as design, procurement, and manufacturing. The large Japanese automakers offer standardized products that allow for some local customization within broad constraints dictated by platform designs that promote cost effectiveness. Thus, although the pressures to localize or standardize are usually felt industry-wide, it does not necessarily imply a cookie-cutter approach to competition. Individual organizations do indeed exercise their choice in designing and executing their unique strategies to address these pressures.

CASE STUDY: COMPETITIVE CHOICES IN THE CONSUMER ELECTRONICS INDUSTRY

The global consumer electronics industry is currently characterized by strong pressures to standardize offerings across the board as a means of realizing important cost savings.[17] Most of the large multinational companies in this market, such as Sony and Samsung, have been using cost advantage as a key weapon in their drive to dominance. Technological innovation and the ability to commercialize new product technologies are equally strong factors at play. Thus, most players find themselves confronting a market that demands a consistent flow of new and improved products at relatively low prices.

The transformation of this industry is reflected in the dramatic upheavals that archrivals Philips of the Netherlands and Matsushita of Japan have faced. Philips, given its small home market, set its sights on internationalization fairly early. In post–World War II Europe, this meant responding to the strong pressures favoring localization. Cross-border trade flows were considerably hampered by tariff barriers and customer tastes were far from convergent. Even standardized products such as television sets were customized to fit local tastes in cabinet design and aesthetics. This gave rise to Philips's subsidiaries, called National Organizations (NOs), which were autonomous profit centers controlling assets, R&D, and local product strategy. There was little effort to create strategy from headquarters because Philips saw its empire as comprising distinctly different country markets; thus, the NOs behaved like national companies in each country. This approach to strategy paid rich dividends for Philips for much of its formative years in the global arena. It was in the late 1960s that the winds of change started to cause concern at Philips.

The 1960s marked the coming of age for Japanese manufacturers in consumer electronics. Championed by Matsushita, Japanese manufacturers relied on cost-structure advantages originating in Japan and designed centralized manufacturing facilities that were capable of capturing significant scale economies. By then, consumer tastes were also converging and there were significant opportunities to build products around common standards that could be adopted worldwide. Matsushita used a fast-follower strategy in technology combined with centralized control of production and procurement functions to grow its share of the global market. The company implemented standardized policies and procedures at the divisional level to promote the ability of headquarters to implement global strategy mandates. These moves resulted in Matsushita's creating a tremendous cost advantage over Philips.

Philips realized the immense magnitude of changes that it would have to adopt to compete against its Japanese rivals. The company tried to change from its decentralized localization approach to a more headquarters-driven centralized approach. This process of change proved to be monumental. It took over three decades and six CEOs to complete. During this period of strategic upheaval at Philips, the fortunes of Matsushita also started to change. Its centralized system of manufacturing was laid bare by the appreciating Japanese yen in the early 1980s. Combined with the threat of local tariffs and the demands for local content voiced by several host-country governments, Matsushita started to restructure its operations as well. It was on a path that sought to transform the company from a centralized structure, where headquarters had the final say on almost all issues, to one of decentralized responsibilities, where divisions would be given more responsibilities to jump-start innovation and creativity at the local level. These changes proved to be equally challenging to implement and took just as long as the changes at Philips. It seemed that both these rivals were looking to mimic one another.

Currently, both companies have taken a more pragmatic view of their strategic choices, shunning both the pure standardization and the localization approaches. They have begun to see value in blending the benefits of both standardization and localization at the same time on a function-by-function basis. In addition, the emergence of Samsung and LG as world-class electronics firms means that the competitive rivalry is even more intense, leaving little room for mistakes by Matsushita and Philips. With the likelihood that Chinese firms will eventually develop a global presence in the electronics industry, the battle between Matsushita and Philips will be only a piece of a much bigger global war.

Configuration, Coordination, and the Design of Strategy

Industry-level forces that create pressures to standardize or localize products play a key role in determining the broad contours of firm-specific strategy in the global arena. These influences are reflected in a wide range of strategic decisions spanning aspects such as location choices, coordination mechanisms that help bridge the divide between headquarters and local subsidiaries, and the specific approach to technology and innovation.

Building on the value-chain framework, Porter argued that one of the most fundamental choices facing organizations that compete internationally is determining the manner in which the firm spreads its value functions across countries (*configuration*) and the mechanisms it deploys to ensure that the far-flung subsidiaries of its global network can be orchestrated to help realize organizational goals (*coordination*).[18] While some activities such as marketing, sales, distribution, and after-sales service lend themselves to a dispersed configuration approach, other activities might benefit more from a concentrated approach. Thus, an automobile manufacturer such as Toyota might choose to locate marketing, sales, and service functions inside each market country and to centralize most of the manufacturing and procurement functions in Japan in order to leverage scale and scope economies. The broad configuration choices reflect the dominant dimensions along which global competition is shaped within an industry. For example, industries in which competitors focus on downstream (i.e., close to the customer) functions to distinguish themselves tend to exhibit more locally oriented subsidiaries. This approach calls for customization of strategy on a country-by-country basis. In industries where firms compete on the basis of efficiency and cost advantage in upstream functions, global players tend to rely on variations of global strategies. This requires that the organization optimize its upstream functions on a global rather than local basis. Thus, sources of location-specific competitive advantage, industry patterns in competitive advantage sources, and firm-specific competencies collectively impact configuration choices.

Logitech, the computer peripherals manufacturer, has located its manufacturing headquarters in Taiwan. This allows the company to take advantage of low manufacturing costs in Asia and harness the manufacturing skills that Taiwanese firms have developed as key producers of electronics components. Logitech's business development headquarters is located in Western Europe, primarily to capture the benefits of strategic alliances established to support the design of peripherals and the development of new data input devices such as optical pens. Many of the alliance partners provide the field of superior design aesthetics that Western Europe has long dominated. Taken together, these configuration choices show how Logitech clearly leverages multiple sources of comparative advantage to build its own competitive edge in a marketplace characterized by intense global rivalries.[19] Along similar lines, many of India's emerging MNEs in information technology have anchored their production operations in Indian cities such as Bangalore, Hyderabad, and Chennai, where they have huge cost advantages in technically qualified manpower (we discuss knowledge resources and emerging markets in chapter 6). However, much of their business development functions are run from offices in the United States, which continue to capitalize on that region's leadership in software design and business process engineering. By tapping into the sources of comparative advantage across both locations, the Indian MNEs can craft viable strategies.

Factors Influencing Configuration Choices

There are various factors that influence configuration choices. These include:

- The ability to leverage sources of country-specific competitive advantage
- The emphasis of industry-level performance drivers (e.g., upstream vs. downstream)
- Competitive parity considerations vis-à-vis dominant competitors
- Cost versus benefit considerations (e.g., logistics costs, factor costs, co-location benefits)
- Transfer pricing and taxation considerations
- Regulatory and trade constraints that help or hinder the free flow of goods and services
- Firm-specific sources of competitive advantage

Coordination

Coordination refers to the manner in which the disparate activities that an organization performs worldwide are managed. In some settings, organizations might benefit from intensive coordination across functions dispersed around the world; for example, coordinating brand-building activities is an integral part of leveraging the benefits of a global brand. Similarly, knowledge developed in isolated pockets can be arbitraged by building cross-functional and cross-border networks that facilitate knowledge flows to areas where benefits may be maximized (this issue is discussed in detail in chapter 5). In the pharmaceutical industry, for instance, it is common for firms to establish formal coordination mechanisms such as joint committees, task forces, or specialized organization structures to orchestrate R&D efforts across multiple locations. Procter & Gamble's best-seller Liquid Tide laundry detergent was created through such cross-border integration of research activities. The cleaning agents were developed by its researchers in Japan, the chemicals that help counteract the damaging effects of hard water came from scientists in Belgium, and the ingredients that help release dirt from the fabric were developed by company scientists in Cincinnati. Each one of these constituent technologies was developed specifically in response to local market conditions such as the hardness of water in Belgium and the dominant use of cold water by Japanese consumers for washing laundry. Thus, through its coordinated efforts, Procter & Gamble was able to build bridges between discrete pieces of knowledge within its network in order to synthesize a blockbuster offering that would not have been possible otherwise.

Close coordination may also be effective in responding to major shifts in location-specific advantages. In an optimally configured network, where each location decision is based on the existence of local advantages, shifts in the availability of such benefits could upset the network equilibrium. Therefore, the ability to shift functions and activities across nodes in the network is valuable. Flexibility to dynamically address changes in underlying sources of location-specific advantage originates by tightly coordinating activities across such locations. Thus, manufacturers can attempt to smooth out fluctuations in exchange rates and input and process costs by incrementally shifting functions to the most optimal locations. The flexibility that comes from a well-coordinated network can be an important weapon in global competition. It offers a firm the opportunity to react differentially to multiple competitors on a country-by-country basis, while at the same time retaining the possibility of coordinated action should it confront a globally connected competitor.

Close coordination can also help firms in building downstream advantages in functions such as marketing. Creation of global brands depends on an organization's ability to tailor messages at the local level while keeping the brand image intact on the global level. To capitalize on local preferences, McDonald's has many country-specific products, such as durian milkshakes in Singapore (durians are a tropical fruit with a particularly pungent odor; in the Singapore subway system there are signs that say "no durians allowed"). Luxury retail houses such as Hermès and Bulgari, which compete in multiple product lines ranging from perfumes and clothing to leather and accessories, closely coordinate brand imagery and positioning across their multiple product divisions. Within product divisions, such coordination is routine at the country level to help maintain the integrity of the brand across markets. Retailers in traditionally localized markets such as food resort to close coordination as a means of maintaining consistency of customer experience across markets. For example, Starbucks, the global coffee chain, ensures that its brand positioning, pricing, store décor, and basic offerings are consistent in all markets. This requires that the strategic decisions relating to these aspects be channeled through the headquarters operation in Seattle. In the cereal industry, one of the more global food categories, Kellogg's has built a powerful global position centered on few brands such as Frosted Flakes and Corn Flakes. Nestlé had a stable of local brands that were really not viable and, as a result, is now a partner with General Mills, with legitimate global cereal brands.

While the benefits of coordinated activities across functions and countries can yield promising results, the costs of intensive coordination can also be significant. These costs encompass a wide range of transactions costs that are often exacerbated by the need to address multiple cultures, languages, business systems, government regulations, time zones, and work ethic. Getting far-flung subsidiaries to cooperate with headquarters in sharing information and resources is a challenging task in itself. Given differences in subsidiary goals and performance metrics, it is a daunting task to direct subsidiaries to work toward common interests at the organizational level. Further, if local markets are indeed different in substantial ways, coordination of efforts across locations might not provide tangible benefits. Having to tailor one's offerings to suit the needs of each market, position the same brand differently in each market to be consistent with important local needs, and customize production operations to suit the legal and regulatory constraints of a given location are all Instances where a loosely coordinated system might be more appropriate than a closely coordinated system.

In the following case we look at Trend Micro, a company that represents a new breed of MNE. Trend Micro operates globally without a real headquarters. In many respects, it represents the ideal of a global firm that can balance global integration and national responsiveness.

CASE STUDY: TREND MICRO—CONFIGURATION AND COORDINATION CHOICES IN THE ANTIVIRUS INDUSTRY

Trend Micro, a software company that focuses on antivirus products, exemplifies some of the crucial benefits of a dispersed configuration blended with tight coordination.[20] The company, founded in 1988 by Steve Chang, a Taiwanese entrepreneur, has consistently beaten global heavyweights such as Norton and Symantec when it comes to responding quickly to virus outbreaks. It is currently a market leader in e-mail and Internet-based antivirus software. A key factor in the company's success is the manner in which it has approached configuration and coordination in crafting its strategy. Trend Micro has spread its management and technical talent across the world without a traditional headquarters operation, although it does maintain a nominal headquarters in Japan where the company's shares are listed. A listing in Tokyo helped ensure that Trend Micro would get far more attention than it would through a NASDAQ listing, where it would be just one of many such companies. The company's main virus response center is in the Philippines, a location that offers an attractive mix of low cost and good technical talent willing to put in long hours. The Philippines operation is complemented by six laboratories, spanning locations as diverse as Munich and Tokyo, that can be called into action depending on the source of the virus outbreak and the technical competency of the specific center. Steve Chang believes that the focus of the antivirus industry is decidedly global. "With the Internet, viruses became global. To fight them, we had to become a global company," he says.[21] Consequently, the organization of Trend Micro's global network reflects the realities of doing business in the industry it has chosen. While much of the financial strategy is crafted from Tokyo, product development is centered in Taiwan, where computer science Ph.D.s are plentiful. Sales and marketing operations are run from Silicon Valley to gain a foothold in the giant American market, which leads Internet-based technologies worldwide. Should any of these geographic centers wane in importance, Trend Micro would be able to retune its operations to closely mirror the changes.

Coordinating these discrete parts of the enterprise has not been easy. "The curse is that national cultures can be very different," says Chang. "We have to figure out how to convert everybody to one business culture—no matter where they're from."[22] At the outset, the company was growing organically and opportunistically, thus paying little attention to coordinating activities across units. For example, the company had multiple images in the markets it served since its advertising agencies were hired locally. It was virtually impossible to develop global strategy mandates that could be implemented by each of the units in their respective countries. So Chang launched a massive internal drive to clarify organizational culture and help promote corporate values at the subsidiary level. He insisted on recruiting the best talent independent of nationality and he built a core of multicultural managers who understood the implications of globalization in their business. He moved to hold periodic meetings in different parts of the world so that managers from the far-flung regions would gain better exposure to markets, technologies, and best practices in the host country. These efforts have helped globalize the company's thought process as well as it products and services. All these efforts have paid off for Trend Micro. The company now functions as a more integrated organization that not only helps further global mandates but also makes sure that local initiatives and best practices are equally valued and protected. In sum, Trend Micro has learned to make local knowledge global.

The Influence of Culture on Strategy

Earlier we referred to the prevalent belief in the 1980s that in a globalizing world, standardization of products and brands would rapidly accelerate, leading to true global brands that could be exploited through enormous economies of scale, common packaging and advertising, and so on. While globalization continues unabated, new ideas about the role of culture are raising questions about the inevitability of global brand and global product dominance. The influential culture scholar Geert

Hofstede argues that culture is more important to international business than ever before.[23] He also argues that the strategy process must acknowledge and incorporate the critical and persistent dimensions of culture. Hofstede cites the work of Dutch marketing expert Marieke de Mooij, who has shown that buying and consumption patterns in affluent countries in the 1980s and 1990s diverged as much as they converged.[24] The argument supporting these data is that affluence creates more possibilities to choose among goods and services and, rather than leading to fewer global brands, affluence leads to greater diversity and a desire for culture-bound variations of products and services found in other countries. The advertising and marketing that support these choices must appeal to a mind that is resistant to simple notions of globalization.

What the previous discussion suggests is that rather than global strategy choices becoming easier in an increasingly affluent world, they will become more complex. Standardization, especially for consumer products, may be something quite elusive and perhaps the stuff of armchair theory only. In reality, firms must incorporate elements of culture in all their global decisions because ultimately those decisions will impact people, and culture and people are inseparable. Take the case of Enron going into India with its Dabhol power plant project (discussed in more detail in chapter 7). The project suffered setbacks and despite an investment of more than $2 billion was eventually shut down (creditors are now seeking to restart the project). Enron faced a raft of accusations from the local press, local governments, and the general population. It was accused, among other things, of bribery, environmental destruction, overcharging for electricity, and improperly linking a gas project in Qatar to the Dabhol project. While some of the accusations were baseless, Enron's failure to understand the local culture played a key role in the company's misfortunes. The electricity industry is highly politicized in India and for much of the population, the electricity itself is viewed as an entitlement. What this means is that many people believe electricity should be very cheap (and free in some cases) and should not be produced for a profit by a non-Indian company. As the Dabhol project unfolded, numerous questions were raised about Enron's motives, return on investment, and commitment to India. Enron bungled its response, generating even greater enmity. "Throw Enron in the Arabian Sea" became a political slogan. Enron never really recovered. Had Enron invested in trying to understand the local culture, many of these issues may have been manageable.

To avoid being surprised when local market and customers reject their products, MNEs must strive to adopt a strategy-creation process that involves cultural assessment. It is not enough to view national responsiveness as tailoring products to local markets. National responsiveness means a deep understanding of the social, political, and cultural values present in a local market, the values connected to goods and services sold in that market, the uniqueness of the local market, and the linkages between strategic decisions and their impact on cultural norms. In Enron's case, the strategic decision to enter India was highly offensive to many Indians.

Among the companies that successfully manage cultural minefields is Mattel, the American toy manufacturer. Since toys fill different needs in different countries, Mattel has had to adapt its marketing strategies to those needs. For example, in some Asian countries, toys are viewed as frivolous and a distraction for children who should be learning and studying. Nevertheless, Mattel has been able to make inroads in countries such as Taiwan by understanding and working within the local culture.

Conclusion

In summary, configuration and coordination choices lie at the heart of global strategic decision making. These choices are influenced by a host of factors, some of which lie outside the domain of immediate influence by an individual firm. Although many of these exogenous factors are common to all firms operating within the same product market context, individual organizations can choose to respond in ways that are uniquely different. Firms can tailor their strategies to address these common external pressures while at the same time leveraging the firm-specific internal strengths and competencies that they possess. Each organization makes these important choices activity by activity and country by country to create the strategic variety that global industries reflect today.

3

Global Strategy and Organization

In the previous chapter we discussed the conflicting environmental pressures for local responsiveness and for global integration. Managing these conflicting pressures means designing an organization that can balance decision-making and resource-allocation processes against the interests of managers, the needs of customers and suppliers, and the political pressures that shape the MNE competitive environment. In this chapter we continue the discussion of strategy choice started in chapter 2. We focus on the organizational demands of global strategies, with an emphasis on MNE structural choices and integrating mechanisms.

MNE Organizational Structures

The basic models of MNE structures developed over the past few decades remain relevant today, although the complexity and sophistication of today's structures continue to evolve.[1] The following case study on Sesame Workshop provides an example of the variety of organizational options available to MNEs. Like many new MNEs, the structure first used for international expansion at Sesame Workshop was an international division that coordinated sales and marketing activities outside the United States. Sesame Workshop's international division was charged with the responsibility of overseeing *Sesame Street*'s licensing abroad. The international division structure has long been used by U.S. firms that move beyond exporting and seek a more significant presence in international markets while recognizing that domestic operations are the main priority for the firm. In the Sesame Workshop case, a reorganization in 1996 created a set of regional divisions with profit responsibility. In 1999 a new international product division was created, although the company as yet had no physical presence outside the United States.

The case illustrates that MNE organizational choices in practice are much more complex than just product versus geography decisions. The case also demonstrates that the organization and strategy for a firm are closely linked to questions such as:[2]

1. What products should be globalized?
2. What markets should be chosen?
3. What mode of entry should be used—export versus alliance versus locally owned unit?
4. How will corporate culture and values be transplanted?
5. How will the firm win local battles against firms with similar products and services?
6. What type of presence is required in local markets and what role will subsidiaries play in MNE strategy creation?

CASE STUDY: MNE ORGANIZATIONAL OPTIONS AND SESAME WORKSHOP

Sesame Workshop, a not-for-profit company based in New York City, is the producer of *Sesame Street*, the highly acclaimed children's educational show.[3] Since its American debut more than 30 years ago, *Sesame Street* has achieved great success in many other countries. In virtually every country where it is has been introduced, *Sesame Street*, or a locally produced version of the show, has become an immediate success. In 2004 the show was broadcast in 120 countries, making Sesame Workshop the largest single teacher of young children in the world. The show was coproduced in the local language in about 20 countries with local actors, writers, musicians, animation, and sets. (Coproduction was a development model in which Sesame Workshop worked with local coproducers, usually a local broadcaster, to develop a new *Sesame Street* program.) In the other countries, the broadcasted show was either the English-language American version or the American version with some segments dubbed in the local language.

Sesame Workshop (originally Children's Television Workshop) was founded in 1968. In 1969 Sesame Workshop created an international division with responsibility for overseeing *Sesame Street*'s licensing abroad. Until 1992, three separate international sales forces were used for the English-language show, coproductions, and product licensing. In 1992, the international television sales group was created to eliminate the problem of having different sales forces targeting the same broadcasters. Also in 1992, markets and customers were categorized as follows:

1. Current customers
2. Broadcasters that had shown a real interest in televising *Sesame Street* (for these potential customers, funding issues were a major element in continuing discussions; about $5–8 million was necessary for a coproduction of 130 half hours of programming that could be used for 2–3 years)
3. Countries that had been in coproduction and had stopped producing, such as Brazil and France
4. Countries that Sesame Workshop would like to enter but where few, if any, established relationships existed

Market-entry decisions through coproduction typically were initiated by a broadcaster that had seen the English version of *Sesame Street* and wanted the show for its country. Various issues would then be considered by Sesame Workshop: (a) What is the level of television penetration? (b) Does Sesame Workshop have a relationship at the government level and if not, can a relationship be established? (c) Does the market have financial viability—that is, is it at least a break-even proposition? (d) Does Sesame Workshop have people available to develop the show? (e) Are Sesame Workshop's license and publisher partners Mattel and Random House established in that market?

Initially, coproductions were funded entirely by local broadcasters. Assuming a decision was made to move forward and a contract was signed with a broadcaster, a coproduction could take from a year to four or more years to produce. During this phase, Sesame Workshop would work with the product partners to develop a product strategy, which would follow the launch of the television show once the brand was established.

1996 Reorganization

A reorganization of international operations in 1996 resulted in a new structure headed by a group president for products and international television. A group vice president for international and two regional vice president positions were created: one for Latin America and Asia and one for Europe, Africa, and the Middle East. There was also a vice president for coproduction. Each regional vice president had profit and return-on-investment responsibility for all Sesame Workshop business. For each region there were regional directors responsible for television and licensing. Given the size and complexity of the China activities, there was also a senior director responsible for the television activities in China. The reorganization resulted in a revised classification of markets and countries. Non-U.S. markets in which Sesame Workshop either broadcast or planned to broadcast could be broken down as follows:

1. Large growth potential markets in which Sesame Workshop had strong recognition—for example, the United Kingdom, Germany, and Japan
2. High-potential markets that could generate more revenue—for example, China and Mexico
3. Maintenance markets: smaller markets that were currently generating revenue but had limited growth potential—for example, Australia, Canada, and the Netherlands
4. Social impact markets—for example, Israel/Palestine and South Africa

The reorganization of international activities resulted in a decision to reduce the managerial time spent on smaller markets and focus on the larger markets with high potential. However, selling the English version of *Sesame Street* or doing a coproduction required roughly the same amount of effort regardless of the market size. Additionally, many of the smaller markets were some of Sesame Workshop's oldest customers, which raised the issue of whether relationships with smaller customers should be scaled back. Within Sesame Workshop the obvious answer was no, but there was consensus that priority markets had to be established. And some market entry decisions did not fit neatly into this model. For example, after the successful launch in Russia, the U.S. Agency for International Development (USAID) asked Sesame Workshop to consider Egypt, which was not initially considered a high-potential market.

1999 Changes at Sesame Workshop

In 1999 a new international division was created to manage projects that involved governments and nongovernmental organizations (NGOs), such as in South Africa, Egypt, and Israel. This division, called Project Management, consisted of four directors and focused on issues such as educational outreach, fund-raising, and government contacts. These projects had limited product licensing opportunities. With the creation of this new division, the products and international television group, which consisted of 16 people, concentrated on developing markets in which both a product license and television businesses could be supported. However, there were close linkages between the groups, as a Sesame Workshop executive explained: "Every market we are in is mission—there is no market where Sesame Street is not reaching and teaching kids. When we go to meetings, we don't say 'how will we make the most money?' We say 'how will we reach the most kids?' This is a concept that is very comfortable to everybody."

In 2001 Sesame Workshop had no offices outside the United States. Agents were used to manage day-to-day business relationships in international markets. The firm began shifting away from having different agents in each country. Sesame Street now had one agent for all of Europe, which helped streamline decision making. The same approach was being implemented in Latin America. Sesame Workshop was considering how to more effectively use alliances to support marketing and advertising while still maintaining control over the brand and program content. Sesame Workshop was also evaluating the pros and cons of establishing subsidiaries in major market countries rather than relying on local agents and extensive travel by employees based in New York.

Patterns in Global Strategy, Organization, and Structure

Research on the structure and organization of MNEs has coalesced around two typical patterns of choices. The choices correspond to the national responsiveness or localization imperative and the global integration or standardization imperative, respectively. The multinational organization, also referred to as multidomestic, typifies organizations that plan and execute strategy on a country-by-country basis. There are few, if any, overlaps or linkages across country markets. Knowledge developed at the local level stays within the subsidiary. On the other hand, the global organization calls for centralized planning and decentralized execution. Organizations adopting this approach usually centralize core functions such as research and development and strategic planning in the home country and rely on subsidiaries in individual country markets to perform downstream functions such as marketing, after-sales service, and, increasingly, manufacturing. In relative terms, there is very little room for the articulation of country-specific strategies in such organizations. Note that the multinational and global approaches are two ends of a spectrum and most MNEs are rarely positioned on the extreme ends.

Multinational Organization

The appeal of a multinational strategy lies in its ability to carefully customize a set of value propositions that match the unique demands of a country-specific market. Typically, this calls for localizing all or most of the value-adding activities in each of the countries where the firm operates (see figure 3.1). Under a

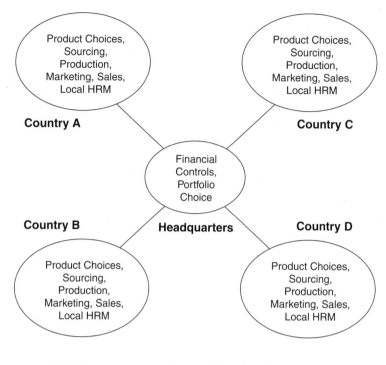

Figure 3.1. Multinational or multidomestic business. HRM = human resource management.

multinational approach, country managers have a significant role in determining the strategic positioning and marketing approaches that they will use. Typically, headquarters has very limited influence in articulating a global mandate of strategic proportions that would be followed by all the country subsidiaries. This approach also limits the ability of individual country operations to benefit from scale efficiencies since the local markets are invariably small and cannot generate enough volume to drive economies of scale. Thus, the multinational strategy represents a trade-off between flexibility and local customization against the potential for reaping scale benefits and other operational synergies.

Fiat, the Italian auto manufacturer, championed the use of a multinational approach several decades ago. Although the automotive industry is a textbook example of a scale-sensitive industry, Fiat was able to operate small-scale plants because it chose to locate in countries where there was limited competition or where country governments offered subsidies to attract a company of

Fiat's stature. Fiat was operating in much of communist Eastern Europe either as a wholly owned venture or through alliances with local manufacturers. Scale benefits were not as crucial given the captive markets, limited pressure to innovate, and the patronage of local governments. Many of the packaged-food companies such as Nestlé (which sells 8,500 brands in 86 countries) and Unilever have in the past used multinational approaches successfully. Given the uniquely localized preferences for food products, these firms have had to customize their offerings on a country-by-country basis. In particularly large markets such as China and India, there might be enough critical mass even at the country level to achieve economies of scale. According to Nestlé CEO Peter Brabeck-Letmathe:

> There is not something like a global consumer in the food and beverage industry. . . . There is only the local consumer. This is fundamental to our thinking. We are saying that everything the consumer can see, touch, feel, or taste has to be local. That means that our products, our brands, and our communications will always stay local in order to stay relevant to the local consumer. On the other hand, of course, everything which the consumer does not see, taste, smell, or feel can be rationalized. It can be centralized. It can be regionalized and globalized. This is basically the balance we're trying to find. . . . The point is simple. . . . We always try to keep the consumer in the forefront of our thinking.[4]

Given the rapid strides toward globalization, the emergence of homogenized market preferences transcending country borders, and the decline in tariff and nontariff barriers, the pressures to adopt pure forms of multinational strategies have declined. For example, many firms now pursue modular product development approaches that allow them to produce localized variations of their products based on a common product platform. As Julian Birkenshaw points out, most MNEs today are moving toward some variant of the global business unit in their international operations, with a dilution of in the power and responsibilities of the country manager.[5] (We discuss this in more detail later in the chapter.) The result is that the national subsidiary with a fully integrated value chain of activities no longer exists in most developed countries. In its place we increasingly see subsidiaries playing a discrete value-chain role, such as manufacturing, R&D, or sales and marketing. In doing so it becomes feasible to harness global-scale economies while at the same time offering just enough flexibility to customize products locally. For example, many of the world's leading car manufacturers build their product range around a small set of common platforms and customize their offerings in each country as demanded by local buyers.

In general, a multinational strategy is ideal in settings where:

- Buyer preferences vary by country context where they are located (e.g., packaged food products).
- Local legislative barriers require a significant local content in the products that are sold locally or they force companies to share a heavy burden by way of customs duties and tariffs that makes importation of products from global plants uneconomic.
- It is feasible to obtain local scale economies owing to the significant size of the local market (e.g., China and India in some consumer products).
- The product does not lend itself to cost-effective shipping across long distances, thus requiring local manufacture and sale on a country-by-country basis (interestingly, innovations in shipping are starting to challenge long-held convictions, such as "furniture and cement are too heavy or bulky and low value to be shipped long distances").

Global Organization

The case for a global organization is invariably related to maximizing efficiency and capturing the benefits of scale. In scale-sensitive industries, efficiency and operations costs are typically the key drivers of competitive advantage. Combined with a context where customer preferences are relatively invariant, a global approach to organization offers firms the opportunity to maximize the benefits of standardization (see figure 3.2). A global organization allows headquarters to orchestrate competitive moves across global industries—a critical advantage in industries that are characterized by competitors seeking to optimize operations across borders. In industries such as semiconductors, software, chemicals, and increasingly even in industries offering semi-localized products, the ability to orchestrate a unified strategy across the entire network of operations is becoming increasingly important. Access to location-specific advantages coupled with globally scale efficient operations offers firms using a global organization the benefit of a superior operating cost structure. In most cases, the vital value-chain activities relating to the core competencies of an organization, such as production methods and research and design skills (although R&D may have to be distributed to capitalize on growing global markets; see the Honeywell case later in the chapter), are located within the home country. Downstream functions such as sales and marketing and after-sales service are located in the country where the customers are located. For example, Japanese automakers have long utilized the benefits of global scale in staying competitive. Many of them got a start in the global automotive business on the strength of manufacturing efficiencies created in large-scale Japanese factories. This

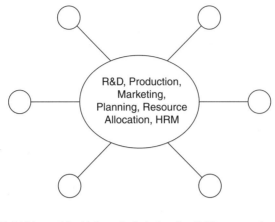

- **Tight hierarchical integrated chain of activities spanning multiple national markets**
- **Production standardized across all countries**
- **Global-scale economies stressed**
- **Country with one approach to markets irrespective of location**

Figure 3.2.   Globally integrated business.

approach seemed to work until some of the importing countries frustrated Japanese advances by either erecting nontariff barriers or requiring local content as a prerequisite for access to their markets.

A similar pattern is emerging among Indian information technology (IT) companies that have started to dominate the landscape for IT services and back-office operations (e.g., call centers, account processing). Firms including Wipro and Infosys have established large-scale operations in India for servicing client needs in areas such as software design and development, inbound and outbound call centers, helpdesk management, and payroll processing. The location allows these players to tap into the advantages of a labor pool that is technically competent while at the same time leverage the benefits of a low labor-cost structure. Thus, while much of the labor and technology-intensive processing functions are carried out in India, client servicing functions such as business analysis, project management, and performance control are carried out partially in the countries where the client is located.

In general, a global organization approach works if:

- The industry is populated by firms with the ability to leverage cross-border synergies, engage in cross-subsidization across country markets, and/or act in ways that allow them to enjoy significantly better cost structures than their local rivals.

- The industry is not subject to limiting tariff or nontariff barriers that inhibit free flow of goods and services across borders.
- It is critical to achieve economies of scale to stay cost competitive (i.e., price is an important driver of competition).
- Customer preferences across country markets are relatively invariant and minor differences across markets can be addressed at the local level without significantly reducing the opportunity to obtain scale economies.

The disadvantage of a global approach to organization is the high level of risk associated with the key country nodes where major operations are located. If disruptions occur in central operations, the entire network is debilitated. Several years ago, Toyota Motors of Japan experienced the fallout of such an event when its large supplier of brakes in Japan was forced to shut its plant due to a fire accident. This left Toyota's plants idle in Toyota City, the major manufacturing hub for the company. A global approach can also lead to increased exposure to risks that cannot easily be mitigated, such as political or economic risks. For example, fluctuations in exchange rates created an adverse condition for Japan's auto exporters when they saw the value of the yen appreciate rapidly against the dollar in the 1980s. Since the Japanese auto companies manufactured much of the product in global-scale plants in Japan, their operating costs suddenly shot up and made their exports too expensive for markets such as the United States. In addition, centralization to achieve scale invariably leads to constraints on flexibility, making it difficult for companies to respond rapidly to changes in the external marketplace, an issue examined in the case study that follows.

From a Multinational to a Global Organization

The following case study describes Warner-Lambert's (WL) transition from a country-centered firm to one with a global strategy based on a line-of-business organizational structure. The motivating factor for the organizational change was the realization that a country-based structure was becoming less efficient and was inconsistent with an increasingly global industry environment, especially in pharmaceuticals. In addition the country-based structure was becoming a limiting factor in the speed with which new products were developed and introduced.

For each of WL's three major product sectors there were conditions favoring both localization and globalization (see table 3.1). For example, the pharmaceutical sector could benefit from global R&D but had to cope with complex local regulatory issues for new drugs. The confection industry could benefit from global purchasing, standardized packaging, and manufacturing economies of scale

Table 3.1.   Globalization and Localization Conditions at Warner-Lambert

	Pharmaceuticals	Consumer Health Care	Confection
Conditions supporting globalization	Nature of the product: same chemical compounds High research and development (R&D) costs Easy to transport Diseases are global Can leverage knowledge/easy to share knowledge Competitors are becoming global Regulatory EOS Supports consumer health-care efforts (consumer health care is more advertising driven)	Consumer health-care drugs: similar arguments to pharmaceutical sector Many consumer needs are becoming global Can rationalize manufacturing Brand-oriented business Purchasing electronic ordering system (EOS) Competitors are becoming global (e.g., Colgate, Gillette, etc.) Advertising can be leveraged across countries Global trend to self-medication	Coca-Cola phenomenon—advertising and positioning can create global food/candy brands Purchasing (e.g., sugar) and manufacturing can be rationalized Global advertising can be leveraged Brand-oriented business Competitors are becoming global (e.g., Wrigley) and becoming global
Conditions supporting localization	Highly regulated on a country-by-country basis Different drug preferences across countries Marketing practices differ from country to country Industry is fragmented with many pharmaceutical firms Incidences of diseases differ across countries	Consumer health care is as much fashion as science Heavy local advertising requirements Purchasing power differs across countries Retail regulations and distribution channels vary widely (from drugstores to supermarkets to kiosks)	Confection is part of the food industry; food industry is very local Is there such a thing as a global food product? Easy for local competitors to imitate, which means fast local response ability is necessary Pricing, packaging, and distribution must be local Purchasing power differs across countries

but still had to deal with the reality that confection is food and, thus, highly local in flavor and taste preferences. In creating a global line of business structure, WL substantially reduced the power and authority of the country subsidiaries and centralized major product decisions involving branding, positioning, and packaging. The end result for WL was very positive. The company successfully introduced a range of new products on a global basis, including the pharmaceutical product Lipitor, which has become the world's best-selling drug. The organizational benefits from the changes included:

- Better coordination of product research and development
- Competition among the affiliates for global resources
- New opportunities to develop regional brands into global brands
- New opportunities to develop confections in Europe and pharmaceuticals in Latin America
- Central control over packaging, flavors, and the like for the major brands like Halls, Clorets, and Listerine
- Rationalization of manufacturing in Europe and Latin America
- Reduction in the number of international staff in New Jersey headquarters
- Increased sharing of knowledge across affiliates
- Enhanced ability to identify and leverage pockets of excellence
- Greater development and promotion opportunities for high-potential managers

Nevertheless, like every organizational change, there was substantial resistance and some legitimate complaints within WL. The latter section of the case provides some comments from a manager who saw the changes as ill conceived and designed to centralize decision making in the United States, to the detriment of the international organization. As the case demonstrates, no MNE organization design will be perfect and the conflicting pressures regarding local responsiveness and global integration will always remain, which means not everyone will be satisfied with the organizational structure.

CASE STUDY: WARNER-LAMBERT COMPANY AND GLOBALIZATION

In 1991, Warner-Lambert (again, WL; now a part of Pfizer Inc.) was organized into four major divisions reporting to the president and chief operating officer (COO): Parke-Davis Group (pharmaceuticals), American Chicle Group (confectionery), Consumer Health Products Group (over-the-counter health care), and International Operations.[6] International Operations was organized as a collection of country units headed by country managers. All four groups had their headquarters in Morris Plains, New Jersey. At that time, there was growing concern that the organization was not optimally structured to compete in an increasingly globalizing world. For example, within WL, the country managers were referred to as "kings." The primary objective of country managers was maximizing the performance of their affiliates with little regard for total organizational performance. There was very little interaction between the senior U.S. pharmaceutical, health-care, and confectionery managers and their international counterparts. In the non-U.S. affiliates, manufacturing and raw materials sourcing was largely done locally, which meant that scale manufacturing and purchasing advantages from being a global firm could not be exploited

In October 1991, WL announced that it was restructuring its worldwide operations and eliminating 2,700 jobs over the next five years. The new structure would be based on a line-of-business model with headquarters for the business lines in New Jersey. The restructuring divided WL's business into three main segments: pharmaceuticals, consumer health-care products, and confectionery. The restructuring immediately involved all of the operations in Japan, North America, and Western Europe and was planned to impact the entire company within a few years (all developed- and developing-country markets).

To implement the reorganization, plants were closed and new products were launched where previously there had been resistance to the products. For example, Listerine, one of WL's leading brands, was moved into Japan and the United Kingdom and later into Germany. In the international affiliates, the country manager position changed significantly. In the new structure, each affiliate had a line-of-business or product-sector head. For example, in France, the former country manager became the head of pharmaceuticals in France. This manager may have seen the country sales volume that (s)he controlled directly drop from 100 percent to 70 percent. A method called the host system was set up to handle the allocation of staff services (HR, finance, manufacturing, logistics, accounting). The largest product sector in the country became the host for the other product lines. The host was responsible for managing and accounting for staff services and providing staff services to the other product sectors when they needed them. Allocation of staff services across country-product sectors was based on a simple allocation method (dollars or head count). There was no attempt to allocate on the basis of time spent on the different sectors. In Canada, for example, there were "condominium rules" for how services were allocated. These were written out and negotiated and dealt with who does what, at what level, and so on.

Comments about WL's Organizational Changes

Not everyone in WL agreed with the changes. Here are some comments after the reorganization from a manager in a large European affiliate:

> The markets are so different throughout the world that globalization from an American perspective is not necessarily globalization from our perspective. In the new structure, we divided our pharmaceutical business into ethical and OTC [over-the-counter] divisions. It doesn't work here. Our OTC products used to profit from the ethical sales force and marketing support. Now OTC is on its own. In the past, 65–70 percent of our biggest selling product used to be sold through doctors' prescriptions. Now it is sold strictly as an OTC product by the OTC division. This means it no longer has support in the doctors' offices. After the first year we found that sales were about the same, even though we added 30 new salespeople who work exclusively on OTC products.
>
> The pharmaceutical business is long term. The Americans think too short term and they are not strategic enough for us. We come up with a plan here and the plan gets reversed by headquarters. The political and market risks are totally ignored. The Americans are flexible but superficial; they don't have much background knowledge. They treat the affiliates too rigidly. Everybody gets treated the same without regard to what is needed in an individual market.
>
> We have an American product manager for Listerine. He doesn't speak any local language and knows nothing about the local market or culture. The drugstore wholesalers who buy Listerine are kings; they will not speak English and the product manager can't go in with an interpreter because that would make him look bad.
>
> I agree with globalizing the development of pharmaceutical products. But, to not take advantage of the existing affiliate products that are already successful is almost criminal. We have products in our affiliate that have huge potential. I understand that resources are not unlimited but the affiliate is more experienced and better able to evaluate the local market.[7]

The Evolution of MNE Organizations

Bartlett and Ghoshal suggested that discernible patterns of strategy and structure were associated with the home countries/regions where the MNE organizations originated.[8] Many of the European multinationals, they observed, witnessed aggressive expansion into foreign markets in the 1920s and 1930s. This period in history was characterized by strife, mistrust between nations, and rising nationalism. These divisive forces gave rise to protectionist trade barriers that were erected by national governments seeking to save their own domestic industries. Thus, competing in such tariff protected fragmented markets meant that European multinationals were forced to adopt multidomestic strategies, loosely coordinating value activities across country borders. This led to a distribution of assets to national entities along with significant local strategy-making responsibilities. The far-flung subsidiaries were consequently managed more as a portfolio of investments than as a well-coordinated set of assets with a common purpose and strategy to compete in the global marketplace.

American firms launched international expansion efforts mostly in the 1940s and 1950s, although some firms such as GM had internationalized much earlier. Since America was relatively untouched by the ravages of World War II, its innovative abilities remained intact. Soon after the war, many U.S. firms were developing novel technologies that they sought to leverage in foreign markets. In establishing a presence overseas, many of them favored a coordinated federation model, a variation of the dominant European model but with far greater coordination across the subsidiaries than was attempted by the European firms. This allowed the organizations to transfer core technology and processes to subsidiaries worldwide, creating copies of the parent in each location for all intents and purposes, albeit with the absence of research and development functions. Although the subsidiaries were relatively free to adopt variations of strategies as dictated by local market conditions, their dependence on the home office for much of the technology inputs effectively limited the freedom to customize their strategy on a country-specific basis.

In contrast to the U.S. and European firms, Japanese organizations emerged as multinationals in the early 1970s on the strength of their automotive and consumer electronics industries. Given the fairly limited exposure to world markets for a considerable period of their history, organizations from Japan tended to rely more on their operations at home to venture overseas. Many of the leading Japanese MNEs adopted centralized structures with very tight control over subsidiaries. Much of the product development and manufacturing was located in Japan, where global-scale plants were set up to serve world markets. Entire cities sprung up around companies in Japan, such as Toyota

City around the nerve center of Toyota's operations. There was very little autonomy for country managers to adopt customized strategies. Given the increased importance of cost-based competitiveness in most of the global industries at the time, the centralized approach fit well with environmental demands.

The Transnational Organization

The multinational and global approaches to MNE organization represent variations on the central theme that seeks to identify an ideal balance between the competing forces favoring integration and scale efficiency and the forces that favor localization and flexibility. Each dominant form has had varying degrees of success depending on the performance drivers at the industry level and the contextual pressures at the country level. In today's context of rapid deregulation, advances in telecommunication and increases in the interconnectedness of the world's economies, many believe that none of these approaches is ideally suited to address the demands in most global industries. Based on an extensive study and analysis of some of the leading corporations across the world, Bartlett and Ghoshal suggested that a new form of organization, the transnational, was emerging as the ideal prototypical strategy to address the demands of globalization.[9] In contrast to the multinational strategy that seeks to maximize responsiveness to local demands and the global strategy that seeks to maximize scale efficiency at the cost of flexibility, the transnational approach attempts to synthesize the salient benefits of both approaches without many of the disadvantages associated with either (see figure 3.3). Leading multinationals such as Unilever, Ericsson, and Philips were identified as firms that were evolving into transnationals (as is discussed later in the chapter, it looks as if Unilever is still struggling to adapt to a global environment).

The transnational approach is characterized by (a) decentralization of assets across subsidiaries, (b) formal knowledge management structures that promote inter-subsidiary sharing of best practices and innovations that leverage centers of excellence, and (c) a blend of formal and informal relationships and mechanisms across the organizational hierarchy to leverage efficiency and flexibility simultaneously. These mechanisms include meetings, conference calls, subsidiary visits, cross-national teams, rotations and transfer of employees, and task forces that utilize inputs from across the firm.

In contrast to the headquarters-centralized approach of the global strategy architecture, or the duplicated, distributed operations of the multinational architecture, the transnational organization seeks to establish world-scale operations outside its home country based on the activity in question and the

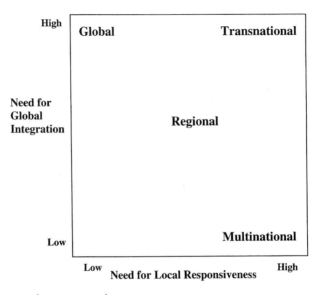

Figure 3.3.   Broad international strategy types.

location-specific advantage that the subsidiary locations offer. For example, routine manufacturing might be performed in a centralized fashion at a location that offers lower labor costs, lower input costs, or better transportation costs. Knowledge-intensive activity such as R&D might be centralized in a country with access to technical expertise, leading research institutes, and a critical mass of innovative talent (see the case study on Honeywell later in the chapter).

In this regard, the main difference between the global-strategy architecture and the transnational is that the operations are not always centralized in the home country. They are decentralized (away from home) should other locations offer benefits that outweigh the advantages of operating from the home country. The decentralization decision is based purely on dimensions such as economics and other location-specific advantages. This approach alleviates the typical limitations of the global strategy, which is an inability to respond rapidly to evolving changes in the marketplace given the centrality of headquarters. The internal communications channels in such organizations are often overloaded with requests that have to be approved by headquarters before the subsidiary is allowed to act. In the multinational strategy, many functions are duplicated at the individual-country level, leading to suboptimal resource utilization. The transnational remedies this shortcoming by having selected subsidiaries provide product or expertise on a worldwide basis to all other subsidiaries in the network. This allows the firm to build scale-efficient subsidiaries without duplication. Further, the optimal location of the subsidiary in the chosen field of activity allows that subsidiary to sense important changes as they evolve in leading-edge markets. In essence, the national subsidiary is no longer viewed as the end of the value stream, charged with delivering the final product or service to the customer. Instead, the national subsidiary is an important source of ideas, knowledge, skill sets, and resources for the entire organization.

In the transnational organization, value-chain activities may be grouped to create international production centers devoted solely to producing a product, international purchasing centers may be geared to ensure optimal sourcing decisions, and centers of excellence may operate where a specific technology, product development, or process expertise forms the central focus. This approach to the division of responsibilities, coupled with well-matched location choices, offers an ideal blend of cost and scale efficiency while at the same time ensuring that the organization is positioned to tap into the best available expertise and thinking in each of its value activities.

In contrast to the decentralized structure of a multinational or the formal centralization of a global strategy, the transnational attempts to blend both formal and informal elements to effectively address changing environmental demands. Formal knowledge flows and expertise transfers are coordinated through hierarchical links between subsidiaries. Given the notorious limitations of such formal relationships, these organizations also use dotted-line and informal relationships to create the ideal blend of flexibility and standardization. Informal relationships are built through periodic meetings between subsidiary managers and job transfers. Thus, in structural terms, the transnational organization reflects carefully managed elements of centralization, well-defined individual roles that encourage formalization, and a set of informal relationships that are encouraged by socialization.

The Strategy and Role of the MNE Subsidiary

An MNE subsidiary is any value-adding organizational unit located outside the MNE's home-country base. Although the scope and role of MNE subsidiaries are evolving away from the country organization's performing a full value chain of activities, the subsidiary remains the key implementer of MNE strategy. As we have seen, the MNE can assign various roles to its subsidiaries. from the stand-alone miniature and fully integrated versions of the parent company to a discrete value-chain activity that supports a global strategy. Subsidiaries may also compete for, and win, global product mandates within the MNE, which means that these subsidiaries become the global supplier for a particular product or service.

An important question associated with the MNE subsidiary is how the role comes about. This role can be shaped by various forces: through the initiative of the subsidiary managers, by decisions made at MNE headquarters, by external forces introduced by competitors or local governments, by the actions of other subsidiaries, and through a combination of forces. Historically, American and European subsidiary managers had a substantial degree of authority. In contrast, the typical Japanese subsidiary manager is closely tied to Japanese headquarters (hence, the name *transplant* for many Japanese manufacturing plants located outside Japan—these plants are replicas of plants in Japan and must conform to strict operational policies set in Japan). In fact, Japanese subsidiary managers typically spend an inordinate amount of time in direct communication with their Japanese headquarters.

Five reasons can be identified to explain why the traditional country-based authority and power of American and European subsidiary managers is waning:[10]

1. Global customers are emerging with demands for consistent products and services on a worldwide basis. MNEs are responding with global account-management systems that provide centralized negotiating for prices, delivery, and so on, effectively taking these decisions out of the hands of subsidiary managers. For example, WPP Group, the large advertising and communications services firm, uses global client leaders to manage a client's affairs across the various WPP entities to ensure consistency in service quality.

2. Global supply chains are being integrated (as we saw in the WL case), which means subsidiary managers may no longer be involved in purchasing and logistics decision making.

3. The Internet is injecting a level of transparency into global markets that makes it both easier and more important for MNEs to become more integrated, especially in their dealings with major customers.

4. As we have emphasized throughout this book, global industries demand global integration, and fewer and fewer companies can afford to operate in a localization mode. Even the major food industry MNEs like Unilever and Nestlé recognize that with some food products, such as ice cream, breakfast cereal, and chocolate, a globally integrated approach is strategically necessary.

5. MNE R&D organizations are under pressure to become more efficient and provide more consistent services to the MNE's primary operating and product development units.

Does Globalization Always Mean Centralization?

One of the paradoxes of globalization and its impact on MNE organizations is that while global industries may demand more integrated customer service, subsidiary managers are increasingly being exhorted to act more entrepreneurially.[11] In addition, as MNEs penetrate more markets, corporate-level or headquarters managers may lack the local market knowledge necessary to make sound strategic decisions for all activities. R&D is a case in point. In order to develop new products for customers around the world, MNEs are under pressure to make their R&D activities more responsive to local customer demands, which may mean a decentralized approach to R&D. They are also under pressure to develop products that can be sold in multiple markets. In the following case study we discuss the R&D issue by looking at Honeywell and its decision-making criteria concerning decentralized R&D. The Honeywell case study illustrates the dilemma facing all MNEs: how should the far-flung international network of subsidiaries, affiliates, alliances, and partners best be utilized in implementing the MNE strategy? Table 3.2 provides a summary of arguments for and against centralized R&D. (See work by Kuemmerle for a more detailed discussion of MNEs and R&D.[12]) Both sets of arguments are persuasive, demonstrating that rarely will MNE organizational issues be solved by using an either/or approach.

CASE STUDY: HONEYWELL R&D AND GLOBALIZATION

In the late 1990s there was a growing consensus that R&D had to become more international to support Honeywell's growth opportunities.[13] R&D was a focal point throughout Honeywell, a large diversified MNE involved in home and building controls, industrial controls, and avionics systems.[14] Technology was seen as the key to marketplace differentiation and about 30 percent of Honeywell's sales were from products introduced in the past five years.

The Honeywell Technology Center (HTC) was Honeywell's primary research organization and it supported the worldwide product divisions. HTC, based in Minneapolis, employed about 575 people, including 300 engineer/scientists. Of these 300, 100 had Ph.D.s, and 180 had bachelor's or master's degrees. With the exception of about 40 employees in Phoenix and 5 in Prague, all HTC employees were in two locations in the Minneapolis area. As a corporate service organization, HTC's mission was to support the product divisions and develop technologies that had the potential to benefit multiple product divisions. This mission was expressed as follows: "In partnership with Honeywell's businesses, we provide world-class technologies, processes, and product concepts that fuel Honeywell's global growth and profitability."

Table 3.2. Arguments for and against Centralized Research and Development (R&D)

Reasons for Centralized R&D

1. The higher the complexity of products and systems, the more important it is to locate a large team of R&D people in one location to ensure that interaction occurs among scientists.
2. A centralized R&D organization can help disseminate ideas around the world. Decentralizing R&D would jeopardize this central dissemination function.
3. When the product is a system comprising various parts, a team can be built using people from different areas. Scattering people geographically would make this difficult.
4. If R&D scientists are too far from the central labs they risk becoming obsolete, migrating from R&D to the product divisions or losing contact with central R&D.
5. If R&D is tied too closely with a local product division, there is the risk that the division will not have the long-term orientation necessary for R&D, which could lead to complacency. Or, after assuming ownership of the R&D, the division may decide that a particular technology is no longer necessary and R&D efforts could decline. A central R&D organization can ensure stability in research efforts and implement controls to keep people motivated.
6. Engineers and scientists interested in R&D prefer to work in a central R&D organization.
7. Multiple R&D sites could mean multiple R&D cultures and a lack of consistency across the R&D function.
8. It may be difficult to replicate the culture in international locations if the R&D culture is well established.

Reasons for Decentralized R&D

1. Central R&D is too far removed from the customer, particularly customers outside the primary home market. It is impossible to develop customer solutions if you do not understand customer problems. Different parts of the world should logically be the focus for problems unique to their area.
2. If the technology does not require interaction with other technologies, it may be better to have it located where the local support structure is strongest. The support could come from the product division or in a geographic area known for a particular technology.
3. Application developments may require close interaction with a customer in the customer's facility.
4. Putting R&D people in geographic business units would increase the relevance of R&D and increase the information flow from business units to R&D.
5. R&D should be located in the regions that represent the fastest growing areas of the business.
6. Rather than tying up R&D people with expensive and time-consuming travel, it would be better to have people on the ground in international locations.
7. Remote R&D facilities would facilitate technology transfers to and from many different countries.
8. Remote locations in countries like China provide a foothold that gives firms credibility and may help in hiring local engineers and scientists.
9. Remote locations show the international product divisions that the firm is serious about a particular region.

Honeywell was involved in two main R&D activities: R&D that supported Honeywell's worldwide product divisions and contract research funded by government agencies and outside firms. Honeywell's R&D organization was centralized in Minneapolis. With respect to the question of international R&D, a Honeywell manager based in Asia raised the following issues:

> There are several reasons for spreading R&D capability around the world. One, time to market in today's world is probably the most significant competitive advantage a company can have. One way to get quicker time to market is to do R&D in multiple locations around the world so you have a 24-hour R&D process. Second, there are talented people around the world and by not taking advantage of those skills and talents that may exist in China or India or other places, a company is putting itself at a competitive disadvantage. Third, in many countries, including China, personal contacts and connections are invaluable in the business world and there is a great loyalty among alumni of certain institutions. American companies that have established relationships with these institutions may get access to alumni in important government positions down the road. Fourth, its much easier to understand the unique product require-ments of a country or region of the world if you spend time there. It's very hard to sit in Minneapolis and figure out the cooling control requirement for a Chinese air conditioning system if you have never been in an apartment building in China that has poured concrete walls that you can't run thermostat wire through.[15]

International R&D and Honeywell

In view of Honeywell's international growth opportunities, the issue of in-ternational R&D was becoming a high-priority issue in HTC. For example, China's economy was growing so rapidly that some sort of HTC pres-ence seemed inevitable. One line of thinking was that HTC should have employees based in China with a broad learning and exploration agenda. Another view was that until there was a clear understanding of the op-portunities in China, it would not make sense to commit to expensive expatriate employees. A further issue was that in China, and Asia in gen-eral, there were no engineering staffs to adapt technologies for the local market. For the most part, products manufactured and sold in Asia were products transferred from American or European Honeywell divisions. Without an engineering staff in Asia, technology could not be transferred.

Further issues with respect to international R&D are evident in the following comments from HTC managers:

By the year 2000, sales outside the United States could be 60% of our business. At HTC we have to start experimenting in other parts of the world. Our mission is to help the divisions understand what they can do with our technology. If you ask them what they want, you will get the most ordinary ideas. If we work with their customers and understand that environment, we can link customers with our technology and come up with something completely different. If we are not out there looking at the world we will never grow the company. And I can't hire someone in China to do this for me; someone from here has to go over there and get the HTC culture going.

Technology is technology; it is physical principles and science—there is nothing unique about the technology needed in Europe or Asia. However, the application needs seem to vary from region to region. Perhaps we should set up application groups around the world. The technology engine will remain in Minneapolis and Phoenix. These groups will be the selectors and appliers of those technologies given their knowledge of the region. If we go this way, we won't need the best researchers in Prague and other regions. We will need people who can apply technology and gain access to technology sources outside the United States. We have really not tapped into these non-U.S. sources.

The notion of distributed R&D is very important to me. I am convinced that HTC is going to become more distributed, not less. How we can create one large, global R&D organization and not 12 small ones is a big issue. Strategically, putting together other R&D centers in Beijing or Eastern Europe is going to become a way of life at HTC.

It is difficult enough making HTC work. Trying to replicate it somewhere else in the world is even more difficult. In the United States, 20 years of evolution has allowed HTC to develop some unique capabilities. Can we wait for other remote R&D centers to naturally evolve over 20 years? What is the best way for a non-U.S. R&D organization to have an impact?[16]

Clearly, before R&D could be internationalized, many issues had to be addressed. How should Honeywell attempt to build effective global R&D capabilities? Honeywell's R&D organization had developed a unique entrepreneurial, interaction-based culture. Could this culture be replicated outside the United States? How quickly should R&D be moved? Who would manage new R&D organizations? How would these organizations be funded? Should international R&D sites be centers of excellence for specific technologies, or should they be application centers using technology developed in Minneapolis, or should they be a combination of both?

How Will the MNE Organization of the Future Manage Complexity?

As MNEs continue to grow in size and reach, new organizational forms will undoubtedly evolve, especially as firms grow larger and more complex. The MNE organization that works today may be inappropriate for a company with $1 trillion in sales and 5 million employees (which Wal-Mart could have in fewer than 15 years if its current growth rates continue). While the conflicting location and integration pressures will remain, firms will need to create new approaches to issues such as global product management, shared service management, and managing the transfer of knowledge and best practices (In chapters 5 and 6 we discuss knowledge-based issues and consider some of the ways that firms are meeting the need to tap into their various pockets of valuable knowledge.)

As an example of a company struggling to manage organizational complexity, consider the case of Citibank, the world's largest financial services company. Citibank has more than 275,000 employees in 100 countries and is involved in just about every aspect of financial services, including retail banking, investment banking, private banking, insurance, venture capital, and many different trading activities. In 2001, Citigroup found itself embroiled in a regulatory scandal in Japan.[17] A few years later, a report on the scandal concluded "Quite simply, this is a situation characterized by a multitude of failure points within the organization. . . . Experience has taught us that a business failure of the kind witnessed in Japan is typically an indication of deeper fault lines in the control structure of the organization as a whole. . . . In hindsight, one may fairly question whether global business and international supervision was close enough to recognize the severity of the management discord in Japan."[18]

It appears that a key underlying reason for the Japan problems was a breakdown in control systems, probably associated with the enormous complexity of Citigroup's global structure. The private banking group brought a variety of Citigroup investment services together to serve wealthy clients. In the pressure to achieve financial goals, and amid complex reporting relationships, efforts to enforce compliance with Citigroup standards failed. More generally, this example suggests that there may be limits to the speed by which firms can globalize. Without the appropriate controls in place, globalization of products and services may result in some major difficulties. More sophisticated control systems will have to be created to support Citigroup and other MNEs' expansion efforts.

Reorganization as a Response to Globalization

Earlier in the chapter we discussed how WL was able to successfully reorganize in a global structure (notwithstanding the inevitable set of complaints, challenges, and detractors). The response to increasing globalization for many companies is to reorganize, under the mistaken belief that changes in the organizational structure will be accompanied by corresponding changes in managerial behavior. More than two decades ago, Christopher Bartlett cautioned companies against resorting to yet another reorganization to solve their international organization challenges.[19] In Bartlett's view, firms would be better off keeping a simple structure and focusing instead on building a complex decision-making process that takes many perspectives into account.

Nevertheless, MNE reorganizations continue to be commonplace, especially by American and European firms. The difficulties of reorganizing huge MNEs can be seen in the case of Unilever. Since 1999, Unilever, the huge food and consumer products company, has been engaged in a reorganization designed to centralize decision making and reduce the power of local country managers. Historically, Unilever relied heavily on local-country managers (mainly British and Dutch) to run country affiliates. These managers had significant autonomy, much like that of the former WL country managers discussed earlier in the chapter. The country managers, called chairmen, were even allowed to make their own acquisitions. The result, according to a *Wall Street Journal* article,[20] "landed Unilever with a confused mishmash of products and a structure ill-suited to the increasing globalization of business." In some countries it had as many as six companies operating independently. Unilever's German subsidiary had four different autonomous companies covering food, ice cream, soaps, and food services and two separate country heads. By the late 1990s, Unilever was buying more than 30 different types of vanilla for its ice cream in Europe.

The 1999 reorganization plan, called Path to Growth, was intended to reduce duplication and focus the company's efforts on key global brands. Unilever eliminated hundreds of businesses, 55,000 jobs, and 1,200 brands. However, much of the confusion in control and responsibilities still remained five years later. The reorganization was supposed to reduce the influence of country heads and phase them out by 2001. In early 2005, Unilever still had country-based executives that coexisted with regional and global managers. An effort to eliminate duplicate back-office operations ran into major problems. The result was that Unilever's profitability lagged far behind that of major competitors such as Procter & Gamble.

A possible message from Unilever's struggles to reorganize is that there are limits to size and MNE complexity. Perhaps the successful MNEs of the future will be those that focus on fewer value-chain activities than giants like Unilever and Nestlé, a sort of Dell Computer–like model that can achieve huge economies of scale but not try to serve all customers across all product segments. Or perhaps the successful MNEs will invent new coordination mechanisms and processes that can tie together networks of affiliates into a seamless global strategy. It could also be that companies with deep cultural and organizational legacies, such as Unilever, will get left behind by newer companies that do not have deeply entrenched cultural barriers to creating innovative new organizations. For example, in the personal computer (PC) industry Dell Computer is winning the global battle, despite being less than two decades old and having to go head-to-head with well-established firms like IBM. Evolutionary theorists would attribute this to the natural order of things. In the world of global business, bigger in size and broader in scope may not necessarily be better.

Conclusion

Because the MNE operates in multiple country environments, the organization of MNE activities is much more complex than that of a solely domestic firm. Not surprisingly, the fundamentals of the strategy and organizing processes are relatively invariant across both domestic and global firms. It is the ability to forge a strategy that blends unique, firm-specific advantages with location-specific competitiveness that distinguishes a global approach from a domestic one. A strategy to address global markets has to carefully consider the internal as well as the contextual factors whose interplay ultimately determines the success or failure of that strategy. These factors represent a wide spectrum, from location-specific advantages, to industry-level performance drivers and competitor abilities, to a firm's own internal stock of resources and skills that allow it to position itself as a unique global player.

As globalization pressures increase and new country markets become viable, MNEs must adapt and develop original means for designing and controlling their organizations. The divisional form of organization found in large domestic firms must give way to more complex structures, variously referred to (somewhat idealistically) as a transnational organization or a heterarchy.[21] Although it remains to be seen how large MNEs will cope with their increasing complexity and scope, there is no doubt that innovations in organization will allow some MNEs to outperform others.

4

International Strategic Alliances

Strategic alliances are an important tool for most MNEs. Although once considered peripheral to competitive strategy, alliances have entered the mainstream and should be viewed as integral and mandatory strategic tools. Alliances are often essential for market entry into new geographic areas and can provide strategic flexibility for new businesses. These alliances are formed for various strategic reasons; indeed, most alliances are formed to serve multiple objectives. Consider the case of Renault and Nissan. In 1999, Renault acquired a 37 percent stake in Nissan, a company mired in financial trouble. Renault provided a much-needed cash injection for the then unprofitable Nissan. Likewise, this allowed Renault to significantly increase its market scope. By 2001, after major cost cutting by Carlos Ghosn, the Renault executive who led Nissan's restructuring, Nissan was profitable once again. In 2002 Nissan acquired a 15 percent stake in Renault, increasing the ties between the two firms. The two companies created a joint purchasing organization that expected to spend $21 billion in 2003; the alliance was also moving toward joint powertrain development and platform-sharing. In January 2003, the Renault CEO commented, "The alliance with Nissan has delivered faster than I expected—and much more than anybody expected."[1] Clearly, the Nissan-Renault alliance has created strategic value for both partners and has been driven by multiple strategic objectives. In this chapter we examine the nature of alliances, with an emphasis on alliances that mutually benefit the partners.

What Is a Strategic Alliance?

A strategic alliance is a link between two or more firms that enhances the effectiveness of the firms' competitive strategies. More specifically, an alliance is a voluntary arrangement between two or more firms that involves the exchange, sharing, or codevelopment of products, technologies, or services. An alliance can be formed by firms located in similar or different positions in their respective industry-value chains. In alliances with scale and cost-sharing objectives, the partners often compete in similar markets and industries and have formed those alliances to achieve economies of scale or to reduce excess capacity. These alliances include joint R&D efforts, joint production of a particular component or subassembly, or the manufacture of an entire product. In the oil and gas industry there have been several alliances involving the oil majors, with the objective of combining their national refining and gasoline marketing operations in order to reduce costs and achieve greater economies of scale. In the airline industry, the major international code-sharing arrangements are an attempt by competitive airline companies to reduce costs and increase load factors. In contrast, alliances can be formed to combine different and complementary skills and resources. In this type of alliance the partners usually have heterogeneous capabilities. For example, the automotive competitors GM and Toyota formed the NUMMI joint venture to assemble cars. Toyota contributed the product design and the manufacturing process; GM contributed the plant and local knowledge of workforce management and business practices in the United States.

Elements of Alliances and the Importance of Trust

In the last decade or so it has become fashionable to term any interfirm relationship an alliance, as in "our suppliers are our alliance partners." In our view, most interfirm relationships lack the requisite elements to be termed alliances. Alliances are more than a price-driven, financial relationship shaped by contractual details. Three distinct elements distinguish alliances from other interfirm relationships:

1. The partner firms worry about themselves and their partners because they know that the success of the alliance depends on collaborative efforts.
2. The relationship involves the exchange of knowledge associated with technologies, skills, or products.
3. Trust plays a key role in the management of the alliance.

When alliance partners exchange knowledge, there is the risk that the knowledge could be used opportunistically by one of the partners. For example, when a major consumer products company entered China through a joint venture, they were surprised to discover that their partner had built a factory a few miles away making similar products and using product and packaging technology clearly appropriated from the joint venture. Although the joint-venture contract would have been replete with nondisclosure and noncompete clauses, theft of intellectual property still happened. This situation illustrates the reality of strategic alliances: a contract cannot predict all the potential competitive and organizational risks that an alliance creates. As a result, any firm going into an alliance must be prepared to deal with risk, which is why trust is so important. Trust is the decision to rely on another party (i.e., person, group, or firm) under a condition of risk.[2] In the absence of risk, trust is not necessary. Many contractual relationships between firms have minimal risk, which means the parties to the relationship have little reason to rely on trust. Strategic alliances, in contrast, are characterized by a complexity that ensures some level of risk and trust becomes a necessary element. Trust is critical in alliances because, invariably, it is impossible to write a contract that anticipates all of the possible contingencies. If it were possible to write an all-inclusive contract, trust would not be necessary and alliances would be simple to manage. Since neither is the case, we suggest that if managers seek to answer the question "Is my interfirm relationship a real alliance?" they ask a follow-up question: "Does trust play a role in the management of the relationship?" If the answer to the second question is no, the relationship is probably not an alliance and does not present the complexities and challenges of the relationships discussed in this chapter.

Types of Strategic Alliances

The term strategic alliance covers a broad array of possible interfirm relationships. The "classic" alliance is the equity joint venture, which is formed when two or more distinct firms (the parents) pool a portion of their resources in a separate jointly owned organization. In the case of two-partner joint ventures, the equity stakes may be equal or one partner may hold the majority. An equity joint venture could be formed via greenfield (i.e., new plant, new employees, etc.) or via a divisional merger whereby the parents contribute an existing division to the alliance. An example of a divisional merger was the one between Molson of Canada and Elders of Australia in 1988. In this joint venture, both companies contributed their existing Canadian brewing operations to the joint venture.

Nonequity alliances involve no exchange of equity and no new company is formed. There are many variations on nonequity alliances, including: licensing and technology exchange, joint research and development, joint product development, and joint distribution or marketing. New forms of nonequity alliances are being created all the time. Unlike equity joint ventures, nonequity relationships are easier to form and dissolve, and they typically involve less complex corporate governance and partner management issues. On the negative side, nonequity relationships often suffer from unclear strategic objectives and a lack of equity signals that the alliance may be temporary. A fascinating example of the speed with which a nonequity alliance can be formed and accomplish its goal is the collaboration that occurred in 2003 to deal with SARS. With oversight from the World Health Organization, laboratories from three continents that normally compete with each other instead worked in a joint effort to discover the identity and genetic code for the disease. The effort took only about two months, an unprecedented development in medical history. Another example is the alliance between electronics companies and contract equipment manufacturers such as Flextronics and Solectron; see the case study that follows.

CASE STUDY: OUTSOURCING ALLIANCES AND COMPETITIVE RISK

Although outsourcing has long been a means for a company to eliminate noncore activities, the rise in the 1990s of electronic manufacturing services (EMS) and semiconductor foundries created new and powerful alliance forms. EMS companies manufacture products according to designs provided by their client companies. They include Solectron (2003 sales $12 billion), Flextronics ($14 billion), and Celestica ($7 billion). Companies like Cisco, Ericsson, Alcatel, Lucent, and Motorola (OEMs) rely heavily on EMS companies for their manufacturing and logistics management. Cisco has never manufactured much of its output, and in recent years, traditional manufacturers like Ericsson have become heavily reliant on EMS companies. In many respects, these relationships go far beyond normal outsourcing arrangements because of the degree to which the parties must collaborate. The risk for companies like Ericsson is that EMS companies might try to move downstream and become original design manufacturers (ODMs). ODMs design products as well as make them, working to specification from their clients. The ODM model is prevalent in the personal computer industry. Once an ODM is designing and manufacturing products, the next question is whether it will move to building its own brand and become its clients' competitor. Historically, EMS companies have lacked the critical R&D and design expertise to pose a substantial competitive risk for the major OEMs. That could change over time, in much the same way as Japanese electronics companies that began as manufacturers under contract and license eventually drove American electronics firms out of business.

For small firms requiring semiconductors, the cost of building a semiconductor plant is prohibitive (close to $3 billion and climbing). This high cost led to the emergence of semiconductor foundries that manufacture under contract. The design work for the semiconductors is done by an OEM such as Sun Microsytems or Qualcomm, and the manufacturing is done by the foundry. One of the largest dedicated semiconductor foundries is Taiwan Semiconductor Manufacturing Company (TSMC; sales of $4.7 billion), which had more than 300 clients in 2003. Texas Instruments, in addition to manufacturing under its own brand, also operates as a foundry. To date, the semiconductor foundries have had limited design capabilities. However, one of the growing areas for semiconductors in 2003 was mobile phone chips. Qualcomm commanded about 80 percent of the CDMA chipset market, with the majority of the chips built by TSMC. In mid-2003, Texas Instruments announced that it would start making its own CDMA chips, threatening both Qualcomm and TSMC in its move downstream. In this case, Texas Instruments was using its foundry and design experience to enter a new market, potentially upsetting the long-established alliance between Qualcomm and TSMC.

As we argue in the chapter, alliances are not permanent, and alliance partners should plan on termination. In the world of contract manufacturing and outsourcing, there is little partner loyalty when a competitive alternative comes along (which is why EMS companies, including Flextronics, talk about developing into ODMs). In 2002, IBM started production on a new $3 billion semiconductor plant in New York State. In March 2003, Nvidia Corporation, a California maker of advanced video chips (including those in Microsoft's Xbox game player), announced that it would use IBM's plant to make its next-generation chips. Nvidia had been a showcase account for TSMC. When the announcement was made, TSMC's stock fell 15 percent. Clearly, the relationship between Nvidia and TSMC was not strong enough to prevent Nvidia from entering into a relationship with IBM when it perceived that IBM offered a better technical solution.

The third category of strategic alliance is the minority equity alliance. The Nissan-Renault arrangement mentioned earlier is an example of a minority equity alliance. In this alliance one parent makes a minority investment in the other, and under this umbrella a variety of deals are made. Minority equity alliances are used quite frequently in industries with high technological uncertainty, such as telecommunications, software, and biotechnology. In these instances a minority equity alliance can be a hedge, in that the larger firm may have an option to later purchase a majority equity stake in its smaller partner. Minority equity alliances are also used when there are government restrictions on full acquisition. Such restrictions exist in many industries and in many countries. In the United States, for example, there are restrictions on foreign ownership of airline companies and television stations.

Alliances may also incorporate various structural elements. Global One is an example of a complex alliance that combined minority equity investment and an equity joint venture. Global One was an alliance among Deutsche Telekom, France Telecom, and Sprint, formed in 1994 (operations began in 1995) and terminated in 2000. The structure of the alliance is shown in figure 4.1. France Telecom and Deutsche Telekom held a 10 percent stake in Sprint and each owned 50 percent of Atlas, the joint venture of the two companies formed prior to the formation of Global One. Atlas held a two-thirds ownership interest in the European operating unit of Global One and Sprint held a one-third interest. France Telecom and Deutsche Telekom, through Atlas, held a 50 percent ownership interest in the Global One World operating unit; Sprint held the remaining 50 percent. The alliance was troubled from the beginning, with financial difficulties and conflicts between the partners. When the alliance was terminated, France Telecom took over Global One.

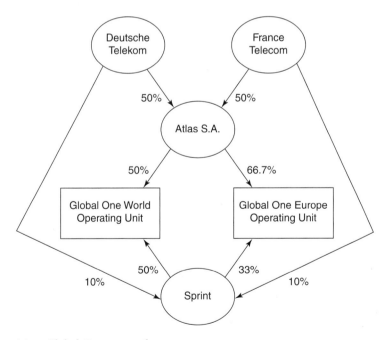

Figure 4.1.   Global One ownership structure.

Why Companies Use Strategic Alliances

The last two decades have witnessed a proliferation of international strategic alliances. There are multiple reasons firms choose to use strategic alliances; indeed, it is unusual for an alliance to be formed for a single strategic reason. More likely, a combination of the following reasons leads to an alliance.

Speed of Action

Alliances can help firms react swiftly to market needs and build leadership positions quickly. In many international-market entry situations, a wholly owned subsidiary may be legally possible. However, the time it would take to create the subsidiary may simply be too long. In China, which has seen several hundred thousand joint ventures over the past 20 years, it is possible in most industries to form a wholly owned subsidiary. However, the complexity of doing business in China has led most firms down the alliance path, deciding that entering China on their own will take too much time. Wholly owned subsidiaries in China may have difficulty winning contracts, getting licenses, and building local relationships. (See work by Wilfried Vanhonacker for an argument in favor of wholly owned subsidiaries in China.[3]) Alliances also play a key role in time-to-market decisions and in allowing firms to quickly access new technology.

Risk Sharing

Many international business decisions entail significant risks, and these risks are often viewed as unacceptable for any one firm to bear on its own. The oil and gas industry has been using alliances in the upstream exploration area for risk-sharing purposes since its inception. In this industry, the financial stakes are enormous and the regional geopolitical environment in which oil and gas exploration occurs is complex. For example, the Sah-Daniz Production Sharing Agreement in the Caspian Sea in Azerbaijan includes seven partners: BP (operator–25.5%), Statoil (25.5%), the State Oil Company of Azerbaijan Republic (Socar–10%), LUKAgip (10%), NICO (10%), TotalFinaElf (10%), and TPAO (9%). This partnership was formed in early 2003 to begin the first stage of development. Risk sharing is also a large concern in other areas, such as R&D, pre-competitive standard-setting activities (such as the next-generation mobile telephony standard), and where there are large uncertainties with new markets and new technologies. In all these cases firms may prefer an alliance to going it alone.

Economies of Scale and Critical Mass

A third and quite straightforward reason to use an alliance is to create economies of scale in a way that broadens scale without broadening the firm itself. For instance, small firms may seek to match the economies of scale achieved by their larger competitors. The benefits could come from manufacturing, distribution, purchasing, or some other value-chain activity. The small firms may participate in networks that create scale to achieve common objectives such as buying power or coordinated foreign market entry. The ease of communication created by the Internet has greatly facilitated creation of networks designed to jointly perform common tasks.

Learning New Skills

In bringing together firms with different skills and knowledge bases, alliances create unique learning opportunities for the partner firms.[4] By definition, alliances involve a sharing of resources. In some cases, the shared resources are strictly financial, limiting partner learning opportunities. In other cases where the firms contribute complementary skills, alliances create an opportunity for firms to access the knowledge of their partners—new knowledge that, in most cases, would not have been available without the alliance. Partner firms that use this access as the basis for learning can acquire knowledge useful for enhancing partner strategy and operations. In chapter 9 we discuss learning and knowledge management in more detail. But as an example of alliance learning here, consider the following statement about interfirm relationships by John Browne, CEO of BP: "Any organization that thinks it does everything the best and need not learn from others is incredibly arrogant and foolish. . . . You have to recognize that others may actually know more than you do about something—that you can learn from them."[5]

Exploration

Alliances can be the basis for exploring new business opportunities. Firms may be interested in new businesses or markets that have already been developed by other firms. An alliance with a first-mover firm can provide the opportunity to learn about the new business. Also, an alliance may be formed to learn about the partner firm, perhaps as a precursor to a deeper relationship or an acquisition. An alliance may also be used to help in the sale of a business. If a business does not have an easily determined market value, a firm may agree to a partnership with a potential buyer as the basis for setting the market value. Finally, an alliance may be used to learn more about a competitor or even as the basis for co-opting a competitor to become an ally.

No Choice

This final reason for the formation of an alliance is not really strategic. "No choice" means that a company is forced to use an alliance for of one of the following reasons: (a) government requirements that foreign direct investment can be made only with a local partner involved; (b) the new market is too complex or difficult for a firm to enter on its own; or (c) not forming an alliance puts the firm in an indefensible competitive position. Although joint-venture requirements have disappeared in many countries, they still exist in certain markets and industries. When GM entered the Chinese automobile industry in the mid-1990s, the Chinese government required a joint venture, regardless of GM's preferred entry mode.

Why the Number of International Alliances Continues to Increase

The reasons provided above explain why firms choose to use strategic alliances. On a worldwide basis, the use of alliances continues to grow each year. There are various explanations for this rising trend in the number of alliances:

- *Deregulation.* Many countries continue to deregulate industries and invite foreign competition, often in the form of alliances.
- *Strengthening of intellectual property laws.* In the past firms have been reluctant to enter new markets in industries such as pharmaceuticals and biotechnology for alliances because of fear of losing intellectual property (IP) to partners. In various countries, the strengthening of IP laws has alleviated that fear, increasing the willingness of foreign firms to collaborate.
- *Globalization.* The continuing spread of global ideas, concepts, and competition creates ever increasing pressure on firms to globalize; alliances are a fast-response competitive weapon.
- *Innovation in alliance design.* New types of alliances are constantly being invented, thus increasing the range of strategic choices that firms have for forming alliances.
- *Strategic importance of speed.* Speed and time to market continue to mandate the need for fast competitive response.

- *Increased skills in alliance management and alliance exit.* Relative to a decade ago, firms are, on average, much more sophisticated in alliance management (both entry and exit). As opposed to the ad hoc approaches that used to characterize alliance management, many firms have learned, often from bitter experience, that alliances cannot succeed without effective alliance management processes.
- *Easier communication across long distances.* The Internet has greatly simplified the ability of firms to communicate with distant international alliance partners.
- *Unbundling of the value chain or "skeleton companies with brains."* As firms continue to focus on core activities, alliances play a key role in allowing them to participate in noncore activities without a wholesale exit from these activities.

Competitive Risks and Problems with Alliances

The reasons for using alliances must be weighed against some potential costs and risks.[6] Although every business involves risks associated with new entrants, demand and supply fluctuations, changing government regulations, and so on, there are several key sources of risk in these alliances. The risk most often considered is that of partner-opportunistic actions. The risk of partner-opportunistic behavior plays a pivotal role in all alliances, not because all economic agents behave opportunistically all the time but because it is difficult to differentiate those that do from those that don't. The risk of opportunism refers to the extent of loss incurred by Partner B if Partner A behaves opportunistically. Opportunistic behavior could result from exposing valuable firm knowledge to another organization. Alliances, and more specifically technology licensing agreements, have been blamed as one of the reasons that the United States lost out to Japan in the electronics and various other industries.[7] Given that knowledge sharing is one of the elements of a true alliance, the risks of sharing this knowledge must be acknowledged.

A second type of risk involves the inability of a partner firm to execute its share of the agreement. When an alliance is formed, the partners must assess each other's competence and decide how tasks will be performed. Before the partners have worked together, they have little information about each other's skills. So if one firm leads the other to believe it can perform certain tasks when it cannot, it may be impossible to achieve the objectives of the alliance.

A third type of risk, asset specificity, is associated with the specific resources and efforts devoted to building a cooperative relationship. These resources and efforts may have no transferable value if the alliance is terminated. A fourth risk is that of a zero-sum game. Although this chapter is based on the objective of creating mutual value (i.e., both partners realize benefits from the alliance), one view is that alliances can become a learning race, with the partner that learns faster becoming the winner.[8] Although we believe this phenomenon is relatively uncommon, zero-sum outcomes do occur and often lead to painful alliance dissolutions. In addition, the firm that gains a reputation for "starting and winning alliance learning races" will find a shrinking pool of potential alliance partners.

Finally, one of the most important costs, particularly for firms that are not experienced with alliances, is the volume of management time required. In many cases, this time is disproportionate to the size and importance of the alliance, leading some analysts to suggest that alliances should be used only for peripheral activities. Although we disagree and believe that proper alliances can yield significant benefits, we acknowledge that they often involve significant coordination costs. The various stages of an alliance, from negotiation to implementation to dissolution, can take a lot of managerial time. The case study that follows illustrates the life cycle of an alliance and the collaborative issues that consume managerial energy.

CASE STUDY: ALLIANCE LIFE CYCLE—MATRA-ERICSSON TELECOMMUNICATIONS

All strategic alliances go through a life cycle with three main stages: negotiation and formation, implementation and operation, and dissolution.[9] This case illustrates a typical joint-venture scenario in which one party brings the technology and the other party contributes the local knowledge.

Negotiation and Formation

Matra-Ericsson Telecommunications (MET) was a joint venture formed in 1987 between the Swedish company LM Ericsson (Ericsson) and the French company Matra S.A. (Matra). The joint venture was formed as part of the French government's decision to privatize CGCT, a French telecommunications manufacturer. The government invited several telecommunications companies, including Ericsson, Siemens, and AT&T, to submit proposals to take over CGCT. As part of the requirements, the bidder would have to partner with a French company. The winning bidder would be guaranteed a 16 percent share of the French PTT business for 10 years starting in 1987. Ericsson won the bid and teamed up with Matra. An equity joint venture called MET was formed, with Matra controlling 50.01 percent of the equity venture and Ericsson 49.99 percent. Other important alliance conditions were:

- The board comprised 10 members, with 5 appointed by each partner. The board was the primary vehicle for strategic interaction between the firms.
- Ericsson was responsible for technical issues.
- MET was set up to produce sell public network switches based on existing Ericsson technology.
- Components for the switches would primarily be transferred to MET from Ericsson in Sweden.
- Ericsson would receive a fee of 7 percent of sales revenues.
- The venture was committed to developing export markets.

Implementation and Operation

MET began operating in 1988 and within a year was profitable. However, not long after its formation, the partners became involved in a series of conflicts. Very quickly, the two senior managers from Ericsson and Matra disagreed over a number of issues, some important and some trivial. Clearly, the relationship between the two showed poor chemistry. After two years, Ericsson agreed to replace the top venture executive appointed from Ericsson. However, the partner conflicts had escalated to the point that in 1990, Ericsson's new executive appointee to MET was refused access to the joint-venture premises. The conflicts involved various issues: the responsibilities of the two partners in managing the alliance, MET top manager roles, technology transfer, licensing fees, transfer pricing, local content, and exports. Despite these conflicts and the significant management time they consumed, MET continued to be profitable. Matra, frustrated at Ericsson's unwillingness to commit to a deeper technological collaboration, formed a relationship with Nortel, a major competitor of Ericsson. Not surprisingly, the formation of the Nortel alliance changed the nature of the Matra-Ericsson relationship.

Dissolution

From 1994 to 1997, revenue at MET continued to grow. Although originally MET was restricted to 16 percent of France Telecom purchases, by 1997 MET's share of new France Telecom orders had grown substantially. In 1997 Matra and Nortel decided to combine the activities of MatraCom (Matra's telecommunications subsidiary, which did not include MET) and Nortel France into a single organization called Matra Nortel Communications, owned equally by Matra and Nortel. This company would have about 5,000 employees and compete across a broad range of telecom products and services. In 1997 Matra also decided sell its share of MET to Ericsson, ending the venture and giving Ericsson a 100 percent owned subsidiary in France.

MET Case Implications

MET lasted ten years—a few years longer than the median life span for an international equity joint venture. Over the period the partner relationship and the alliance went through various significant changes and weathered some challenging issues. The MET case illustrates several key strategic alliance issues:

- Partner conflict is normal and should be expected in strategic alliances. Conflict does not necessarily mean that the business cannot be profitable.[10]
- The alliance relationship evolved in ways that neither partner could have predicted at the outset.
- The alliance continued for 10 years because it was profitable and because it met the strategic needs of both partners. When the strategic objectives of Matra changed, Matra agreed to sell the business.
- Although Matra and Ericsson were partners in MET, they were competitors outside the narrow scope of the joint venture, as seen in Matra's decision to partner with Nortel.

Unavoidable Issues with Alliances

From the discussion of alliance risks, we suggest that there are several issues that are unavoidable when it comes to alliance management:

- *Alliances involve uncertainty and ambiguity.* This uncertainty and ambiguity add to the managerial challenge and are one of the main reasons alliances involve significant coordination costs.
- *The partner relationship will evolve in ways that are hard to predict.* Alliances are formed for strategic reasons and as strategies and competitive environments evolve, so must alliances.
- *Alliances remain vulnerable to many types of destabilizing factors regardless of the strategic logic underpinning their formation.*
- *Today's ally may be tomorrow's rival.* As one article said, "Successful companies never forget that their new partners may be out to disarm them."[11]
- *The partners will eventually go their separate ways.* All alliances eventually will end, which means firms must be realistic in considering alliance longevity.

Avoidable Issues with Alliances

Apart from the unavoidable issues, there are two additional issues or risks that can be circumvented:

- *Alliances do not have to be very difficult and expensive to manage.* Alliances can involve significant managerial time, especially when a firm has little experience in managing alliances or when the prior experience between the partners is limited. However, the last decade has seen growing competencies in alliance management. As firms gain experience with alliances and build effective control systems, these partnerships do not have to be viewed as expensive and difficult to manage. See table 4.1 for a list of key questions that should be considered in a strategic alliance development process.
- *Core competencies will not necessarily be appropriated by your partner— that is, "sleeping with the enemy."* As we have acknowledged, alliances do create competitive risks and there are enough cases of knowledge theft to suggest that companies must be aware of these risks. Fortunately, a firm can take a few easy steps to protect intellectual property in strategic alliances (see table 4.2).

Table 4.1. Strategic Alliance Development Process

A strategic alliance development process should include a series of checkpoints that must be satisfied before the process moves forward. The process should be designed to ensure that key questions are posed and debated as the alliance moves through the formation process. The questions that should be addressed during strategic alliance development include:
- Are there clearly understood and agreed-upon objectives before alliance formation?
- How will the alliance be integrated with the parent firm's strategy?
- Will there be cultural compatibility and organizational fit between the partners?
- Does the alliance leverage the complementary strengths of the partners?
- Will an exit strategy be defined upfront?
- Is there a monitoring process for new alliances?
- Have all the partnering risks been identified and accounted for?

Properly implemented, a systematic alliance development process will ensure that:
- Projects are strategic to the firm.
- Projects meet financial objectives.
- Projects move quickly through required corporate approval processes.
- Project risks and challenges are identified and understood by all parties involved in the alliance formation process.

Table 4.2. Protecting Intellectual Property in Strategic Alliances

---

Steps that an alliance partner can take to help protect its intellectual property from partner appropriation include the following:

1. Anticipate partner's learning intent and learning ability.
2. Design the joint tasks to "wall off" certain aspects of the business.
3. Transfer older technologies to the alliance.
4. Locate the alliance close to the facilities of the parent to provide easier monitoring.
5. Limit the number of managers a partner can contribute to the alliance.
6. Limit personnel transfers from the alliance to the partner organization.
7. Limit the number of partner visitors to the alliance.

Partner Selection Criteria and Managing the Alliance Relationship

Partner selection is one of the most important decisions in the formation of a strategic alliance. Choosing the wrong partner can result in years of interfirm conflict and failure to achieve alliance objectives. In some cases, a firm may have only one candidate. For example, when GM entered the China market in the 1990s, the partner had already been selected by the Chinese government. GM competed with Ford and won the right to form a joint venture with Shanghai Automotive Industry Corporation. GM did not get to choose its partner; its only choice was whether or not to bid for the project. In most cases, firms choose their alliance partners from several possible partners.

In partner selection, there are two key considerations: strategic fit and organizational fit. Few managers would question the importance of strategic fit; indeed, strategic fit is typically the focus of most analysis. Alliances are formed for strategic reasons and, therefore, firms seek a partner that helps accomplish those strategic objectives. An analysis of strategic fit addresses questions such as "What are our competency gaps?" and "What are the options for filling these gaps—alliances, acquisitions, or internal greenfield development?" If it is determined that an alliance is the appropriate choice, a partner must then be found that has the complementary skills. There may be many such partners; there may be only one; or there may be none. Regardless of how many potential partners are identified, strategic fit requires that the partner selected help accomplish the strategic objectives.

Further, finding good strategic fit is necessary but not sufficient for success. The partners must also be able to work together and achieve a strong organizational fit.[12] Together, strategic fit and organizational fit represent the focus of partner-selection decisions. Ignoring organizational fit in favor of strategic fit can lead to serious implementation problems. The organizational fit is crucial because, as John Browne of BP argued, you never build a relationship between your organization and a company or a government—you build relationships between people.[13] Many alliances fail in implementation because the people working together make or break the deal, and many organizations wait until after the deal is struck to address such organizational issues.

What Is Organizational Fit?

Strategic fit refers to the strategic complementarity between the partners: does the combination of skills and resources allow the alliance entity to perform a task that could not be performed as well by the partners acting alone? If the answer is yes, then an alliance could be justified. However, the success of the alliance depends on whether the partners are able to work together organizationally. Quite simply, organizational fit refers to the ability of the partners to work together. Without this ability the alliance cannot function.

There are various factors that promote good organizational fit:

- Common or similar corporate cultures and values
- Convergence of strategic goals
- Good chemistry between key managers—senior executives and key operating personnel
- Partners that value public reputation
- Compatible control and decision-making systems
- Common time horizons
- Partners that discourage secretive behavior in their own operations

All of the above are quite straightforward in their connection to organizational fit. However, for firms forming international strategic alliances, identifying a partner with the above characteristics can be difficult because of the company's possible inexperience in the market and/or lack of local knowledge about possible partners. Moreover, measuring variables such as "common or similar corporate cultures and values" or "common time horizon" can be difficult and time-consuming. For example, many firms entering China end up forming alliances with companies about which they know very little. Consider the case of Standard Industries (disguised name), an American firm that entered the Chinese market in 1996. Standard negotiated a joint venture between June 1995 and late August 1996. The venture equity split was 60 percent for Standard and 40 percent for the Chinese partner. The Chinese partner was a large diversified Chinese company that contributed its automotive division. That division, which had more than 700 employees, represented about one-third of the Chinese company's total business. The Chinese partner was a Chinese Township Enterprise company that was, as far as Standard knew, family controlled.

At times the Chinese partner deferred to higher authorities, but throughout the life of the venture, the Standard managers never truly understood who owned and controlled its partner.

In the above case, Standard did not have a good understanding of partner organizational issues before the joint venture was formed and, ultimately, there were many problems involving financial performance and partner interactions. The joint venture was terminated prematurely, and Standard used its experience (and that from several other failed ventures) to redesign its international joint-venture formation process. In another case in China, GM and SAIC were able to establish a strong working relationship in their successful Shanghai General Motors joint venture. The first president of the venture was Hu Mao Yuan; he was subsequently made head of SAIC. Hu made the following statements in an interview: "In many other places GM won't listen to its local partners. That made my job more creative. It's not easy to change the attitudes of GM people. They [legal contracts] were just to meet legal requirements, and we never had time to look at them afterwards. . . . My relationship with Phil [Philip Murtaugh, the senior GM manager in the joint venture] is a secret weapon . . . both of us had bad tempers. In negotiations you're allowed to lose your temper, but it shouldn't happen in a partnership."[14]

With Shanghai GM, the two firms were able to establish an organizational fit that worked. One of the reasons for this success was the personal bond that developed between the two senior managers. Without this bond, it is questionable whether the organizational fit would have been so strong.

Why Many Companies Overlook Organizational Fit

In the case above, Standard management would agree, in retrospect, that the company should have devoted more effort to understanding organizational fit. Standard is far from alone in having focused more on strategic issues than on organizational issues. Why does this happen? We can identify various reasons many companies overlook or downplay organizational issues:

- Alliances are designed to meet strategic rather than organizational objectives.
- Investment bankers, analysts, and consultants find strategic issues easier to quantify and measure than qualitative issues.
- Few operating specialists are involved in the process.
- Issues of organizational fit are viewed as able to be postponed.
- There is pressure to close the deal quickly because managers and analysts charged with alliance formation are isolated and under stress;

consultants or business development managers are paid to "close" the deal; and the dealmakers strive to complete the deal before news leaks out.

All of these reasons are exacerbated when the alliance crosses borders. Time pressures become greater and cross-cultural issues complicate the evaluation of organizational fit. Nevertheless, as we have emphasized, organizational concerns must be taken seriously in any alliance.

Alliance Management and Design

In considering alliance design and management structure, the prospective partners should, quite obviously, try to create an entity that allows them to achieve their collaborative goals. One key issue is how the alliance will be controlled. Control refers to the process by which the partners are involved in the decision making and the extent to which they have active roles in the strategy and operation of the alliance. In some cases, a partner may play a limited role because it lacks relevant managerial skills or knowledge. In many international joint ventures, local partners provide the access and government connections but act as silent partners when it comes to day-to-day operations. In other cases, all the partners play meaningful managerial roles. In an independent venture (a relatively rare phenomenon), the alliance operates autonomously from its parents.

Many firms believe that they should not enter the alliance unless they get control. What these firms often fail to understand is that there are different levels of control. At one level, there is strategic control, which refers to the ability of the partners to control the strategy of the alliance, shaped primarily through the alliance's board of directors. At a different level, there is operational control, which involves control over the actual operation and functioning of the alliance. For operational control, the key question is whether one of the partners has been designated as operator. In most oil and gas alliances involving exploration, one of the partners is the designated operator and the other partners will have agreed to this arrangement. Other operational control questions are concerned with who controls the technical processes and who controls market access. A third level of control, applicable only to equity-based alliances, involves equity ownership. Specifically, how will the equity be divided? One school of thought says that equal ownership is preferable because it forces the partners to agree, since none of the partners can outvote the others. Another view is that majority ownership is the best option because majority ownership means control. Our view is that majority ownership in an equity joint venture provides some control but should never be the sole lever of control. Control can be exercised in various ways beside equity stake, such as managerial selection, contribution of key technologies, and responsibility for key alliance tasks. We have observed numerous cases in which the majority owner was frustrated by an inability to influence certain aspects of the alliance. The example of Standard Industries discussed earlier is one such case.

Given the different types of control possible, there are several questions that firms should consider as they design their alliances and plan for alliance management and operation:

- What elements of the alliance are most important to its success (e.g., market access, technology, financing)?
- Of these key elements, is one of the partners better suited to have control? Or should control be shared?
- What are the most powerful levers of control and which partner has them?
- In the event that the partners wish to share control, can a shared-management alliance succeed?
- If one of the partners is designated as operator, what role do the other firms play as nonoperators?
- How will an operator handle a nonoperator that tries to be a hands-on partner (i.e., "you operate or we operate" does not work as expected)?
- How will the firms control and protect their technology?

Alliances and Stability

The primary problems in managing alliances stem from one cause: there is more than one parent. The owners of alliances are often visible and powerful; they can and will disagree on just about anything.[15] Contractual agreements between alliance partners are often executed under conditions of high uncertainty, and it is unlikely that all future contingencies can be anticipated. As alliances grow they may develop an identity and culture distinct from the parents, adding to problems of coordination. These problems are compounded when the parents are from different countries.

Several definitions of alliance instability have been used. One perspective considers both a shift in alliance control and alliance termination as evidences of instability. A narrower view uses alliance termination as the sole indicator of instability. However, an alliance cannot be considered unstable simply because its life span is short. All relationships between firms face challenges that threaten to change or eliminate the basis for cooperation. Sometimes alliance terminations have been anticipated and planned for. Ventures may also be terminated as a matter of policy, such as when there is a change in parent ownership or management. In other cases, the difficulties associated with ending a relationship may create a rationale for maintaining an alliance that would otherwise be terminated.

We maintain that instability should be linked with unplanned ownership changes or major reorganizations in the alliance. Usually, instability results in premature alliance termination, either when one partner acquires the alliance business or the venture is dissolved. A complicating factor is that alliance termination is not always a mutual decision. Premature termination may be precipitated by the actions of one partner. For example, we have observed several cases where one partner was clearly trying to learn from another partner in order to eliminate dependency. The "learning" partners and "teaching" partners had very different longevity objectives. These ventures would be classified as unstable because termination was premature from the perspective of the "teaching" partner. Thus, if at least one of the partners anticipates a long-term relationship, premature termination constitutes instability.

In most alliances the partners do not have a specific plan for termination of their ventures. Also, it is important to emphasize that we do not equate the longevity of an alliance with alliance success. Many firms view alliances as intentionally temporary. If an alliance termination is orderly and mutually planned, the relationship may well be evaluated as extremely successful. In fact, an alliance that is prematurely terminated may also be evaluated as successful, depending on the criteria used.

Managing Partner Conflict and Adjustment by the Partners

There are many possible areas that can contribute to partner conflict. One of the realities of alliances is that the partners rarely have common goals for collaborating. Those goals should be mutual and complementary but that does not mean they will be the same goals. When Ericsson of Sweden joined with the French firm Matra, the primary strategic goal was entry in a major Western European market. Ericsson's partner had a very different strategic objective; Matra was seeking entry into the telecommunications industry and needed Ericsson's experience and technology. The life cycle of the Matra-Ericsson joint venture is described in the case study "Alliance Life Cycle—Matra-Ericsson Telecommunications." In this case, the strategic goals were complementary and were the basis for creating a profitable alliance. However, there was significant conflict between the partners. The problems originated with the organizational fit and with the partners' different strategic objectives. We would argue that

Matra-Ericsson, far from being atypical, illustrates the problems in many alliances. Managers must grasp the reality that the nature of alliances almost guarantees some conflict. The following is a list of possible areas of partner conflict in an equity joint venture:

- Dividends
- Exports
- Financing of venture alliance expansion
- Transfer pricing for products supplied by the partners
- Choice of suppliers
- Divestments
- Role of each parent
- Product pricing
- Growth versus return on investment (ROI) for the alliance
- Criteria and evaluation of management
- Selection of alliance managers

In addition, various other things can go wrong. Trust can break down, strategies can change, alliance champions may leave, collaborative value may not materialize as expected, the cultures of the partners may not mesh, their systems may not be effectively integrated, and so on. In short, the potential for alliance problems will always be high.

Table 4.3 provides some statements from a manager in an international joint venture with 50:50 ownership. These statements illustrate the difficulty of reaching a common frame of mind in a collaborative setting, and convey a sense of frustration for one of the partners. While it is true that this alliance had a rocky start, it went on to become very successful and several large capital expansions were undertaken. As the partners gained experience working together and learned more about each other, they developed the ability to manage conflicts and channel their energies in a constructive manner. Conflict did not disappear totally, but it became manageable. Thus, we reiterate a key point made earlier: alliances evolve in ways that the partners cannot predict at the outset. Learning and adjustment are key elements in that evolution.

Yves Doz and Gary Hamel have argued that learning and adjustment are keys to alliance longevity and the avoidance of premature dissolution.[16] In another study, Doz described the process of partner adjustment as follows:

As the partners enter the cooperation, they start observing each other through the interface they have created. In other words, while formal, or explicit even if unilateral, reevaluation is a periodic rather than continuous exercise, the information gathering that feeds that exercise

Table 4.3. Alliance Comments and Partner Interactions

"We spend a lot of time dancing around issues. We are juggling dozens of issues and they are all ambiguous. Our partner thinks issues are resolved and we don't because we don't have it in writing. Some of our managers think we are being lied to because our partner keeps changing its mind. The problem is that our partner gets told one thing by the government and then the next day the government tells it something else. Then our partner comes back to us and we think it is going back on its word."

"Every single issue with our partners involves a protracted negotiation. If we say ten, they will say five. It doesn't matter if the issue is significant or not. If we say let's do 'x' because 'x' makes sense, they will challenge us. It is as if they must leave a meeting with a lower number than we proposed even if our first number was the right one. When we go to meetings we talk for two hours *211* to see who will turn the lights on. Often we will agree on something on Monday and then on Tuesday they will deny that we had an agreement. They will even sign off on an issue and then want to renegotiate. Or they will keep delaying until it is too late to do what we want to do and we have to do it their way. Even minor decisions require senior management approval. There is a tremendous unwillingness for anybody in our partner to accept risk. When we try to explain to our people in Europe or the United States why things are moving slowly, they just say 'What is the problem—make a decision!'"

"I am used to following a system and being evaluated on performance. Our partner gets assessed on relationship building. There are certain objective steps that must be followed to achieve an outcome. Our partner finds the objective steps very difficult to understand."

"We are dealing with talented people in the negotiations. The top people assigned to the project are the best they have. Unfortunately, when you get below these people the talent leaves a lot to be desired. The depth of management is a function of relationships. And the senior people don't know how to delegate. As a result, lots of things fall through the cracks. When things go wrong, we are not sure if our partner is deliberately trying to mess things up or if it genuinely don't know how to get things done but won't tell us because it would lose face."

Source: Compiled from original research by the authors.

is continuous and starts early. Partners watch each other for unexplained divergence between what they see as the task requirements and the behavior of the partners vis-à-vis those requirements. . . . In other words, they read in the behavior of the partner clues about the partners' competencies, capability to adjust, and trustworthiness.[17]

Cross-Cultural Dimensions and Alliance Stability

International strategic alliances, like any type of international activity, require that the managers and firms of different national cultures work together. Thus, in addition to learning how to work with a different organization, alliance partners must learn how to deal with a different national culture. According to Carlos Ghosn, "In cross-border acquisitions or alliances, cultural differences can be viewed as either a handicap or a powerful seed for something new."[18] Cultural differences can provide an opportunity to learn and innovate in a new environment. Cultural differences can also lead to serious partner conflict and the failure to achieve collaborative objectives.

For MNEs experienced in working in many different countries, the cross-cultural aspect may be immaterial. Research has shown that managing organizational culture issues can be as, or more, significant than managing national culture challenges.[19] However, for companies entering new markets, learning about national cultures can involve significant time and resources. For example, when Toyota entered the United States in 1984, the firm chose to partner with GM. A primary reason for this decision was to learn how to work in the U.S. environment and, in particular, how to manage a U.S. workforce.

The cultural differences between alliance partners often contribute to managerial issues and may contribute to alliance instability. Certainly, cultural diversity makes alliance management more difficult.[20] However, the relationship between cultural diversity and stability really depends on whether "stability" is viewed from the local or the foreign partner's perspective. As a foreign partner gains local experience and builds its knowledge base, the cultural gap decreases. When that happens, instability becomes more likely because that local knowledge was probably one of the key reasons for the alliance (as it was for Toyota in entering the United States). Conversely, if the foreign partner does not adapt to the local environment, continuing cultural differences between the partners can foster stability.

From the perspective of the local partner adapting to the foreign partner, however, the situation is somewhat different. When the local partner increases its understanding of its foreign partner's culture, alliance stability may increase because the partners have gained greater understanding of each other's behavior. In our research on Japanese-American joint ventures, we found that it is particularly difficult for American managers to understand pricing decisions for Japanese customers. Consequently, the pricing structure of joint-venture products is often a source of major conflict. By increasing its understanding of the Japanese approach to pricing, the American partner could eliminate that conflict, which in turn could reduce the potential for instability.

Alliance Performance Measurement

Even if there is an attempt to establish objective alliance-performance measures at the formation stage, there can be formidable challenges to completing those measurements once the alliance is formed.[21] Alliances are often shaped in highly uncertain settings and involve partners with different and often competing agendas. There may be a failure to develop clear performance measures, for various reasons: unfamiliarity with alliance measurement, unwillingness to deal with partner conflict over performance issues, asymmetric views on performance measurement, multiple constituencies with input in the performance issues, and unclear managerial responsibility for alliance outcomes.

We recommend that alliance managers keep the following three factors in mind when considering alliance performance measurement:

1. Alliances should be evaluated using a combination of factors: objective measures, such as financial performance (ROI, cost structure, process improvements) and market share; subjective measures, such as relationship between the partners, alliance stability, and technological learning; and survival of both the partnership and the alliance business.
2. The weight of each measure should vary over time. In newly formed alliances, objective measures should be discounted. In older alliances, objective measures will receive greater attention.
3. The weight of each measure should be consistent with the strategic intent of the alliance. If the intent is to learn, objective measures should be discounted. If the intent is market share or profits, strategic measures may be discounted. Finally, subjective measures will always be difficult to assess.

As we mentioned earlier, it is a mistake to equate longevity with success. Longevity can be a rough indicator of success. As long as alliances serve the strategic objectives of the venture, the alliance should be safeguarded, nurtured, and kept alive. However, when alliances fail to fulfill their promise or outlive their usefulness because partner objectives have been accomplished, they must be terminated. Therefore, managers involved in alliances must be prepared to critically assess performance and recognize when performance is poor and unlikely to improve.

Alliance Assessment: Creating Successful Alliances

We conclude this chapter with some specific suggestions as to how to create successful alliances. (Also see chapter 8 for a discussion of emerging-market strategic alliances.) First, we identify a series of issues that firms should consider after an alliance has been identified as a possible strategic option but before negotiations begin. These issues, if properly dealt with, provide the foundation for creating viable collaborative relationships. Table 4.4 provides a list of questions that should be addressed in order to consider all the issues. The questions in table 4.4 are generic in the sense that they should be asked for any proposed alliance. If a firm cannot answer these questions, it is not ready to enter alliance negotiations. Alternatively, the answers may suggest that an alliance is not the best course of action. Of course, the answers to the questions are contingent on various factors, including the firms involved, the nature of the proposed alliance, the anticipated impact on firm strategy, and the collaborative experience of the firms involved.

Our second suggestion involves assessment and follow-up subsequent to alliance formation. Once an alliance is formed, firms need to regularly review the alliance and ask some fundamental questions about performance and partner interactions. These questions include the following:

- Is the strategic logic of the alliance grounded in reality? What will each partner gain and how will the alliance continue to create value?
- Do the partner firms pursue a set of mutually beneficial and agreed-upon goals? Has a climate of openness between the partners been established? Do you understand your partner's competitive position?
- Is the organizational fit between the partners based on trust?
- Do the partners contribute more than money and contribute on a continuing basis (technology, products, ideas, etc.)? All partners need an incentive to remain in the alliance. Are the partners equally committed to remaining in the alliance?
- Will there be managerial continuity between the partners?
- Are the partners willing to review and readjust the governance systems? Don't assume that degree of ownership equals control.
- Are the alliances performance measures consistent with the alliance strategic intent?
- Is the expectation of alliance longevity realistic? Are exit provisions well thought out?

Conclusion

The cliché "same bed, different dreams" is often evoked to describe the reality of alliance management. This phrase gives the impression that alliance partners should expect problems in their alliance efforts. We agree that international alliances can be challenging to manage and, in some instances, lead to serious partner conflict and painful termination. However, many international alliances survive and prosper for many years, with both sides becoming more competi-

Table 4.4. Key Planning Issues for the Success of an Alliance

Mutual Value Creation

- Have both short- and long-term collaborative objectives been clearly established? Will an alliance help you achieve those objectives?
- Will the alliance negotiation be focused on joint economic success and mutual value creation or will it lead to a one-sided outcome?
- What will happen if an agreement cannot be reached in your alliance negotiations? Besides an alliance, what are your options for achieving strategic objectives?

Initial Partner Knowledge

- What do you really know about your partner and your ability to work together? What are the partner's strengths and weaknesses? How much experience and success does the firm have with alliances?
- Has your prior experience with the potential partner created a strong level of interfirm trust? Can that trust play a key role in current negotiations and will the individual managers who built the trust be involved in the planned alliance?
- Is your partner a competitor or likely to become a competitor at some point in the future? What role will your firm's knowledge play in determining whether or not your partner becomes a competitor?

Risk

- How much risk are you willing to bear? What are the implications if the alliance is terminated and the business is sold to your partner?

Essential Terms

- Have you clearly determined the issues that are nonnegotiable? Are you willing to compromise on these issues in the case of unique collaborative opportunities?

Individuals' Roles

- Do you know the role that your counterpart negotiators will play in the future alliance?
- Will these individuals be the managers you have to work with when the alliance is formed? Or will a new set of managers be assigned to operational roles?
- Do your counterpart negotiators have personal incentives associated with a successful alliance negotiation?
- Will operational managers be involved in the negotiations? Have these managers initiated the potential alliance?
- What will the alliance top management team look like? Will your partner have any objections to your choice of managers? Based on the relationship between partner and the competitive environment the alliance faces, what skills should the alliance managers have?

Alliance Governance and Trust

- Do both parties understand that successful alliances will undergo a series of transitions as the partners learn more about each other and competitive dynamics shift?
- Do venture partners recognize that the alliance negotiation is a means to an end? No matter how well the alliance is negotiated, issues of organizational fit and implementation will be critical in contributing to alliance success.

(continued)

Table 4.4.   (*Continued*)

Alliance Governance and Trust (continued)

- Do all partners understand the importance of flexibility in the negotiation process and the contractual agreement?

Cross-Cultural Issues

- Are the managers who will be involved in the negotiation and venture management familiar with the national culture of the partner? If not, are there other internal or external advisors who can be consulted?
- Is your partner skilled in cross-cultural management?

Flexibility and Review

- Is review time built into the alliance formation and negotiation plan?

Source: Andrew C. Inkpen and Kou Qing Li, "Joint Venture Formation: Planning and Knowledge Gathering for Success," *Organizational Dynamics* 27, no. 4 (1999): 33–47.

tive in a win-win relationship. In this chapter we emphasized mutual value creation as the foundation for successful alliance management. While some alliances may result in a zero-sum game of winners and losers, if alliances are to be an integral element of global strategy, firms should seek partners with whom they can achieve an effective working relationship that links complementary assets. In the international arena, national culture adds a dimension to the challenge of partner selection and building successful alliances. But it is important to remember that cultural differences do not arise just from differences in nationality. All alliances involve the combining of organizational cultures that may be vastly different. Firms that are skilled in alliance management recognize that successful collaboration requires a commitment to the collaborative task and a willingness to tolerate some ambiguity and flexibility. When properly managed, alliances create the foundation for global opportunities that may be difficult or impossible to exploit independently.

5

Global Knowledge Management

To emphasize that valuable knowledge often exists at the geographic periphery of MNEs, Gary Hamel wrote that "the capacity for strategic innovation increases proportionately with every mile you move away from headquarters."[1] While this comment was intended to be provocative, the essential argument is valid and important: the MNE is a repository of valuable knowledge that often goes unexploited. In this chapter we explore how that knowledge can be managed and transferred in the global organization.

A key assumption underpinning the discussion is that knowledge, like money, has velocity: the more it gets used, the greater the potential effect. More important, unlike physical assets that depreciate over time, knowledge can increase in value when used, whereas neglect will destroy it. Along these lines, John Browne, CEO of BP, said: "Learning is at the heart of a company's ability to adapt to a changing environment . . . In order to generate extraordinary value for shareholders, a company has to learn better than its competitors and apply that knowledge throughout its businesses faster and more widely than they do . . . No matter where the knowledge comes from, the key to reaping a big return is to leverage that knowledge by replicating it throughout the company so that each unit is not learning in isolation . . . The wonderful thing about knowledge is that it is inexpensive to replicate if you can capture it."[2] As Browne says, knowledge is valuable *if you can capture it.* The reality is that there are significant transactional difficulties associated with exploiting organizational knowledge.[3] Quite simply, organizational knowledge is hard to capture, transfer, and make usable. Because knowledge is embedded in organizational structures, processes, procedures, and routines, it is not easy to separate it from the context in which it has been created. In addition, when knowledge is tacit, it is difficult to transfer without moving the people who have the knowledge.

Thus, even though many studies have argued that the ability to transfer knowledge is a primary source of a firm's competitive advantage and growth, we know relatively little about how to transfer knowledge within and across organizational boundaries.[4]

MNEs that can effectively tap into their various pockets of valuable knowledge have the potential to outperform competitors that rely on one-way knowledge flows from headquarters to subsidiaries. Not too long ago, it was rare for an MNE to think much about knowledge transfer from subsidiaries to headquarters or from subsidiary to subsidiary. More typically, a U.S. or European firm either acquired or established a subsidiary as the means of market entry. In many cases, local production was necessary to avoid tariffs and other barriers. If the business was acquired, it would usually be left alone, aside from the introduction of headquarters' policies. If the subsidiary were a greenfield site, the headquarters would transfer the appropriate knowledge based on how things were done in Europe or the United States. In the case of a manufacturing subsidiary, the transferred knowledge would consist primarily of product design and manufacturing technology. When Japanese firms began to aggressively enter new markets in the 1960s, their internationalization model resulted in the term *transplant*, which is applied to the replication of a home-country production model in a new geographic market. The Japanese MNEs rarely acquired firms, preferring to transfer their own management systems to the new markets.

In most instances, the knowledge transfer models used in the previous century can be called *projection models:* the knowledge was projected from headquarters to the distant realms of the corporate empire.[5] Under the right conditions, the projection model can work quite well. One of those conditions is that the firm projecting its knowledge should have a clear and sustainable advantage with few threats from other firms in its global markets. Obviously, firms of this sort are few and far between. As a result, firms in today's competitive environment must exploit their total knowledge resources and abandon the idea that the headquarters or a primary subsidiary has the most valuable knowledge. Increasingly, firms are tearing down the boundaries that prevent knowledge from crossing borders and cultures. This can be seen in GM's 1998 decision to move the headquarters of its international division from Switzerland to Detroit. Given the need to design and engineer vehicles for the entire world, using common parts and components, the move was essential for greater integration of GM's international and U.S. operations. Keeping valuable knowledge isolated in geographic areas no longer makes sense in the global automobile industry.

In today's global economy, knowledge moves around the world at a faster and faster rate. Indeed, via digital means, some types of knowledge can be moved quickly and at virtually no cost. MNEs must develop their strategies by tapping into the repositories of knowledge that exist in all parts of their organizations. However, this knowledge is context dependent: the more valuable the knowledge, the more difficult it is to replicate in other parts of the organization. Moreover, innovation is critical for competitiveness. The knowledge source for innovation cannot be exclusively in the home country. Firms must find and exploit valuable knowledge from inside and outside their organizations in all the geographic markets in which they operate.

Organizational Knowledge

What is organizational knowledge? Let us first consider how knowledge differs from other firm assets.

Unlike assets such as raw materials, plants and equipment, and buildings,

- Knowledge is not depleted (and does not depreciate) during production. Additional use will probably enhance knowledge.
- Knowledge can be possessed by multiple "owners" simultaneously.
- Knowledge is embedded and cumulative.
- Knowledge transfer cannot easily be governed by contracts.
- Giving value to knowledge is problematic and few companies have adequate systems to measure knowledge.

So, knowledge is an asset that differs from traditional hard or tangible assets, and the difference is a function of its nature. One study defined *knowledge* as cognitive perceptions as well as the skills and expertise embodied in products or services.[6] Other studies divide knowledge into two types: information and know-how. Information, or knowledge of what something means, includes facts, axiomatic propositions, and symbols. Know-how, or awareness of how to do something, is the accumulated practical skill or expertise that allows a person to do something smoothly and efficiently. A simpler, and perhaps more useful, view is that organizational knowledge creates the capacity for repeatable action by the organization's members. In other words, people link the knowledge to a meaningful application within the organization. The notion of repeatable is important because nonrepeated and idiosyncratic pieces of knowledge are not valuable; organizations are interested in reusable knowledge. This distinction separates organizational knowledge from facts that have little value for the organization.

For organizational knowledge to be valuable, it must be usable at some point in the future. Value is derived from use, and as we have said, the more knowledge is used, the more valuable it may become.

Tacit and Explicit Knowledge

The distinction between tacit and explicit organizational knowledge is a critical one. Tacit knowledge is intuitive and unarticulated, and not capable of being verbalized. It is knowledge that has been transformed into habit and made traditional, in the sense that it becomes "the way things are done around here." Tacit knowledge is highly context specific and has a personal quality, which makes it difficult to formalize, communicate, and transfer. For example, tacit knowledge may originate from an organizational story or unique experience. From that experience, such as an organization's establishing its first international subsidiary or overcoming significant geographic barriers to market entry, personnel may have developed unique knowledge about international markets. If this knowledge is not written down, if it exists solely in the heads of these individuals, then the knowledge is tacit. Should those individuals leave the organization, the knowledge would be lost.

Knowledge may be *seem* tacit because no one has yet articulated the key ideas. For example, when a large American firm entered the China market and experienced significant problems with its joint ventures, the tacit knowledge of the experiences eventually gave way to development of a codified joint-venture development process. In this instance, tacit knowledge was translated into explicit knowledge.

In contrast to tacit knowledge, explicit knowledge is knowledge that is transmittable in formal, systematic language and may include facts and symbols. Examples of explicit knowledge are a document describing how to connect the components of a personal computer or direction on how to utilize an e-mail system. Explicit knowledge can be codified or articulated in manuals, computer programs, training tools, and so on. For example, much of the success of McDonald's can be attributed to the company's ability to articulate and codify its process of fast-food delivery to ensure consistent quality around the world. Some of the company's more recent problems can perhaps be attributed to the fact that competitors also understand the McDonald's process and have improved upon it. As a result, making knowledge explicit is a double-edged sword: on one hand, explicit knowledge can be transferred and replicated easily; on the other hand, it is much more subject to competitive spillover and appropriation than tacit knowledge.

Other dimensions of organizational knowledge have been identified, including complex versus simple, teachable versus not teachable, and observable in use versus not observable in use.[7] For all these dimensions, it is important not to create a false dichotomy. Knowledge exists along a spectrum, and the endpoints are mainly descriptive devices. Although the distinction between tacit and explicit is important, it does not allow us to consider any gray areas. Thus, explicit and tacit knowledge types can be classified on a continuum that ranges from the explicit knowledge embedded in specific products and processes to the tacit knowledge acquired through experience and use, and embodied in individual cognition and organization routines.

A key challenge for organizations is to convert tacit knowledge to explicit knowledge.[8] Tacit, personal knowledge has little value until it can be converted into explicit knowledge that organizational members can share. However, as we have mentioned above, this conversion process risks imitation by other firms. Therefore, firms must be cognizant of the trade-off between the need to share and transfer knowledge internally and the risk of exposing the knowledge to competitors.

Knowledge Management

Verna Allee (1997) defined knowledge management as "much more than managing the flow of information. It means nothing less than setting knowledge free to find its own paths. It means fueling the creative fire of self-questioning in organizations. This means thinking less about knowledge management and more about knowledge partnering."[9] Knowledge management involves processes such as sharing individual knowledge and its evolution to a collective state, embedding new knowledge in products and services, and transferring knowledge across organizational boundaries. The success of knowledge management depends on whether that new knowledge improves organizational actions or creates the basis for new action. A study of 31 knowledge management projects in 24 global companies identified eight key factors for success, including culture and processes, common purpose, and common language for knowledge identification and selection.[10]

In the MNE, successful knowledge management ensures that the various subunits of the firm are capable and willing to seek opportunities to create, share, and transfer knowledge. For example, Dell Computer Corporation searches for business practices that can be applied consistently across the globe. Managers are expected to cooperate in establishing operational processes that can become repeatable and reliable. For this to happen, Dell devotes significant resources to developing a culture that supports knowledge partnering and knowledge management.

How Is Organizational Knowledge Transferred?

From the previous discussion comes the notion that organizational knowledge has value when it can be used in repeatable applications. This suggests that organizations should be constantly searching for new applications for existing knowledge and also for new knowledge outside their boundaries. The difficulty is that very often what might be repeatable in one organization is foreign, different, and highly suspicious to another organization, or even to another division of the same organization. Unfortunately, much research in the area of knowledge transfer does not help managers struggling to move sticky knowledge. As Paul Carlile explains, the concept of knowledge transfer has its roots in technical information-processing research, where the primary focus has been on the storage and retrieval of knowledge.[11] However, information-processing approaches tend to assume that a common language underpins the transfer process. Carlile uses the term *novelty* to explain the difficulties of transferring knowledge across boundaries. Individuals involved in knowledge transfer are often reluctant to abandon existing knowledge for something new, or novel. When these individuals must communicate across boundaries, the circumstances are often viewed as novel because there is no common language or context. Individuals can differ in their cognitive knowledge and specialization, language, social norms and identities, and type of sense-making used to analyze problems.[12] When the circumstances are novel, knowledge transfer becomes sticky and prone to failure. Knowledge that is deeply embedded in the context in which it was created tends to be resistant to both movement and receipt.[13] For example, information about doing business in a foreign market is a combination of tacit and explicit knowledge that is usually quite difficult to extract from its foreign-market context. As a result, firms often rely on local partners for assistance in entering new markets. Even after establishing themselves as viable competitors in the local market, organizations may be unable to acquire and transfer the local knowledge, which means that local partners may become permanently necessary. In addition, knowledge rooted in organizational values and cultures can be difficult to transfer in a manner that leads to a desired change.

The transfer of organizational knowledge can occur through a variety of mechanisms: personnel movement, training, communication and personal relationships, observation, transfer of goods and services, patents, scientific publications, presentations, and interactions with suppliers and customers. Regardless of the method used, the transfer manifests itself through changes in the degree of knowledge or the performance of the recipient unit. As a framework for understanding these different mechanisms, Argote and Ingram distinguished between moving knowledge itself and modifying the knowledge of the recipient unit.[14] That is, when knowledge itself is moved it must be adapted to a new context. The knowledge can be moved by transferring the people possessing that knowledge or by moving the tools in which the knowledge is embedded. In technology-based alliances such as licensing agreements, knowledge transfer may be a quite straightforward movement of software, product design, or manufacturing systems. If the knowledge is moved via people, the transfer will be most successful when the knowledge is not overly complex and when the individuals have the ability to influence those receiving the knowledge.

For knowledge modification at the recipient to occur, there must be intensive social interactions involving managers at various organizational levels, along with consensus building among the managers involved. Alternatively, if knowledge at the recipient end is not modified or no consensus on the value of the knowledge is reached, the transfer of context-specific knowledge will be difficult. There is evidence that knowledge transfer is facilitated by intensive communication and social interaction. Indeed, knowledge transfer has been described as "individuals within one organization communicating on specific problems and procedures with individuals from another organization."[15] Through communication, managers can develop an understanding of the value of knowledge and how an existing knowledge base needs to be modified to absorb new knowledge.

To illustrate organizational knowledge transfer in practice, we provide two case studies. The first case is China-Singapore Suzhou Industrial Park. In this case, knowledge transfer from Singapore to China was an explicit objective of both parties involved in the development of the industrial park. More important, China was interested in acquiring Singapore's knowledge (referred to as "software" in the joint venture) of doing business and managing industrial parks. To quote a manager involved in the transfer, this knowledge represented the "mindset and administrative experience accumulated in Singapore over the past 30–40 years."

The second case study example is that of GM, Toyota, and NUMMI, which deals with a joint venture between GM and Toyota. In this case, the value of the knowledge transfer was not initially apparent to GM. Learning was a GM goal, but there was no consensus within GM about the value of the particular learning opportunity. Over time, the value of that opportunity became better appreciated and knowledge transferred from NUMMI had a significant impact on GM.

CASE STUDY: CHINA-SINGAPORE SUZHOU INDUSTRIAL PARK

In February 1994, the China-Singapore Suzhou Industrial Park (SIP) alliance was created in an agreement between the Chinese and Singapore governments and their agencies. A key objective was for Singapore to share its efficient economic management and public administration experience with its Chinese partner. The Chinese partner would then be able to formulate pro-business policies in SIP and govern with transparency and efficiency. The knowledge transfer program covered land-use planning and development control, building control, environmental regulation, planning and management of industrial estates, new towns and public utilities management, and human resource management.

Singapore formed the alliance with the view that it would be in Singapore's long-term economic interest for China to prosper. For the Chinese, the main objective was to learn how to build and operate successful industrial parks. SIP was expected to share its knowledge with other industrial parks in China, adding the dynamic that SIP would help create industrial parks that would compete with SIP. By 2004, SIP had become one of the most competitive development areas in China and investment in the industrial park was growing rapidly.

The Knowledge Transfer Objective

SIP was formed with an explicit knowledge-transfer objective. Under the agreement, Singapore would help provide Suzhou officials with the public administration and management skills needed for industrial township development. The Singapore side coined the term *software*. As described in the project prospectus:

> Software transfer refers to the sharing of Singapore's successful public administration and economic management experience with the Chinese authorities so that they can formulate pro-business policies in the CS-SIP [SIP], and govern with transparency and efficiency. . . . Mutual visits and training attachments help Suzhou officials understand the Singapore way as well as international practices. Together with Singapore government officials, Suzhou officials decide how best to adapt Singapore's practices to suit local circumstance by selecting and modifying appropriate elements. Singapore sends its government officials to Suzhou to assist in this adaptational process.[16]

The objective was to transfer knowledge from Singapore to China. Singapore Senior Minister Lee stressed that both sides must keep in mind their common purpose, which was not solely the construction of housing and the establishment of high-tech factories. The project involved "the transfer of experiences that Singapore has into the minds of SIP officials, so that they can adapt their experiences to China and spread the ideas, the model, across China. Even if we succeed in having a beautiful industrial park, with housing [and] high-tech factories, if we have not transferred the ideas, the concepts, in the mind of officials, we would have failed. Once the Singapore element-the Singapore officials leave, then nothing is left."[17]

From the Singapore side, the key objective was to transfer tacit knowledge of the Singapore way of doing business and managing industrial parks. The software shared by Singapore covered three aspects: (a) planning, development, and marketing of a modern township (e.g., urban planning and development, infrastructure development, land development, housing development); (b) economic management and social administration of a township (e.g., economic development strategy, labor management, customs, pension fund system); and (c) honest and clean government, legal system, and spiritual civilization (e.g., education, culture, labor unions).

Software related to specific areas such as labor management and a pension system was termed "small software" and contained mostly explicit knowledge. The fundamental principles that connected the small software areas and the systems and policies that ensured implementation was termed "big software"; this contained primarily tacit knowledge. The essence of big software was pro-business thinking, proactive attitudes to business development, financial discipline, long-range vision, efficiency, transparency, openness, fairness, and credibility.

Knowledge Transfer Mechanisms

SIP relied on various knowledge-transfer mechanisms. The transfer of expatriates from Singapore to China played a key role; between 1994 and 2002 more than 120 Singaporean managers were rotated through China, transferring valuable experience and expertise to their Chinese counterparts. For example, officials from Singapore's Urban Redevelopment Authority imparted their knowledge of master planning to the Suzhou officials.

Another knowledge-transfer mechanism was the training program. In 1994, the Singapore government began providing training programs in urban management and other aspects of public administration for Suzhou officials. In the same year, Singapore's Economic Development Board (EDB) set up the Singapore Software Project Office to coordinate the transfer of to Suzhou. The ministries involved included those of Labour, Trade and Industry, and National Development. Statutory boards and other agencies were also involved, including the Housing Board, the National Trades Union Congress, the Trade Development Board, and the Urban Redevelopment

Authority. In 1996, the EDB continued the transfer of public administration and management software to Suzhou by appointing a deputy director to head the newly set up Suzhou Software Project Office. This office and its Chinese counterpart, the Office of Adapting Singapore's Experience, chose and coordinated the relevant software to be transferred. By 2003, more than 1,500 experts in various areas had instructed Chinese trainees. Senior Singapore civil servants who conducted these courses also served as consultants to Suzhou officials. For example, after the Chinese returned home, they could seek advice by e-mail or phone; for more elaborate consultations, Singapore officials visited Suzhou for up to two months at a time. In addition, Singapore sent teams of experts to Suzhou to train SIP officials and those of Suzhou city. Additionally, more than 900 Suzhou officials attended training courses in Singapore. After returning to Suzhou, these officials wrote reports on the knowledge acquired, as well as ideas that were successfully implemented.

In the initial years of the alliance, various conflicts between the partners impacted the knowledge transfer. As the conflicts were resolved and cooperation strengthened, the amount of knowledge transfer increased. Singapore's investor-friendly ideas pervaded SIP and other development zones in Jiangsu province and were gradually spreading across China. Singapore's experience in economic development and public administration was probably the most valuable product of the bilateral agreement. By 2004, SIP was widely viewed in China as the best industrial park in the country. Thousands of Chinese managers and government officials had visited the park since its inception to learn about the Singapore model.

CASE STUDY: GM, TOYOTA, AND NUMMI

Over the past few decades GM has significantly improved its manufacturing productivity and product quality. GM's joint venture with Toyota, called NUMMI, has played a key role in GM's organizational improvements and knowledge has been successfully transferred from the joint venture to other parts of GM. This case study examines how the knowledge transfer from NUMMI occurred and how it has impacted GM.

In the early 1980s, GM and Toyota began negotiating a 50:50 equity joint venture to assemble small cars in the United States. After a year of negotiations, the two companies announced a partnership based at GM's plant in Fremont, California, which had been closed in 1982. Toyota put up $100 million and GM provided the plant (valued at $89 million) and $11 million in cash. The companies also raised $350 million to build a stamping plant. For Toyota, the main alliance objective was to counter Honda and Nissan with minimal financial risk and to learn how to work with an American labor force.[18] The primary goals for GM were to get a small car replacement and to utilize an idle plant. Learning was also a goal for GM, but there was no consensus within GM about the value of this learning opportunity. It was well known in the automobile industry that Toyota was much more productive than GM, Ford, and Chrysler. Some managers at GM were very interested in learning about Toyota's cost structure and how Toyota managed its plants. The CEO, Roger Smith, spoke about the joint venture as a "learning experience—why not take the opportunity to get an insider's view of how the Japanese do what they do?"[19] Many of GM's manufacturing managers were confident of their own capabilities and strongly opposed to an alliance with Toyota.

Toyota was given overall operating responsibility for the plant. The first CEO of NUMMI was Tatsuro Toyoda, son of the founder of Toyota, Kiichiro Toyoda. The chief operating officer also came from Toyota, and the general manager was from GM. The agreement allowed GM to assign up to 16 managers to the joint venture (the actual number has sometimes been higher). A number of managers were also hired from outside GM and Toyota. One of the most important early decisions was to seek a different union agreement with the United Auto Workers (UAW). The union agreed to adoption of the Toyota production system, with its flexible work rules and broad job classifications.

The Joint-Venture Operation

Prior to its closure in March 1982, the GM plant in Fremont had about 800 pending union grievances and absenteeism regularly exceeded 20 percent. When the plant reopened as NUMMI, about 50 percent of the former workers were rehired, which made up about 85 percent of the total production workforce. After about a year of operation, the pending grievances were down to about 15.[20] More important, within a short time, productivity and quality were the highest in the GM organization. Total hourly and salaried workers per vehicle averaged 20.8 at NUMMI in 1986, as opposed to 18.0 in Takaoka, Japan; 40.7 at the comparable GM-Framingham plant; and 43.1 at the old GM-Fremont plant in 1978. Absenteeism was about 3 percent during the period 1984 to 1992. Participation in the employee suggestion program increased to over 90 percent by 1991, and internal surveys of worker attitudes showed steadily increasing satisfaction from 1987 to 1991.[21] All of these results became important triggers for learning and knowledge acquisition.

In 1993, GM and Toyota agreed to extend the life of the joint venture beyond the original termination date of December 1996. The Federal Trade Commission approved an indefinite extension of the original GM-Toyota agreement. In 2002, NUMMI built almost 370,000 vehicles, the most in its history. In 2005, NUMMI entered its 20th year of operation. Employment at the plant was at its highest level ever (about 5,500), and the plant manufactured four vehicles: Toyota Corolla, Pontiac Vibe, Toyota Voltz (a version of the Vibe for export to Japan), and the Tacoma pickup.

Knowledge Transfer

When NUMMI was formed, GM found itself in an interesting position. As 50 percent owner of NUMMI, GM now had access to a largely Japanese-managed plant. Interestingly, Toyota was quite open in providing internal access to GM, even though GM and Toyota were major competitors on a global basis. Although GM had excellent access to knowledge, acquiring the knowledge proved to be a significant challenge.

In the early 1980s, U.S. automakers had limited knowledge of Japanese manufacturing processes and the concept of lean manufacturing was not yet developed. When GM was first exposed to NUMMI, there was only moderate understanding of the potential value of that Toyota knowledge, and only limited understanding of the complexity associated with the Toyota production system. Thus, GM's initial efforts at knowledge transfer were not very successful because the underlying reasons for the differences in knowledge were not well understood. Although partner openness created accessible knowledge for GM, the complexity of the knowledge significantly increased the difficulties of acquiring the knowledge. The Toyota knowledge was deeply embedded in Toyota's history and culture.

In particular, GM needed to learn about the Toyota production system and its emphasis on cost efficiency, quality, flexibility, and innovation, but the Toyota knowledge was deeply embedded in the company's history and culture. GM's challenge was to transfer the "sticky" knowledge of the NUMMI community to the GM manufacturing community. Various GM managers were exposed to NUMMI through assignments and visits, and there was a community of shared understanding and practice. Managers were expected to be the "brokers" who would carry the message from NUMMI back to the parent organization. However, the NUMMI knowledge did not move easily. Initially, the knowledge connections, or organizational mechanisms, that create the social interaction necessary for knowledge transfer were missing. Over time, GM put into place a variety of mechanisms and a systematic approach to knowledge acquisition and transfer emerged. These mechanisms include a more systematic approach to selection and management of GM managers assigned to NUMMI; extensive visits by GM personnel to NUMMI; and establishment of a NUMMI technical liaison office to manage knowledge acquisition. As well, GM leadership increased their commitment to knowledge acquisition from NUMMI.

As the number of managers exposed to NUMMI increased, a GM learning network emerged that readily accepted the NUMMI knowledge and accelerated its distribution. As these NUMMI-experienced managers gained seniority in the company, the distribution of knowledge became easier. In addition, GM's management of NUMMI (in part supported by GM's experience with other Japanese automakers such as Suzuki and Isuzu) can be viewed as a broadening experience that added to the firm's capacity to assimilate new knowledge and increase its absorptive capacity.

Knowledge Movement over Time

When GM first formed NUMMI, expectations of learning were unclear. Although initially some senior managers in GM had the mistaken belief that the learning could be finite, by the late 1990s, there was an understanding that the learning opportunity was continuous. The learning challenge faced by GM was in the nature of the knowledge sought. It was not a set of explicit guidelines or tools; it was tacit and deeply embedded in the Toyota Production System (TPS).

For the knowledge originating in NUMMI to be internalized at GM, a slow and time-consuming socialization process had to occur. The NUMMI knowledge was first directly applied in 1992 to a greenfield site in Eisenach, Germany. NUMMI also was the basis for a major turnaround effort by GM do Brasil. The Eisenach application was followed by greenfield plants in Argentina, Poland, Thailand, and China. As the international greenfield plants were built, knowledge of lean production methods increased and the network of knowledge expanded. Manufacturing efficiency kept growing, with each new plant more efficient than the previous one. Also, within North America, in the late 1990s lean production methods began to impact all aspects of GM manufacturing. The most visible outcome of this knowledge transfer was the new Lansing Grand River plant, which opened in early 2002.

By the late 1990s, the impact of this increasing knowledge was also being felt in brownfield GM sites. Old plants were being improved and the Global Manufacturing System (GMS), GM's standardized approach to lean manufacturing, was being developed. By 2002, GMS was viewed as a core competence. Although its roots were in the Toyota production system, GMS evolved as a unique approach to manufacturing.

Insights from the Case Studies

These two case studies demonstrate that complex tacit knowledge *can* be successfully transferred across organizational boundaries. The knowledge transferred to SIP and to GM had positive knowledge sharing outcomes. In GM's case, the knowledge gained revitalized the company and allowed it to close the quality, reliability, and cost gaps between GM and Japanese products. For SIP, the imparted knowledge supported the creation of a world-class industrial park.

Several key insights from both case studies are as follows:

1. If firms are committed to capturing knowledge, they must create innovative collaborative mechanisms to support the generation and transfer of that knowledge. In both cases, after various missteps, an innovative and systematic approach to knowledge transfer emerged. Both GM and the Singapore government were heavily criticized for not producing faster knowledge-transfer results. There is no question, in retrospect, that GM made numerous mistakes trying to learn from NUMMI. The years 1984 to 1992 were not very productive from a learning and knowledge transfer perspective, because GM leadership discounted the learning opportunity, GM managers assigned to NUMMI were not properly prepared for their assignments and GM reentry, GM did not initially understand the underlying principles of the Toyota production system, and so on. Thus, if knowledge creation and transfer efforts receive only limited and sporadic attention, the payoffs will also be minimal.[22] GM's initial experience with NUMMI resulted in limited impact. Both experimentation and greater investment in organizational knowledge transfer mechanisms had to happen before the NUMMI knowledge was able to start contributing to real change in GM. To GM's credit, sufficient slack time was allowed to ensure that knowledge networks and communities could emerge. Similarly with SIP, both partners had to get beyond the notion that the transfer would be a simple one-way flow of knowledge. Specific

organizational innovations were necessary, such as the Singapore and Suzhou Software Project Offices and the Adapting Singapore's Experience Office to assist and expedite the knowledge transfer.

2. Knowledge activists play a key role in ensuring that knowledge gets transferred. As Käser and Miles suggested, firms are increasingly relying on activists to facilitate the flow of knowledge.[23] The more complex and valuable the knowledge to be gained, the greater the role that innovative and entrepreneurial knowledge activists will play in the transfer. For example, one of the early GM managers to move from NUMMI to GM became frustrated because there was no plan for using the knowledge gained. As he described the situation, "There was no plan for any of us and the reception was not good when we returned [to GM]. In 1990 we decided to quit preaching about NUMMI and got the leadership to agree to let us use the concepts in teaching. We designed a class with leaders teaching. The workshops snowballed and took off. We realized that we had to grow the knowledge and were paving a highway for change." This manager went on to help design GM's global approach to lean manufacturing. Another former NUMMI manager was recruited into GM's European organization. He then hired other NUMMI alumni, and collectively this group helped drive lean manufacturing concepts in Europe (beginning with the Eisenach plant). With SIP, the original knowledge activist was former Singapore Prime Minister Lee Kuan Yew. In both cases, there were knowledge activists who started off as lonely voices and over time founded a community of shared understanding. Within this community, there was a mutual understanding based on practice and experience that allowed the knowledge to transfer easily. But until the community has sufficient critical mass, changing the traditional knowledge base is bound to be difficult.

3. There are a variety of potentially effective knowledge-transfer mechanisms, including people transfers, training programs, and interpersonal relationships. The choice of mechanism depends on the type of knowledge involved and the transfer objective. Some explicit knowledge can be transferred quite easily, although often companies mistakenly believe knowledge is explicit and then discover it is otherwise. GM initially thought that videotapes of the Toyota production system would support knowledge transfer. It took a few years to realize that the most valuable knowledge could not be transferred without some face-to-face interaction, such as training, teaching, visits, and on-the-job experience. The company also learned that it was necessary to supplement the personnel transfer with specific learning assignments

and training. In the SIP case, the initial managers returning to China were only partly successful because the knowledge they were expected to transfer included complex concepts of political confidence, pro-business thinking, and economic productivity. To counter initial resistance to knowledge transfer, in the early years (1994–1996) the Singapore Software Project Office focused on changing the mindset of its Chinese partner and teaching the values of the Singapore system. As Chinese thinking evolved, and as Chinese responsibility for managing the alliance increased, there was a need to modify the knowledge-transfer mechanism. In 1996 the Suzhou Software Project Office was set up to assist and expedite the knowledge transfer.

4. The complexity of the knowledge significantly increases the difficulties of acquiring that knowledge.

5. Social interaction between partners in a joint venture is critical for knowledge to be transferred. Knowledge acquisition is enhanced when the knowledge is related to what is already known and when there is a common language for interpreting experience. Unrelated knowledge is difficult to acquire and may have limited value. Within a community, there is mutual understanding based on practice and experience that allows knowledge to move easily. But between communities, as in the case of alliance partners, there are different standards, different priorities, and different evaluating criteria that must overcome for knowledge to move. Likewise, unrelated knowledge is difficult to transfer and may have limited value to the recipient because there is no common language for understanding and integrating that knowledge. For unrelated knowledge to become valuable, modification of the knowledge at the recipient may be necessary.

6. As knowledge gets transferred and put to use, its value increases and the network of individuals using the knowledge also expands, which creates further opportunities to exploit the knowledge.

Transferring Knowledge in MNEs

We now shift the discussion to consider the particular case of MNEs and knowledge management. By definition, an MNE must transfer knowledge between various parts of the organization. Without knowledge transfer of some sort, the MNE would cease to function. That said, knowledge transfer is not just a simple process of identifying the knowledge and making the transfer. As the Suzhou and NUMMI case studies illustrate, there are various approaches to transfer knowledge. Successful knowledge transfer also involves a significant commitment of resources.

In a study of how MNEs transfer knowledge, Kevin Desouza and Roberto Evaristo found evidence of three approaches.[24] First, in the *headquarters commissioned and executed approach,* the home office sets the tone for knowledge-management initiatives and provides technology solutions and support, training, and policies and procedures. Standardization of interfaces, procedures, and policies was the overriding principle. This approach was found in companies with standardized global products and services, and was used to take advantage of economies of scale. For example, this approach might be used by a software company designing a new marketing strategy. Since the software is technically the same in each geographic market, a common approach to marketing may make sense (although that will depend on many factors, such as whether the target is an individual consumer or an enterprise).

Next, the *headquarters commissioned and regionally executed approach* involves headquarters initiation and broad guidelines and policies. The regional centers then execute the knowledge transfer. In this case, the regional centers are major hubs in each continent where the organization operates. This approach allows tailored solutions for meeting regional requirements and is common for organizations involved in global consulting efforts and manufacturing. Headquarters sets the knowledge-management initiatives, objectives, and tools; the regional centers are allowed to customize aspects of the management such as language and interface mechanisms.

Last, in the *regionally commissioned and locally executed approach,* the vision and initiatives for knowledge management come from the regional offices. The impetus for regional involvement is recognition of a need to exchange knowledge on a frequent and local basis. Each office in a region can execute knowledge transfer to achieve the goals and policies it has set. The benefit of this approach is speed, while the downside is that knowledge transfer is confined to a region and globalization of these efforts may not happen.

The Sharing of Best Practices

The most typical example of global knowledge management in MNEs is knowledge sharing along functional lines, such as marketing or operations. This type of knowledge sharing is often referred to as *the sharing of best practices.* The Suzhou example involved the transfer of Singapore best practices in industrial park management to the joint venture with China. A similar example can be seen in the case study that follows. In this case study, the headquarters successfully replicated in a new market a unique culture and set of operational processes.

Beta Company had four strategic objectives for its knowledge transfer and internationalization: (a) reestablish its brand name in a Latin American country; (b) build an efficient manufacturing facility; (c) export to other Latin American countries using the new production capacity; and (d) establish the new production facility as a worldwide benchmark for efficient production.

The technology transfer involved both process and product technology from other parts of the organization. One main product incorporated about 70 percent U.S. technology and about 30 percent Latin American technology. The other main product was largely European technology. The manufacturing process technology was transferred from another plant in Latin America and a plant in Europe. Transferred knowledge also included both marketing knowledge and the overall Beta Company culture. The objective was to build a new, sustainable organization that would survive for many years. Some of the specific nonmanufacturing-process best practices that Beta Company attempted to transfer from other parts of the organization included a customer-satisfaction measurement program, a distribution network, team building (unfamiliar to most of the local employees), market research methods, various human resource practices such as an internship program, cell structure in the plants, plant dress codes, and a collective bargaining process.

Beta relied on various knowledge-transfer mechanisms, including (a) a large team of expatriates from various parts of the world; (b) an advisory system of visitors from other Latin American and international locations; (c) local and international training for managers and line workers; (d) videos from other locations; (e) extensive e-mail communication; (f) visits outside the Latin American country for Latin American managers and supervisors; (g) international coordination of the manufacturing plant construction; and (h) company manuals.

Exploiting Local Knowledge for Product Innovation

In a sense, the transfer of best practices, especially home-country practices, is often about replication, not innovation, although the best practices themselves may be improved upon by the recipient. A different knowledge-transfer situation occurs when the MNE uses local knowledge as the basis for product innovation. Kazuhiro Asakawa and Mark Lehrer[25] studied this issue and identified two ways to leverage locally embedded knowledge: local-for-regional and regional-for-global. The *local-for-regional approach* is the exploitation of local innovation for regional application. An example is Shiseido cosmetics company and its Paris-based subsidiary, BPI. BPI acts as a regional "innovation relay" to create products for European markets. The subsidiary works with local knowledge for new product development, production, bottle design and image creation, and marketing expertise.

The *regional-for-global approach* involves mobilization of regional knowledge on a global basis. When this happens, innovation often occurs at the local level and then the regional office helps identify its greater potential application. The regional office bridges the gap between innovations developed in local units and strategy creation by headquarters in the home country. The regional office identifies the potential for innovation, then implements the procedures for extracting the relevant knowledge and diffusing it throughout the global MNE network. In this way, the regional office acts as a knowledge broker for the rest of the organization. In assessing the likelihood of local knowledge diffusion, Asakawa and Lehrer concluded that few local innovations become global without active corporate management because local managers are generally not in a position to impact global operations and strategy.

Creating a Knowledge-Oriented Culture

There is little doubt that for the MNE, knowledge exploitation is critical for long-term success and thus will become even more important in the future. The projection model from headquarters to subsidiary as the MNE's sole means of transferring knowledge is a dying concept. Thus, a key question for MNEs is how to create a knowledge-oriented culture. An initial step is to understand the barriers to knowledge transfer and learning.

One barrier to knowledge transfer is the nature of knowledge itself. As we have discussed, valuable knowledge is context dependent. As the NUMMI case study showed, successful transfer of context-dependent knowledge cannot occur until the knowledge source and recipient units are aligned regarding the value and potential impact of that knowledge on the organization. When knowledge is embedded in a unique culture and/or context, its transfer becomes difficult. According to Joseph Badaracco, when knowledge is embedded, "particular problems arise. The knowledge is not available in simple, unitized packages that can be bought for cash. For one organization to secure embedded knowledge from another, its personnel must have direct, intimate, and extensive exposure to the social relationships of the other organization."[26]

A second barrier to knowledge transfer is the not-invented-here syndrome. Managers and organizations tend to be highly resistant to knowledge that originates outside their sphere of activity and understanding. For example, we found that American firms in partnership with Japanese firms tended to initially discount the learning opportunity. Consider the following comment from a senior manager of an American firm that began its alliance with a low assessment of the value of alliance knowledge: "Initially, we thought there was nothing to learn from our partner. When we first went to Japan we thought our partners wanted a joint venture so they could learn from us. We were shocked at what we saw on that first visit. We were amazed that they were even close to us, let alone much better. We realized that our production capabilities were nothing [compared with the Japanese firm]. Our partner was doing many things that we couldn't do."[27]

The case study that follows illustrates how another American firm was unable to capitalize on a unique learning opportunity. Despite a wonderful chance to gain valuable knowledge, Alpha was stuck in the not-invented-here syndrome and squandered its learning opportunity.

A third example concerns a packaged-food-products firm headquartered in the United States. This firm achieved modest success in the highly competitive Japanese food market. Although the business was quite small, its potential for organizational learning, according to American managers working in Japan, was enormous. Since Japanese consumers are so demanding (some would argue that Japanese consumers of packaged products are the most discriminating in the world), these managers believed that there were important lessons in areas such as packaging, distribution, and customer service that could impact other parts of the organization. Unfortunately, there was limited interest at the U.S. headquarters and effort to exploit the Japanese-based knowledge.

CASE STUDY: A FAILED LEARNING OPPORTUNITY

Hito, a Japanese firm, and Alpha, an American firm, formed a 50–50 equity joint venture in the United States. For several reasons, this alliance created a high-potential learning situation. Alpha had the opportunity to acquire knowledge directly associated with Hito's technological and strategic capabilities. The joint venture's manufacturing plant was established in vacant space in an existing Alpha plant near Alpha headquarters. The plant was designed as a close replica of a Japanese plant, largely to satisfy a major Japanese customer. This arrangement provided Alpha with the opportunity to gain firsthand knowledge of Japanese manufacturing processes. Hito was willing to share its technology with Alpha. Because of its proximity, Alpha managers could easily visit and interact with the Japanese managers. Also, because the joint-venture products were functionally similar to Alpha products, Alpha managers were familiar with the technology. Soon the joint venture was achieving greater productivity and lower defect rates than had Alpha's operations. By its fourth year, the joint venture had become one of its primary Japanese customer's most reliable suppliers, indicating that the plant was producing very high-quality products. Also, Alpha served as an intermediate processor, allowing for interaction between parent and joint-venture manufacturing personnel.

Alpha management had indicated that its primary objective was to learn about Hito's manufacturing and customer service, yet few learning systems were implemented. According to senior Alpha managers, the learning experience was less than satisfactory. In fact, Alpha's manufacturing vice president dismissed the opportunity with the comment: "What the joint venture does would never work in our company." Alpha management saw the joint venture as an autonomous subsidiary rather than a closely related division. There were few interactions between venture personnel and Alpha at the managerial level. Top management at Alpha seemed unwilling to initiate learning efforts. For example, Hito offered to share some proprietary-process technology at no cost. Alpha was not interested, or at least made no effort to acquire that knowledge.

Overcoming the Not-Invented-Here Syndrome

What should firms do to overcome the liabilities of the not-invented-here syndrome? The first step is to assess the degree to which the firm is knowledge oriented. In a recent book concerning a new MNE concept called *metanational*, Yves Doz and colleagues identified several questions that managers should ask about their organizations:[28]

- How good is your company at uncovering opportunities for knowledge transfer among different parts of the company? How enthusiastic are your subsidiaries to share knowledge with other units?
- How eager are your subsidiaries to learn from other parts of the company? How good is your company at codifying the innovations generated by your subsidiaries?
- Has your company built efficient communication mechanisms for sharing the codified know-how across locations? How good is your company at keeping codified knowledge proprietary to your company?
- Has your company built effective mechanisms (e.g., people transfer, face-to-face interchange) for the transfer of tacit knowledge across locations?

A second step to consider is the organization culture and the need for a global knowledge orientation. Drawing again on Yves Doz and his colleagues' work on knowledge management in the MNE, we offer the following suggestions:

- Steal with pride (i.e., "great artists steal") and copy with passion.
- Think about competition from a global perspective.
- Recognize that the periphery of the organization has valuable knowledge.
- Learning and knowledge transfer rarely happen spontaneously; firms must be willing to invest in learning.
- Develop cosmopolitan managers who understand that headquarters does not have all the answers.
- People movement should not be one way: people should be moved to and from subsidiaries.
- Develop a culture in every part of the organization that says "Here is not better than there."

The questions in table 5.1 are designed to help MNE managers identify and leverage valuable subsidiary knowledge. The table is based on the assumption that every subsidiary has valuable knowledge that should be shared with other parts of the organization. The challenge is to identify the most valuable knowledge and then develop a process for capitalizing on it.

Conclusion

Knowledge management and the ability to create, transfer, assemble, integrate, and exploit knowledge assets are critical for a firm's success. And to be successful in a global knowledge economy, organizations must not only process information but also create new knowledge. For the MNE, the source for new knowledge should be the world. This means that all units of a global firm should bear responsibility for finding and capturing new knowledge. In turn, headquarters must recognize that its local bases are real assets in discovering knowledge and that knowledge-transfer mechanisms must be established to ensure that local knowledge is not relegated to a peripheral role.

Table 5.1.　Leveraging Subsidiary Knowledge

1. Assess and value subsidiary knowledge
   - What are the core competencies of the MNE's subsidiaries?
   - What specific knowledge does the subsidiary have that could enhance the competitive strategy of other parts of the company?
   - What are the core subsidiary skills relevant for product/markets in other parts of the firm?
   - Reality check: Are the subsidiary skills and capabilities relevant to the strategy and capabilities of other parts of the firm?

2. Determine subsidiary knowledge accessibility
   - Is learning and knowledge transfer a priority for local managers?
   - Do you have easy geographic access to the subsidiary operations?
   - Is there any reason why access to knowledge in subsidiaries is restricted?

3. Evaluate the tacitness and ease of transfer for knowledge of interest
   - Is the local knowledge tacit or explicit?
   - Where in the subsidiary does the knowledge reside?
   - Is the knowledge strategic or operational?
   - Reality check: Do you understand what you are trying to learn, how the knowledge can be used in other parts of the organization, and the ease (or difficulty) of knowledge transfer?

4. Establish knowledge connections between subsidiaries
   - Do headquarters managers visit subsidiaries on a regular basis? Do local managers visit headquarters?
   - Has a systematic plan been established for managers to move between subsidiaries and the headquarters?
   - Have subsidiary initiatives been incorporated into headquarters strategic plans and do local managers participate in parent strategic planning discussions?
   - What is the level of trust between headquarters and local managers?

5. Draw on existing knowledge to facilitate learning
   - Have the managers seeking to learn from each other worked together in the past?
   - Are experiences with other subsidiaries being used as the basis for managing current learning opportunity?
   - Are you open-minded about knowledge that does not have immediate short-term applicability?

6. Ensure that headquarters and local managerial cultures are in alignment
   - Is subsidiary knowledge viewed as a threat or as an asset by headquarters managers?
   - Is there agreement at the headquarters on the strategic rationale and value for sharing knowledge between various parts of the organization?
   - In the subsidiaries, do managers understand the importance of the headquarters learning objective?

6

Leveraging Knowledge Resources Globally

In the previous chapter we explored the challenge of managing knowledge in the global organization. We concluded with the thought that to be successful in a global knowledge economy, organizations must not only process information but also create new information and knowledge. For the MNE, the source for new knowledge should be the world. In this chapter we continue the discussion of knowledge but shift the focus to the global allocation of knowledge-based resources. This chapter argues that the current wave of globalization promises to change the way MNEs choose the preferred locations for their value-added functions and activities. Consider the following snapshot of the new realities in the globalization of knowledge in a digital world:

> Cut to India. In dazzling new technology parks rising on the dusty outskirts of the major cities, no one's talking about job losses. Inside Infosys Technologies Ltd.'s impeccably landscaped 55-acre campus in Bangalore, 250 engineers develop IT applications for BofA. Elsewhere, Infosys staffers process home loans for Greenpoint Mortgage of Novato, California. Near Bangalore's airport, at the offices of Wipro Ltd., five radiologists interpret 30 CT scans a day for Massachusetts General Hospital.... Seven Wipro Spectramind staff with Ph.D.s in molecular biology sift through scientific research for Western pharmaceutical companies.... Cut again to Manila, Shanghai, Budapest, or San Jose, Costa Rica. These cities—and dozens more across the developing world—have become the new back offices for Corporate America, Japan Inc., and Europe GmbH.[1]

The first major evolutionary step toward globalization was the shift from a demand focus to a supply focus, when MNEs actively began seeking locations where they could source inputs and/or manufacture products at lower costs. This migration heralded the rise of manufacturing powers such as South Korea, Taiwan, and more recently China. Until then, most MNEs were either focused on their home countries for the bulk of their manufacturing or had moved some of their processes closer to their markets to be more responsive to customer needs. This decentralization approach has evolved further to embrace critical service processes that usually had been earmarked for the home office. Today, many large MNEs routinely decentralize those activities. For example, air carriers such as Lufthansa process their ticketing transactions through partners in India. Financial service firms from the United Kingdom and the United States manage large retirement and pension plans through operations in the Philippines. Leading U.S. computer hardware manufacturers rely on call-center representatives in India and South Africa. The list goes on. The next wave of globalization is upon us, one that promises to change the way we view the typical value-added functions that, historically, MNEs preferred to keep at home. This shift has important implications for the manner in which global strategy is formulated and executed and is the subject of this chapter.

Various reports suggest that, in the next decade, millions of U.S. jobs will migrate to low-wage countries. Similar predictions have been made about jobs in other countries of the developed world, which together with the United States are home to a dominant majority of the world's MNEs. This migration, labeled *offshoring,* is fueled in part by the widespread availability of a reliable information infrastructure coupled with advances in telecommunications that make distributed control of operations feasible in real time. In global industries such as pharmaceuticals, financial services, business consulting, and software engineering, offshoring is no longer a matter of choice but of competitive necessity. When a competitor is able to leverage a lower cost base for the manufacture of products or provision of services, there is tremendous pressure on the other competitors to follow. Thus, most of the large MNEs are forging ahead with offshoring irrespective of the implications for home-country unemployment and the social and economic turmoil that such a radical redistribution of jobs leaves in its wake.

In many developed countries, the rise of offshore operations has sparked serious threats of strikes and worker unrest by white-collar workers. Some governments in these countries have responded with restrictive legislation that insists on products with locally produced content or imposes a ban on offshoring any work done as part of a government contract. The long-term implications of the migration of high-value-added, high-paying, technical jobs are far from clear. Nevertheless, in the words of a software firm executive we interviewed, moving technical jobs to India was an easy decision to make: he had to do it to keep his business solvent. He acknowledged the controversy regarding offshoring but also said that there was no controversy in his company. Had he kept all the work in California, the company would never have survived. (As it turned out, the company did go bankrupt after the tech bubble burst and it had to undergo a painful restructuring.)

What Are Knowledge-Based Functions and Processes?

Philip Evans and Thomas Wurster captured the central arguments that have favored the outsourcing of knowledge-based functions and processes.[2] They said that every business is essentially an information business. A manufacturer of automobiles must be aware of demand and supply patterns, technology developments, changes in sources of supply for inputs, inventory levels, trends among its loyal customers, and its after-sales service record. According to Evans and Wurster, information is what makes value chains and supply chains work. By extension, they argued that it is entirely possible to separate information from the physical aspects of the manufacturing process. For example, although an inventory of raw materials encompasses a range of goods that have monetary value, the process of inventory management relies on information about that inventory rather than the physical inventory itself. Thus, it is possible to manage and control inventory from a distant location using personnel who may never see the goods themselves. Similarly, at the customer end, market research, customer demographics, and customer support are all examples of processes that are rich with an information component.

Separating the physical component from the information component allows organizations to rethink, reengineer, and reconfigure their value chains to maximize added value. For example, in Britain, the Association of Train Operating Companies has contracted with British Telecom and its partners Ventura and Client Logic to handle customers' rail inquiries. The information line is one of the most widely used by the traveling public to access information about train departures, arrivals, and routing. Ventura, based in India, will deploy its call-center operations in Mumbai (Bombay), India, and Yorkshire, in the United Kingdom, to handle the contract. Client Logic will use its centers in New Delhi, India, and Derby, United Kingdom, to do the same. This is a classic illustration of an organization's ability to separate the information aspects of its business from its core processes. Figure 6.1 offers some examples of knowledge-based functions and processes associated with primary value-chain activities.

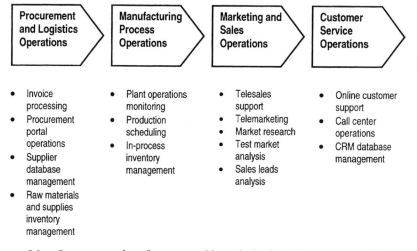

Figure 6.1.   Some examples of outsourced knowledge-based processes and functions in an organization's primary value chain. CRM = customer relationship management.

Offshore Operations—Old Wine in New Bottles?

The migration of jobs with a strong service or knowledge component is quite consistent with the progress of globalization and the disaggregation of value chains. Thus, the phenomenon can hardly be thought of as a radical departure from the way global business is conducted or has been conducted for centuries. Just as China, Taiwan, and Mexico were recipients of manufacturing jobs from U.S. companies seeking more favorable labor and production costs, India, Hungary, South Africa, and the Philippines are witnessing significant inflows of service and knowledge jobs given their attractive cost position. However, although the reasons underlying the migration of knowledge and service jobs parallel earlier waves in manufacturing, the driver of this shift is quite different. It is the transition to knowledge-based competition in most of the industries that has in large part fueled this change.

Classical theories of foreign trade, such as those of absolute and comparative advantage, were predicated on the immobility of key resources such as labor and physical-factor endowments (e.g., availability of raw materials). Since these critical factors of production could not be moved, buyers seeking to take advantage of these resources established operations in countries where the resources were plentiful. But for knowledge-based industries, this reasoning doesn't apply, since knowledge workers (such as computer programmers and systems analysts) can migrate to companies in developed countries where their skills are in demand. Thus, many companies have recruited significant specialized labor resources in countries such as India and China. Having breached the mobility barrier, companies now can locate headquarters, design, manufacturing, and other elements of business almost anywhere feasible. Developments in technology, especially the growing sophistication of telecom networks, have allowed organizations to access knowledge resources in faraway locations without a need to physically transplant such resources to the home country. Companies such as Microsoft and Intel, which have relied on foreign talent for engineering and development services, now operate full-fledged knowledge centers and research facilities overseas, linking these outputs to home-country sites through real-time communication networks. This not only allows them to take advantage of low-cost skilled labor elsewhere but also to leverage time differences to maintain a continuous work flow spanning a 24-hour day.

The decentralization of business processes and knowledge creation offers enormous benefits that transcend mere cost savings (although these savings are quite critical). McKinsey researchers estimated in 2004 that a U.S. software programmer costs the company $60 per hour while her counterpart in India costs only $6—a labor cost advantage that even the most fiercely nationalistic firms would find extremely hard to overlook. McKinsey also found that while about 16 percent of the work in IT services is done remotely, away from the location where the services are consumed, only about 6 percent of software engineering is currently done remotely and only 1 percent of banking services.[3] McKinsey suggests that as much as half of the work in these industries could be moved abroad. Other service industries are also ripe for significant change, including legal services, market research, architecture and drafting, construction design, and insurance.

The urge to move activities offshore is, in significant part, driven by cost pressures and the need to stay competitive and maximize shareholder value. Beyond direct cost savings, the less visible benefits of using offshore locations include:

- Access to better-skilled manpower
- The potential to generate cost savings at home to fund expansion
- Redeployment of home-office personnel to more higher value-added jobs
- The ability to stay competitive in markets where price pressures are significant
- An improvement in the range and responsiveness of customer-centric activities
- The ability to offer 24-hour service
- The ability to offer better jobs for people in emerging markets

Location-Specific Advantage and Access to Manpower

The prominent country destinations for value-added functions with a relatively high knowledge quotient and back-office processes that entail analytical skills have some fundamental similarities. All of these countries offer a qualified labor pool with strong technical skills, high fluency in English, a reliable Internet infrastructure, and competitive labor costs. India, for example, has twice the number of technical graduates as does the United States and has recently accelerated the number of graduates in technical disciplines (see table 6.1).

The plentiful supply of technical graduates in these countries has helped meet the shortage of such talent in the developed world. Countries such as India and China have a relatively well established educational infrastructure that emphasizes analytical skills and numerical ability. India has the added advantage of an education system geared to English as the main language of instruction, making its graduates ideal candidates to take charge of MNE back-office processes. Although the same could be said for South Africa, Ireland, and a few other English-speaking locales, the wage rates in those countries are much higher and, hence, may not offer a value proposition as enticing.

While cost is certainly an important consideration in decentralization decisions, many of the knowledge-related functions cannot be outsourced purely on cost considerations. For example, one of the factors motivating offshore radiology is the need for rapid responses in emergency situations. For emergencies that happen at night there needs to be a radiologist on call—a situation that is becoming increasingly difficult because of a U.S. shortage in radiologists. Use of offshore radiologists during a hospital's evening hours, a practice called "nighthawking," has become much more common in recent years.

The Key Success Factor for Offshoring

For offshoring to be successful, the quality of the overall package (i.e., error-free work, ironclad guarantees of privacy, etc.) has to be superior. Similar to the widely adopted standards in most manufacturing industries, global standards have emerged in knowledge operations as well. For example, software development service companies are rated on the Capability Maturity Model (CMM) developed by the Software Engineering Institute at Carnegie Mellon University. Comprising several achievement levels of organizational expertise and capability, CMM certification is viewed as the gold standard of global software buyers who are in the market for software development services. Of the 14 companies worldwide that have achieved the highest level of certification, seven are based in India—an attribute that is emblematic of the quality

Table 6.1.   Number of Science and Engineering College Graduates

Country	Undergraduate Level		Master's and Doctoral Level	
	1989	1999	1989	1999
China	127,000	322,000	19,000	41,000
India	165,000	251,000	64,000	63,000
Philippines	40,000	66,000	255	937
Mexico	196,000	220,000	61,000	77,000

Source: Data are from *Business Week*, February 3, 2003.

that can be achieved when some knowledge functions are outsourced to that location.

Thus, the decision to decentralize functions with a large knowledge component is mostly based on country-specific considerations that leverage the unique location-specific characteristics to add superior value to the function. Much like the decentralization of manufacturing processes, the decentralization of knowledge-based processes is valuable only when the benefits outweigh the costs. Although there has been a remarkable trend toward greater levels of offshore activity in recent years, some analysts believe that the costs often outweigh the benefits. They cite the costs associated with rectifying error-prone processes and software products, the costs of travel to far-off locations to ensure smooth progress, and the significant adjustments to large time-zone differences—all take a toll on home operations and often lead to costs that exceed promised benefits. However, the trend to shift processes offshore is unlikely to abate anytime soon since lower costs and reasonable quality are powerful lures.

CASE STUDY: KNOWLEDGE OUTSOURCING—THE INDIA ADVANTAGE

India has come to symbolize the new frontier in IT services, much like China is viewed today as the world's factory. Indian companies have been able to leverage some crucial location advantages and build new ones to cement their position as the premier provider of outsourced services spanning software development, design, back-office processes, animation, and graphics design. IT-related products now constitute 27 percent of India's overall exports—a record climb from ground level in less than a decade.

Factor Advantages

India's advantages lie primarily in its skilled labor. The country is projected to expand its labor pool of technically qualified personnel to 17 million by 2008. Although access to local capital markets is severely limited, most of the Indian companies that have established a foothold in IT services have been able to obtain significant capital flows from outside the country. Given the emphasis on this sector as a means of enhancing export revenues, India's central government has undertaken a substantial drive to modernize the telecommunications architecture, opening its doors to foreign competition. A sound telecommunications infrastructure, at least in the nerve centers where IT-related operations are located, has allowed foreign and local companies to access labor at relatively low cost.

Demand Conditions

Much of the Indian IT sector owes its competence to a policy regime that emphasized local self-sufficiency over expensive imports. When IBM was forced to leave the country in the late 1970s, many Indian corporations had to look for alternative local providers who could both maintain existing systems and develop new ones. This gave rise to a new generation of IT firms that were cost-efficient. This competency, nurtured under crippling constraints that limited imports, now offers India a distinct advantage. Overseas buyers are more value conscious than ever, a paradigm that is not new to Indian companies that have operated under similar principles for a long time. It should be no surprise that 225 of the Fortune 500 companies use India as a base for IT services.

Related and Supporting Industries

Educational institutions form the core supporting industry for fueling growth in IT. The well-regarded Indian Institutes of Technology (IITs), established in the 1960s, graduate some of the best and brightest engineers in the field. Entry into these institutes is extremely selective, largely based on entrance examinations that are taken by 200,000 students each year. Only 10 percent of the applicants are admitted. The IITs are complemented by the national universities, technical training schools, and computer training institutes. Many of the large MNEs that have established IT operations in India have now begun supporting these educational institutions to ensure the constant flow of talent to meet their own needs.

Firms, Strategy, Structure, and Rivalry

A wide range of specialized Indian service providers compete for market share both locally and globally. Leading providers such as Infosys, Tata Consultancy Services, and Wipro have established operations in multiple locations worldwide, both for executing contracts close to client facilities and for seeking new business opportunities. Beyond the top tier of blue-chip companies patronized by the world's leading multinationals is an emerging second tier that is equally well stocked and caters to medium and large-scale businesses ranging from architectural consultants to customer service operations. The sheer number of competitors sets up a scenario where only the most nimble and innovative organizations survive. This heightened competition and the concomitant variations in strategies have only helped polish the arsenal of competencies and business acumen that Indian IT firms now bring to the global arena.

What Knowledge Functions Can Be Outsourced?

Decentralization decisions that involve knowledge-based resources or the intellectual capital of the company are often extremely difficult to make. They are inextricably linked with strategic, operational, political, legal, social, and financial considerations. They transcend the simple logic of monetary gains and differential cost advantages. Since intellectual capital is the lifeblood of all organizations, these decisions have to take into account issues such as privacy, security, potential loss of vital competitive information, political hazards, and infrastructure-related risks that routine manufacturing outsourcing decisions may not entail. Beyond the typical considerations of cost, quality, and ability to deliver, the outsourcing decision will be impacted by the need for secrecy and limited access in order to avoid leakage of competitive information, infrastructure reliability, exposure to political hazards, and legal considerations. The characteristics of the process to be migrated, such as transferability, criticality of the business function, extent of client contact entailed, and need to maintain competitive control all impact knowledge-offshoring decisions. Table 6.2 offers an example of the types of decision parameters involved in crafting an offshore strategy. For ease of illustration, the dimensions have been divided into external and internal parameters. External parameters relate to location-specific aspects and, hence, are largely beyond the domain of influence of an individual company, while internal factors relate to parameters that are controllable by the company.

Determinants of the Ideal Processes and Functions That May Be Offshored

There are several process- and function-related parameters that must be weighed in determining the optimal mix of activities that can be decentralized. Although there is a wide array of services that can be obtained through arms-length rela-

Table 6.2.   Decision Parameters in Creating an Offshore Strategy

External Decision Parameters	Internal Decision Parameters
• Country location—access, time zone • Nature of host government policies toward businesses • Stability of host government • Corporate tax laws and the legal institutional framework • Patent protection and enforcement • Hiring and firing practices—incidence of labor unions • Infrastructure—transportation, communications, accessibility • Labor pool characteristics including cost, education level, skill level, trainability, availability, and size of the pool • Language proficiency—level of familiarity with the dominant language that will be used to transact business • Cultural compatibility in terms of social characteristics as well as work behaviors • Level of familiarity with professional management approaches	• Business function characteristics such as criticality of the function, frequency of the process, and need for competitive control • Ability to manage the public relations issues that accompany large-scale job transfers to other countries • Previous experience with foreign ventures especially from a project management perspective • Prior experience with vendor selection and management in foreign locations • Availability of managerial manpower internally to spearhead the move to offshore • Commitment of senior management to an offshore strategy • Ability to implement organizational structures and reporting relationships to maximize the benefits of an offshore strategy ranging from knowledge acquisition and learning to cost containment and quality enhancement

tionships with service providers in low-wage countries, it is imperative that the decentralization decision be driven by sound business logic. Typically such an analysis will encompass the following dimensions:

1. Criticality of the business process or function to overall value creation
2. Extent of direct client contact that the function entails
3. Frequency of transactions
4. Extent of managerial intervention required by the process or function
5. Extent of competitive control that is required over the process
6. Ease of transferability of the function or process

The criticality of a business function refers to the extent to which the function plays a central role in an organization's day-to-day decision making. In a manufacturing firm, functions such as inventory management and production scheduling are critical functions that have a crucial bearing on the implementation of operational strategies. Thus, such functions might inherently be difficult to process at distant satellite locations, cost benefits notwithstanding. On the other hand, industries such as consumer electronics and telecommunications equipment have largely outsourced their manufacturing activities to companies such as Flextronics and Solectron. When this process began, many observers doubted the wisdom of outsourcing manufacturing, since it was believed that manufacturing was a core activity. Now, some years later, it is widely accepted within these industries that manufacturing activities remain critical but can be adequately performed by contract manufacturers.

The extent to which a function closely depends on direct client contact is also an important factor driving the decentralization decision. Functions and processes that require frequent client contact, such as many marketing and sales-related processes, typically will not lend themselves to offshoring. In many of these functions, it is feasible to identify processes that do not require intensive client interface; for example, processes related to customer relationship management entailing the analysis of data could easily be outsourced while the actual customer interface cannot.

The frequency of the transaction is a crucial determinant of the economic benefits of offshore processing. In organizations such as airline companies, financial services companies, or banking institutions, there are many high-frequency business process transactions that are quite routine, such as processing airline tickets and reconciling corporate accounts. These routine transactions require very little managerial intervention, thus such functions often benefit from the significant cost savings that arise from offshore processing. Once the basic processes and control systems are in place, the actual country site where the processing takes place is fairly inconsequential. Thus, almost all the major airline companies have significant back-office operations in countries such as India, where routine functions are handled cost-effectively. In addition, some airlines like British Airways have set up independent processing companies that offer services to other airlines.

Competitive control is another primary determinant of the potential for offshore success. Since many offshore ventures are structured as arms-length or contractual partnerships, they carry all the complexities of traditional firm relationships, including the risk of loss of competitive information. The incidence of information leakage is accentuated by the context within which offshoring is pursued. Typically, the countries where much of this work takes place lack adequate legal infrastructures, raising significant questions about the protection of intellectual property and data privacy. In circumventing this potential risk, some firms have sought to establish wholly owned subsidiaries to undertake offshore functions like back-office operations. However, this decision is one that obviously has significant economic implications, calling for a disciplined cost versus benefits analysis.

The Offshore Decision: Location, Structure, and Ownership

Once the decision to offshore has been made and the offshore functions identified, the organization has to plan its entry strategy. The three major decisions at this stage involve (a) the location where the offshored functions will be performed, (b) the organization structure that will be deployed to maintain oversight of the functions, and (c) the nature of ownership that the organization seeks to exercise over the operations. Although these three decision points address different facets of the process of moving functions to other locations, they are not mutually independent. For example, the choice of ownership structure could be determined by the specific country location being considered and vice versa. The control structure will likewise be influenced by the ownership structure and the location. Thus, given their contingent nature, these decisions must converge on a set of mutually feasible options.

Near-Shore versus Far-Shore

A fundamental choice that organizations confront when outsourcing knowledge functions is between near-shore and far-shore locations. Near-shore locations typically are closer to headquarters and, hence, more politically and socially palatable to its target audience and immediate community than far-shore locations (although not always; moving from Germany to Poland or Hungary is short in miles but often long in attitude). There could be added advantages of cultural similarities that might dampen concerns about the management problems that usually arise in arms-length transactions. For example, companies headquartered in the United States often choose Canada for some of their call-center operations, given their heightened sensitivity to the political and social backlash from far-shore operations in locations such as India. While this choice might help the company maintain an even keel with respect to public relations, it could quite easily have a negative impact on the organization's bottom line, especially because the wage differentials between the United States and Canada are not as significant as those between the United States and China or India. The near-shore option might also offer the benefit of maintaining closer control over quality-of-work processes and forge closer relationships with headquarters. However, the closer the two countries are in terms of economics and geography, the greater the likelihood that they will share constraints such as manpower access, infrastructure limitations, and the like. The far-shore option, on the other hand, brings several advantages, such as lower labor costs and a better skilled labor pool. The disadvantages are in the immense coordination challenges, management of multiple cultures, and the political and social storms that recur periodically. Table 6.3 presents the major advantages and disadvantages of near-shore and far-shore locations.

Many organizations pursue a blend of near-shore and far-shore locations. Their choice is invariably driven by the nature of the function being outsourced and the pressures for leveraging cost efficiencies. The "right source" options emerge from a careful evaluation of the costs, benefits, constraints, and challenges associated with the array of location choices measured against key facets of the function targeted for offshoring.

Structuring an Offshore Entity

Structuring an offshore entity to take over routine business processes is a complex maneuver. It entails aligning organizational goals and strategies with on-the-ground realities. While some organizations prefer to structure their offshore

Table 6.3.   Major Advantages and Disadvantages of Near-Shore versus Far-Shore Location Options

Near-Shore	Far-Shore
• Easier for organizations to pursue in light of potential backlash against the migration of jobs • Cultural similarities with the near-shore location might help minimize operational problems, especially in customer contact functions • Might be a better option for projects and functions that are by definition loosely defined and require frequent intervention • Carries a reduced perceived business risk given potential similarities in economic, legal, and social systems • Coordination and control become easier due to geographic proximity • Might be cost-effective in terms of travel and hands-on contact time spent by headquarters personnel • Might not be able to leverage significant cost savings since the costs of doing business may not be substantially different across locations	• Far-shore locations offer significant advantages in labor cost, access of skilled manpower, and overall operations costs • Since far-shore locations do not share many similarities with the home base, it is likely that business risk factors will not co-vary • Some far-shore locations such as China and India have qualified and technically competent workforces, making it feasible to hire people with advanced skill sets at relatively lower costs; this improves output quality • The control and coordination costs could be prohibitive if they entail significant intervention from the home base on an ongoing basis • Might be less suitable for evolving projects that do not have clear work specifications • Managing a culturally different workforce often poses additional challenges that limit the ability to implement a unified headquarters system of beliefs and practices

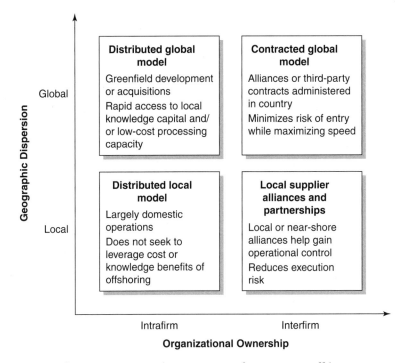

Figure 6.2. Alternative structural arrangements for managing offshore operations.

knowledge operations as wholly owned subsidiaries, others prefer either an arms-length relationship established through a third-party vendor or an intermediary or alliance relationship. While each choice comes with its own advantages and disadvantages, the decision on structure is usually driven by the specifics of the function or process. Figure 6.2 shows the various options.

Establishing de novo operations in the form of a wholly owned subsidiary provides the obvious advantages of control over the operation, an ability to implement corporate policies and procedures, and some safeguards against poor work quality. On the other hand, an arms-length relationship or an alliance helps overcome local obstacles such as managing a local workforce, handling cultural differences, and overcoming local regulatory roadblocks, all of which require considerable experience and learning for a newcomer to do on its own. For example, organizations such as GE, Microsoft, and Intel have chosen the de novo approach in India. Others such as Cisco Systems, Lloyds TSB, and Barclays have chosen to partner with third-party vendors to execute their offshore strategy in the same country.

CASE STUDY: GENERAL ELECTRIC

General Electric (GE) has been one of the leading proponents of offshore outsourcing, both in the area of manufactured products and in its knowledge-based services.[4] GE went to India in 1902, when it installed India's first hydroelectric plant. Over time India has become an important market, generating about $1 billion per year for GE. Along the way, GE realized that India had particular competencies in science and mathematics, and so it established a major research campus in Bangalore to leverage the abundance of skilled engineers. GE also developed a successful world-class outsourcing operation in India employing 22,000 people in operations spanning call centers, back-office processing operations, software development, product design, and R&D. This made GE the largest foreign MNE engaged in the offshoring of knowledge-based products and services in India. GE even designed a virtual plastics plant in India based on its real plant in Spain, where Indian scientists and engineers could monitor real-time operations in Spain and offer advice to their Spanish counterparts on increasing efficiency. Given the wide-ranging nature of GE's knowledge-based services, the company has emphasized de novo operations instead of relying on third-party vendors. About 50 percent of GE's software is developed in India. The network management functions of GE Medical Systems are largely controlled from India. GE's $80 million John F. Welch Technology Center in Bangalore works on projects that feed into all 13 major businesses under the GE umbrella.

The de novo approach was the most appropriate choice for GE for a variety of reasons. First, its operations in India involved crucial knowledge functions such as nonstandard software development, critical network management, real-time systems monitoring, and global product design and development. These functions have a large proprietary component with important competitive strategy implications and hence need to be internalized. Second, given its long history in India, GE is obviously much more knowledgeable about managing an Indian workforce, adapting to the local culture, and navigating local governmental regulations. Third, GE used a blend of employees from its U.S. operations—typically Indian expatriates who have relocated to India to help infuse GE's hallmark culture and management practices among the new employees.

In 2004 GE decided to sell a majority stake (60%) in its Indian outsourcing arm, GE Capital Services, for $500 million to two private equity firms. According to GE, the reason for selling the stake was to "unleash a new entrepreneurial spirit" in the company and to pursue new business with firms outside GE.

Cisco Systems (Cisco), the network products manufacturer based in San Jose, California, has used a blend of both de novo operations and third-party vendors to manage its R&D requirements.[5] Cisco operates its own R&D center in Bangalore, India, and complements this resource by partnering with three Indian vendors who are among the leading offshore service providers in the country. Along with its partners, the company employs about 2,200 people in India, of which 600 work directly for Cisco at its development center. The partners operate stand-alone offshore development centers (ODCs) with a dedicated set of employees and communications systems explicitly for serving Cisco. This arrangement allows Cisco to ensure that competitive information enters the ODCs and that the products designed there stay secure. Samu Devarajan, the head of the Cisco development center in Bangalore, suggested that Cisco chose a partnership option because the company was planning inorganic growth that could not have been achieved by Cisco's development center alone.

The blended approach with an emphasis on partnership seems to be an ideal solution for Cisco because it helps leverage location-specific advantages such as access to cheap and highly skilled labor and also access to large third-party vendors well versed in managing successful partnerships with U.S. MNEs. The blended approach gives Cisco the ability to scale up its product development operations very quickly without having to make significant capital investments for new start-ups. The company is obviously quite comfortable with the controls it has in place to prevent the misuse of competitive information.

A Third Approach for Structuring Offshore Operations

A third and newer option for structuring offshore operations involves a variation on the conventional partnership arrangement with a third-party vendor. Unlike the conventional partnership arrangement, whereby contract services are performed by the vendor at preset fees and charges, the new form includes an element of risk and revenue sharing. For example, Wipro, the Indian offshore service provider, develops software products for its telecommunications network management clients for a development fee that includes a proportion of revenues generated by the sale of these products. This seems a unique way by which the embattled telecommunications companies can sustain new product innovation without bearing all the risks associated with such complex product-development ventures. The upside for the third-party vendor is the potential to leverage its captive access to low-cost labor and technological expertise and to ride the wave of success should the product balloon into a major innovation.

Wholly Owned Subsidiaries versus Contractors

While the intensity of management challenges faced in a de novo wholly owned venture could indeed differ from those presented in a contractual partnership, it is very likely that the crucial aspects of handling a diverse workforce, ensuring service quality, and managing virtually will remain prominent. The proximity of the offshore operation and the nature of the company's relationship with the offshore operation (de novo versus alliance or partnership) are among the two most crucial variables. A fully owned offshore facility will offer the best potential for close operational control and quality monitoring, allowing the company to imprint its value systems and belief structures on its employees in far-flung locations. However, this does not always happen on it own. For example, when Siemens set up a regional development facility in India to leverage native software talent and a low-cost labor pool, it launched a fully owned venture.[6] This development center was charged with creating software solutions for applications in the telecommunications segment, primarily for a European clientele. Despite implementing the best project management practices that Siemens had distilled from years of experience with 16 other global development centers, the company found that its learning curve was rather steep. Coordination costs skyrocketed by 15 percent because of the sheer number of expatriates who had to be deployed in India, the travel costs associated with supervising projects in India, and the constant teleconferences between headquarters in Munich and the Bangalore facility. Siemens had to patiently solve significant cultural, technical, and motivational problems, as well as deal with government regulations to make Bangalore a productive node in its network. It took over five years for the process of acculturation and resource acquisition to run its course before the center was able to take independent responsibility. Currently, Siemens uses its Bangalore facility to spearhead all its 3G-based software development efforts.

The benefits of using a third-party provider to orchestrate the migration of processes from home office to offshore facility are manifold. These independent service providers are likely to be entrenched in the local economy and well versed in navigating the cultural, political, and economic realities. For example, many companies find that employee retention is a significant management challenge. The competitive labor market not only drives wages constantly upward but also gives rise to routine poaching of trained talent. Thus, retaining employees requires a careful blend of compensation and development opportunities challenging enough to hold employee interest. Independent providers are experts in these matters and have significant advantage over de novo operators. In the fierce political debate over the migration of jobs to emerging countries, some companies feel it in their best interests to stay out of the debate by using independent providers to handle the business, circumventing political fallout at least in the short term. The independent service provider functions much like any other contract vendor of goods and services. Indeed, a new genre of intermediary companies (e.g., NeoIt, a specialized consulting firm) has emerged to counsel multinational firms on the process of leveraging benefits from offshore processing. Some of the world's largest consulting companies, such as IBM and Accenture, are already major players in this area.

The key downside to using an independent service provider is the risk of loss of competitive information. While contracts can be structured to ensure that adequate controls are in place, there is no failsafe method to prevent competitive information from falling into the hands of competitors. There is also the very real possibility that increased reliance on contracted offshore services could ultimately damage the innovative capacity of the organization and undercut its ability to add value in any meaningful manner. There have been numerous stories in the business press that tell about the wrongful use of private data by an offshore provider as well as attempts by offshore programmers to sell software designs to their clients' competitors. Table 6.4 summarizes some of the key costs and benefits of using a wholly owned approach and a contracted provider approach.

Successfully Managing Offshore Relationships

Whether the arrangement is a wholly owned subsidiary, a contracted partnership in the form of a vendor, or a third-party services intermediary, managing an offshore relationship requires some unique skills and competencies. Geographic distance, cultural dissimilarity, and variations in employee skills at the offshore location make for a challenging management environment. When offshore facilities take on the routine tasks of fundamental business processes, they need to be integrated into the organizational network on a real-time basis. Decisions to be made in one part of the network rely on data originating in a different part of the network, and most often in real time. Take the example of Lufthansa, the German flagship carrier that processes most of its ticketing functions in India. The Indian facility maintains all information systems pertaining

Table 6.4.   Key Costs and Benefits of a Wholly Owned Model and a Contracted Provider Model

Wholly Owned	Contracted Provider
• Offers the best possible level of competitive control over operations • Internalizes all the cost benefits associated with offshoring since it eliminates intermediary margins • Allows the firm to establish its own value structure and belief system over the offshore facility to ensure a seamless migration between home office and the subsidiary • Provides excellent channels to ensure that output quality meets established standards and complements the process with a well-tested system of checks and balances developed at the home office • Could provide global career development opportunities that transcend subsidiary borders—an important tool in increasing employee retention • Normally takes a longer period of time to realize cost benefits since the start-up will require substantial coordination costs • Often a challenge to establish home office norms (e.g., policies and procedures) • Often challenging to maintain reasonable levels of employee retention in a market that is very competitive and where noncompete contract clauses are not easily enforceable	• Offers the quickest solution to entering the offshore labor market in order to gain cost benefits with the least amount of project gestation time • Leverages the expertise of the provider that is likely to include an in-depth understanding of important dimensions such as local labor market conditions, skills availability, and regulatory restrictions • Builds on the experience curve and learning advantages that the contract provider would have already internalized • Offers some limited protection from the negative public relations fallout that invariably accompanies the migration of knowledge-based jobs to offshore locations • Provides flexibility in ramping up and scaling down operations on an "as needed" basis, a prospect that would be difficult in the case of a wholly owned subsidiary model • The firm that is buying contracted services needs to be able to enforce contracts in emerging markets should there be a leakage of competitive knowledge, often a very costly proposition • Long-term reliance on the contract provider model has to be limited to noncore functions, forcing the firm to forgo cost and quality benefits that could arise by outsourcing some of the core functions

to routes, seat availability, and fares. Managers in Lufthansa's Frankfurt office routinely scan the data to make decisions regarding projected passenger and revenue yields on the thousands of daily departures, adjusting fares to make sure that optimum yields can be realized. Thus, the geographically distant offices need to perform their functions in a synchronous manner calling for management skills that transcend geographic, cultural, and technological boundaries. Thus, success turns on the ability of the managers to marshal virtual teams.

Virtual teams are new entities that sprang up with the advance of offshore outsourcing. These teams encompass members who may or may not work for the same company, who may or may not belong to the same culture, who may or may not possess the same functional skills. Yet this geographically dispersed network has to be closely choreographed to ensure that organizational objectives are met. Apart from the usual demands originating in geographic and cultural diversity, a new set of challenges arises: these networks often involve members of third-party organizations such as specialized service providers. Leadership of virtual teams consequently demands a blend of skills ranging from persuasion and technological competence, to the ability to manage high levels of ambiguity and cross-cultural communication.

Best Practices in Leveraging Offshore Locations

Organizations that compete at the frontiers of globalization are quickly beginning to understand the need to access knowledge-based advantage across borders. What typically started out as routine back-office processing, as in the case of GE, has blossomed into a research and development center in India that develops most of GE's proprietary software systems, performs significant design functions in areas ranging from aerospace to medical imaging, and processes much of GE's routine accounting transactions. The experiences of Microsoft and Intel, among others, have been quite similar. Synthesizing some of these experiences into best practices offers insights into approaches to handle offshore knowledge-based functions.

Successful companies have shown that there is considerable value in thinking about outsourcing and offshoring along strategic lines rather than as tactical moves to match prevailing demands for increased efficiency and cost-effectiveness. American Express, for example, has been using offshore facilities in India for business process transactions for over a decade. This exposure evolved into operating call centers both in both near-shore and far-shore locations and using of a blend of independent service providers and wholly owned facilities to manage its critical software development projects. Much of the company's success has been predicated on careful strategic analysis of the value fundamentals of offshoring. This helps the firm guard against what could sometimes be a herd response to what others have done.

Analysis must supersede expediency. The analysis must encompass exhaustive cost versus benefits estimates that account for all real and imputed costs, such as the costs of coordination, travel, and use of expatriate managers overseas. Although most organizations factor in obvious costs such as wages and benefits, they often do not factor in the largely invisible costs of coordination.

The benefits that can be expected, such as improved quality levels in output, cost savings, reduction in development cycle time, and so on, must also be appropriately captured. A thoughtful audit of skills and competencies required for successfully moving some business processes offshore is a key milestone. This audit includes detailed analyses of the strength of the local talent pool and productivity comparisons. The evaluation of intended strategy, along with a comprehensive analysis of costs and benefits, will help address issues relating to ownership structure and questions of wholly owned facilities versus using contracted services.

Clear articulation of objectives and expectations should shape the work undertaken by the offshore facility. This process involves setting realistic goals for the offshore facility and ensuring that the resources required for meeting those goals are readily available. There must be a strong commitment from senior management to the offshore strategy as a prerequisite for success. Often this commitment takes the form of in-person visits, cross-company meetings, and communiqués from top management about the role of the offshore facility in the overall strategy of the organization. The deployment of resources must be matched with a robust monitoring system of checks and balances to optimize the use of offshore resources. It is a necessity to periodically examine the fundamental logic behind the offshore venture to make sure that the rationale fits new market realities that might have emerged. This should encompass the often difficult questions of cost of delivered services, especially for in-house operations compared to market prices. This disciplined comparison with market prices focuses the organization on the value proposition of its offshore facilities.

Conclusion

While offshoring has generated substantial controversy and antiglobalization activists excoriate companies for using offshore locations, the reality is that most industries and value-chain activities remain solidly nonglobal. Diana Farrell argues that, to date, few businesses have recognized the full scope of performance improvements that globalization makes possible.[7] She suggests that globalization creates opportunities for step changes in performance, and that firms can save enormous money by globalizing their value chains. To do this, firms must use global assets effectively and efficiently, and they must understand the benefits and risks associated with building a global value chain. Moreover, firms that do not exploit these opportunities will be left behind.

To be successful in leveraging offshore activities, firms are institutionalizing the following best practices:

- Articulating a clear, defensible strategic rationale (both short and medium term) for engaging offshore facilities in moving knowledge-based functions and processes.
- Providing a comprehensive assessment of costs and benefits that explicitly accounts for hidden transaction costs, such as the deployment of expatriate managers or the use of special coordination devices. These assessments also include a realistic estimation of the benefits in terms of cost savings, new knowledge acquisition, and enhanced output quality.
- Choosing between wholly owned and contracted provider models on the basis of strategic need rather than expediency and cost consideration.
- Cultivating excellent partnering skills, cross-border management skills, and virtual teaming skills among employee cadres across all levels of the organizations that are likely to be come into contact with offshore operations.
- Setting clear and explicit goals and expectations for the offshore facilities while providing the resources needed to accomplish the assigned tasks. This calls for a comprehensive audit of skills and competencies and the creation of long-term staffing plans and career development paths.
- Creating adequate monitoring systems that are not too onerous but at the same time rigorous enough to provide a snapshot of performance and progress on an ongoing basis. The system must offer enough flexibility for local management to demonstrate initiative within the broad contours of expectations articulated by the home office.

7

Global Strategy in Emerging Markets

The forces of globalization, technological development, economic growth, and trade liberalization have defined the next arena that will make or break corporate reputations. Gone are the days when established MNEs could seek solace in commanding market positions in the developed world. Emerging markets represent the next big growth opportunity for the world's multinationals, and the race to dominate this rapidly evolving terrain is under way. The emerging economies have not just been transformed into fertile markets for the products and services that the developed-country multinationals have to offer but also have evolved into reliable suppliers for a wide range of goods and services. Indeed, the next wave of global players is rising from these very markets. Emerging-market multinationals such as Haier and Huawei of China, Taiwan Semiconductor Manufacturing and Acer of Taiwan, and Embraer of Brazil are emblematic of this new breed of competition. The end of corporate imperialism, as Prahalad and Lieberthal have proclaimed, may well be at hand.[1]

The growth of the big emerging markets (usually defined as Argentina, Brazil, China, India, Indonesia, Mexico, Poland, South Korea, and Turkey) has been carefully documented by several scholars over the last decade. Much discussion has centered on the economic potential being unleashed in countries such as India and China, which historically had been handicapped by poor infrastructure, regulatory constraints, and a bleak economic landscape. While there is undoubtedly significant potential in much of the developing world, it has proved difficult for many of the leading multinationals to effectively tap into local demand. The business press is rich with stories of companies that have faced significant financial reverses following jubilant entries into emerging markets. In this chapter we examine these emerging markets from a strategic perspective, with the goal of developing an understanding of the opportunities and challenges that lie ahead. A fundamental premise here is that the obstacles to success in emerging markets are greater than the typical international business dimensions of cultural differences and geographic proximity. The barriers that firms encounter in emerging markets are fundamental and often call for radically new thoughts on defining and implementing corporate strategy.

What Is an Emerging Market?

Despite popular use of the term, there is no such thing as a typical *emerging-market* country. The term itself is used rather loosely to refer to markets in countries that have significant potential for growth following a prolonged period of infrastructural, economic, institutional, and/or political weakness. Thus, a significant number of countries in the developing world are often characterized as emerging markets. However, those are quite different from *less developing countries* (LDCs). Although the two groups may share endemic weaknesses, emerging markets typically reflect significant propensity for growth while LDCs do not. In reviewing the broad domain of emerging markets, it is helpful to examine some of the physical and institutional characteristics of immediate relevance to the strategy maker.

The defining features of an emerging market are the developmental status of its physical infrastructure (i.e., communications, transportation, electricity, ports, etc.), its institutional infrastructure, its sociopolitical fabric, and its economic performance record and potential. Table 7.1 provides a synopsis of the key differences between these characteristics when comparing emerging markets with developed-country settings.

Physical Infrastructure

One of the distinctive challenges facing the strategy architect in an emerging market is a relatively weak physical infrastructure. While there are indeed significant variations in infrastructure quality even across emerging markets, in general the reliability of the telecommunications networks is spotty; the availability of surface transport is constrained by a poor roadway network; and the supply of energy is a continuing challenge. Consider the following from a 2004 *Wall Street Journal* article:

> The traffic is so bad on the road to India's busiest port here [Mumbai] that local truckers measure speed in hours per mile instead of miles per hour . . . With container traffic surging as India's economy booms,

Table 7.1.   Characteristic Differences in Physical Infrastructure between Developed and Emerging Markets

Characteristic	Developed County	Emerging Market
Communications	Typically well developed. Significant inflow of investment into creation and maintenance of nationwide communication systems. Very little incidence of systems failures. Reliable technology that is constantly renewed and updated. Very visible private-sector involvement.	Usually directed by national policies that set priorities. Weak inflows into creation of nationwide networks given capital shortages. Often relies on outdated technology. Unreliable performance with potential for frequent systems failures. Historically owned and operated by the government but may be privatizing.
Transportation	Well-established system of roadways, waterways, ports, and air traffic systems connecting most of the country.	Limited transportation network that links key cities. Reaching secondary and tertiary markets may be difficult given inadequate transport networks. Many of firms are likely to be directly or indirectly operated by the government.
Energy	Well-designed and operated national power grid. Power shortages are either nonexistent or very rare. Many privately owned and operated power providers.	Inadequate power supply often constrains manufacturing sector productivity. Power shortages are rampant. Very little private-sector involvement.

hundreds of trucks—10 abreast in places—are sometimes stuck in five-mile lines for as many as 30 hours before they can unload their cargoes of towels, tea and tractors to be shipped around the globe. . . . It can take six to 12 weeks, for example, to deliver products to the United States from India, while Chinese exports can move from the factory floor to U.S. stores in as little as three weeks.[2]

Much of the weakness in physical infrastructures originates in the capriciousness of governmental policies that are changed with each election cycle and the concomitant changes in priorities. It is exacerbated by significant constraints of available capital and competing demands for scarce resources. In most of the emerging economies, significant portions of the physical infrastructure remain under the control of the government. The level of private-sector involvement is limited, although this may be changing, given the massive privatization programs under way in much of the developing world. China, for example, spent close to $1 trillion over a five-year period (1995–2000) to improve its roadways, build dams to augment power needs, and construct bridges to improve surface transport. Similar massive infrastructure improvements are in progress in most of the emerging markets, and indeed these may represent some early opportunities for developed-country multinationals in the construction, power, and extraction industries (although MNEs have learned to be cautious when it comes to involvement in government-owned infrastructure projects—see the discussion of Enron later in this chapter).

The prevailing weakness in physical infrastructure can impact global strategy in many ways. For example, subsidiaries of U.S. multinationals in Prague, Warsaw, or Budapest often find it easier to route their intercountry calls through the United States because of the poor telecommunications infrastructure in these cities.[3] Also, the inability to transport products by road adversely affects location choices. For example, refrigerated trucking is not widely prevalent in India, making it a challenge for ice cream manufacturers to penetrate rural areas. The non-standard railway lines originally used to ward off foreign invasion in Russia have resulted in a patchwork system of tracks that is incompatible with Russia's neighbors, making it difficult to move goods across those borders. These are but a few of the innumerable examples that veterans of emerging markets are familiar with.

Given the nature of these obstacles, firms seeking to enter emerging-market countries might be forced to use costly alternatives, such as private communications networks, captive power-generation plants, and multiple manufacturing locations closer to key market regions (some emerging markets have been referred to as BYOI markets—bring your own infrastructure). Many of the infrastructure companies, as well as those in the extraction industries, are all too familiar with these demands. ExxonMobil, the oil and gas major, often builds entire towns around its key sites to provide reliable captive services. On occasion these services are even made available to the local population, which may not have safe drinking water or reliable electricity. While these additions might be considered value-destroying in a developed country, they often ease the entry of multinationals into emerging markets.

The infrastructure challenge in emerging markets requires organizations to be innovative in their approach and to overcome the typical tendency to implement standardized solutions. For example, Hindustan Lever (see case study on the next page), the Indian subsidiary of Unilever, maintains one of the best retail distribution networks in India. The network uses a variety of transportation modes ranging from rail and road, and even small boats, to reach remote settlements in the southern states. Bertelsmann, the German publishing company, runs a book club through a joint venture in China. Given the inability of the Chinese postal system to handle bulky packages of books, the company limits membership to those in cities and uses cycle rickshaws instead of the post to deliver its books.

CASE STUDY: HINDUSTAN LEVER LTD.—TACKLING THE CHALLENGE
OF DISTRIBUTION IN RURAL INDIA

Over 70 percent of India's 1 billion people live in rural communities that are often very small and isolated.[4] Given the vast geographic spread of these communities and the weak physical infrastructure, companies are forced to think of novel ways to reach this sizable market. While retail distribution systems combining rail, road, bicycles, and even small boats are fairly common, Unilever's Indian subsidiary—Hindustan Lever (HLL)—implemented a unique approach to tap the economic power in rural India. Called Project Shakti, which means "strength," HLL launched a direct marketing scheme along lines similar to that of Amway and Avon to sell bath products to Indian villagers. The company organized self-help groups of 10 to 15 women each; these groups access micro-credits through nongovernmental organizations that partner with HLL to buy bath products in small volumes. HLL offers free management and sales training to the groups, and the women go door-to-door selling the products. Most of the women are successful in creating a micro-business, which earns them roughly $20 a month, doubling their household income to make a tangible difference in their quality of life. The program has been extremely successful and HLL reports that over 6,000 groups are currently active. This has proved to be a win-win situation for both HLL and the rural villagers. It offers the company a cost-effective way of reaching critical rural markets that are otherwise difficult to penetrate and it affords the average villager an opportunity to gain economic strength.

Institutional Infrastructure

The institutional infrastructure encompasses the legal system, the banking system, and the capital markets that have a significant bearing on the ability of firms to raise money for their activities, conduct businesses, and enforce contracts. Emerging markets often do not have the robust institutional systems that developed countries have established over time. Thus, organizations operating in emerging markets have to design alternative approaches to remedy these institutional deficiencies.

Capital Markets

In the next chapter we discuss international corporate governance, and argue that in many emerging markets there is a poor degree of legal protection and enforceability of investors and stakeholders' interests. As La Porta and colleagues have argued, opaque systems and the lack of adequate safeguards for investor rights give rise to weak and badly functioning capital markets.[5] In turn, this situation reduces the propensity of investors to back new ventures and creates a limited market for risk capital. Private venture-capital funds are equally scarce. The few venture-capital funds that operate are typically set up by international development banks and financial institutions such as the International Finance Corporation (IFC), which are risk averse to begin with. Further, many of these countries have archaic tax laws that discriminate against equity investments and favor debt capital.[6] If a company manages to overcome these formidable obstacles and access equity financing from the capital markets, it will have to contend with a regulatory burden that can often be crippling. The listing and reporting requirements can be quite extensive, although the accompanying monitoring is weak. In most emerging economies, there is often a dual standard with respect to regulatory compliance; that is, most often the subsidiaries of foreign firms are held to a higher standard. For example, foreign banks that operate in India have historically been subject to much more intensive reporting requirements than have local banks. (Table 7.2 presents rankings of the big emerging markets and the United States on key capital-market indicators.)

Despite the differences in reporting, transactional transparency is hardly the norm. Since many of the emerging markets are built either on the "insider" model or the "family/state" model of ownership and governance, there is very limited flow of information to the public on company performance.[7] Insider-model

Table 7.2. Ranking of the Big Emerging Markets and the United States on Key Capital Market Indicators

Country	Financial Market Sophistication	Access to Loans	Venture Capital Availability	Financial Regulation	Equity Market Access	Reliance on Retained Earnings
Argentina	31	56	65	24	66	5
Brazil	12	29	27	28	34	24
China	64	60	49	60	53	33
India	36	25	26	39	21	36
Indonesia	55	48	62	68	49	43
Mexico	34	64	63	55	48	49
Poland	37	27	37	30	28	27
South Korea	46	38	20	61	44	13
Turkey	35	38	72	64	33	54
United States	1	6	1	4	16	40

Source: Data in above table taken from annual survey by Michael E. Porter, Jeffrey D. Sachs, Peter K. Cornelius, John W. McArthur, and Klaus Schwab (Eds.), *The Global Competitiveness Report 2001–2002* (New York: Oxford University Press, 2002).

countries are usually bank centered and organizations show a significant dependence on banks and allied institutions for their funding. In lieu of arms-length lenders, the banks tend to have personal, complex working relationships with their clients and are often extensions of the governmental bureaucracy. Thus, confidential sharing of information and lack of public disclosure are more the norm rather than the exception. Personal relationships with banks and other financial institutions assume far greater significance than they do in developed countries.

Access to both long-term and short-term debt can be equally daunting. Most emerging-market banking networks are owned in part or in full by the government, which sets priorities for lending. There is a strong likelihood that organizations with preferential access to government-owned banks will be able to obtain more favorable terms than firms that don't have such links. This situation places the MNE subsidiary in a quandary since the likelihood of its leveraging personal relationships with the local banks is rather low. Private financial institutions are usually outnumbered by their public-sector counterparts and may not be able to meet the entire needs of the foreign subsidiaries. Thus, many companies become less ambitious in their growth and expansion objectives since much of it has to be funded through capital infusions from the parent company or through retained earnings at the subsidiary. And capital infusions from the parent company can be a daunting proposition when political risk is high and private property rights are questionable—or subject to the whims of the government.

In response to corporate governance weaknesses in capital-market infrastructure, many local firms rely on diversified portfolio holdings to finance their operations and expansion. As Khanna and Palepu observe, many of the conglomerates perform the role of venture capitalists and direct their investment resources to various parts of their portfolio, thereby overcoming the institutional voids.[8] This also raises their potential to sustain weaker margins or even losses in parts of their portfolio in order to establish a firm footing in newer business areas, a strategy that is seldom supported by investors in countries with vibrant capital markets. The attractiveness of these conglomerates is also accentuated by the fact that there is often a marked absence of alternative investment opportunities, thus making conglomerates the beneficiaries of whatever meager capital resources the external markets can spare. Typically, they have preferential access from the local banks with which they enjoy longstanding relationships. The banks are normally reluctant to counsel management against unrelated diversification since they owe a large part of their lucrative noninterest income to such organizations and perhaps due to the rationale that diversification in such economic contexts can actually yield positive results.[9,10] Taken together, the conglomerate in an emerging market is a creation of progressive attempts to remedy institutional voids and one that has a fairly wide array of capital resources sufficient to cause significant concern to the newly created MNE subsidiary.

Subsidies and Distortions

Governments in many emerging markets provide explicit or tacit support to local firms through subsidies or other means of regulatory control that handicap the MNE subsidiary in its ability to compete. For example, local-content regulations, tax subsidies, and direct purchase price supports are all forms of the visible hand of government. In the realm of capital resources, many emerging-market firms are state-owned organizations. Therefore, by virtue of their ownership structure, they have very little incentive to engage in proactive competitive strategy. When they do compete aggressively, they are helped in large part by the government. While this is not limited to emerging markets, it tends to occur with more frequency in developing-country contexts than it does in developed markets. Coupled with regressive tariffs, these subsidies might all but render the products and services of the MNE subsidiary uncompetitive.

Consider the case of Singapore International Airlines (SIA). SIA has been heralded as one of the most competitive carriers in civil aviation worldwide. Its approach to competitive strategy has been built around excellence in customer service and ground operations, and an overall emphasis on effective and efficient management of its cost structure. However, many observers believe that the critical difference in SIA's ability to compete effectively is its ownership structure. SIA was originally incorporated as a wholly owned subsidiary of Temasek Holdings, an organization set up by the government of Singapore to oversee all government holdings in companies such as SIA. Today, Temasek holds 56 percent of SIA and the rest of the shares are publicly traded (the majority owned by institutional investors). Some industry analysts argue that the high level of government ownership allows SIA to experiment in ways that market-owned companies cannot replicate. Temasek Holdings maintains that it operates much like any other institutional investor and does not afford any protection or unfair advantage to the companies it owns or controls. It is easy to see why competitors may believe otherwise.

Legal Infrastructure

The legal infrastructure in many emerging markets without market-oriented institutions is often inadequate. The judicial system is at times hijacked by political goals and in general there is limited stock placed in its efficacy. The legal framework in some of these settings offers very little protection in critical competitive areas, such as intellectual property protection and transfers of property rights. This is one of the primary reasons many of the leading companies in pharmaceuticals, high technology, and biosciences are reluctant to make investments in emerging markets. Labor laws are equally difficult to navigate. Often these laws are designed to ensure continued employment of workers even to the detriment of the organization's viability. Since layoffs and plant closures are extremely difficult, organizations are forced to look for alternative ways to achieve workforce flexibility. Conglomerates are well placed to sidestep some of these drawbacks since they can shuttle employees from one division or business to another without running afoul of the law.[11]

Perhaps the most critical aspect of legal infrastructure weakness that should concern the subsidiary of an MNE is its ability to enforce contractual arrangements. Absent a strong legal system, contracts are very difficult to enforce. There are numerous examples where companies operating in countries such as China have been forced to exit because they have been unable to seek recourse when local entities have failed to uphold their end of a contractual agreement. (Chapter 9 describes the case of a Chinese company that went far beyond trademark piracy and was attempting to steal a U.S. company's identity.) To complicate matters further, identifying the jurisdiction of each legal entity is itself fraught with problems. Some issues fall within the purview of the federal or central government; others within the purview of the state, provincial, or municipal authorities; and many other matters are jointly acted upon by the center, state, and municipality. It is not surprising to find the legal system plagued with inconsistencies among the various levels of enforcement, making it difficult for an organization to obtain redress in cases of contract infringement. Developed-country MNEs often find it useful to cultivate personal relationships in such contexts so that they can explore alternative channels of conflict resolution rather than be bogged down by a weak judicial system.

In chapter 8 we provide two case studies (BP in Russia and Thai Petrochemical) involving corporate governance and legal issues in emerging markets. The following case study on Enron also illustrates some interesting legal entanglements.

CASE STUDY: ENRON AND THE DABHOL POWER COMPANY

Enron Development Corporation, the infrastructure subsidiary of Enron Corporation, the now-bankrupt Houston-based energy company, signed an agreement with the government of India to build a massive power plant (Dabhol Power Company) with an installed capacity of 2,184 MW at a cost of $2.8 billion. Structured in two phases, the project would be the biggest foreign direct investment India had seen and the largest power plant that Enron had built anywhere in the world. Given the nature of this venture, Enron negotiated very carefully to mitigate the risks of default. Enron obtained a "take or pay" contract with the local state electricity board to ensure that there would be a captive buyer to purchase power at the prices agreed upon. Enron also obtained a second guarantee against default from the central government of India. The government promised that it would indemnify Enron against default by the state electricity board and make good any payments that might be due.

Even as the project was coming on line, there were allegations of corruption and bribery, which, although never proven, generated significant public controversy. The World Bank issued a report saying that the deal was heavily skewed in favor of Enron and bad for India. After the local elections, the new party in power decided to unilaterally abrogate the contract and issued a notice to Enron telling it that the project was suspended. Enron threatened legal action but also tried to build bridges with the local politicians to renegotiate the contract. After several months of negotiation and protracted legal battles with various parties, the project was restarted. Phase 1 was completed in 1998 and the plant began generating power.

In 2001, as the second phase neared completion, the local electricity board could not make its payments to Enron. The government of India stepped in to bear the cost of the default, but then indicated that it could not honor the contract for an indeterminate period. Ken Lay, the CEO of Enron at the time, threatened economic sanctions against India for reneging on a contract but the government refused to budge. The power plant was shut down on the basis of a legal technicality enforced by the state electricity board. The matter remains tied up in the Indian courts with the Indian creditors seeking an injunction against the sale of the assets in India to pay off Enron's creditors in the United States and elsewhere. Although many argue that the initial contract was lopsided in favor of Enron and that a breakdown was predictable, the situation nevertheless demonstrates the difficulties in enforcing contracts in emerging markets. Enron thought it had an ironclad central-government guarantee and events turned out much differently. Unfortunately, Enron's 2001 bankruptcy muddied the waters to the extent that it is impossible to know how this situation's legal outcome might have been resolved.

Politics and Corruption

Political instability is a common feature of emerging markets. Since industrial policy is closely linked to the party in power, governmental priorities can change dramatically within a short time. Corruption, defined by *Transparency International* as "the abuse of entrusted power for private gain," is a major concern, especially when organizations are forced to navigate a regulatory labyrinth to obtaining approvals for all major strategic actions such as new capacity creation, licensing foreign trademarks and brands, obtaining foreign investment from the parent firm, and repatriating profits.[12]

In most of the emerging-market countries, complying with arcane regulations can be a major challenge in itself. For example, a report on daily commerce in the city of Mumbai, India, observed that an average shopkeeper who owns a small corner store has to obtain 30 different approvals and clearances before commencing business. According to a study reported by the World Bank, it takes 152 days to start a business in Brazil and 151 days in Indonesia, compared to 3 days in Canada and 2 days in Australia.[13]

Foreign investments usually are funneled through a central oversight agency that has to approve all inflows. These agencies approve or disapprove investments based on a variety of considerations, many of which tend to be opaque. For example, India relaxed investment limits for foreign investors in the pharmaceuticals sector, allowing them to increase their holdings in the country. In response to this relaxation, Merck and Glaxo had their affiliates issue them preferential shares to increase their holdings to majority levels. When the government clamped down on this practice, firms such as Hoechst and Pfizer applied to the government to set up wholly owned subsidiaries. While the government approved some of these applications, others were denied for no transparent reason.[14] This differential treatment, shrouded by the veil of bureaucratic and regulatory control, raises the level of uncertainty that MNE managers routinely face in emerging markets.

The bureaucratic nature of these regulatory approvals is often a fertile breeding ground for bribery and corruption. While corruption is certainly not the exclusive domain of emerging markets, it plays a far more visible role in such settings than it does in developed countries. Institutional dishonesty can be linked to the relatively low levels of income and poor living standards among a large segment of the population.[15] Whatever the cause, the pervasive and often highly arbitrary incidences of corruption increase the costs of doing business and render the strategy–performance link fairly tenuous since performance outcomes could be determined largely by factors outside the control of management.

The U.S. Department of Commerce estimates that between May 1994 and April 2002, as many as 437 large contracts worth $237 billion could have been tainted by bribery. It also claims that U.S. companies lost 110 of the contracts—about $36 billion in value.[16] It must, however, be pointed out that despite the Foreign Corrupt Practices Act (FCPA) of 1977, which makes it illegal for American firms to offer bribes, fewer than 50 cases have been prosecuted as a result of this act in the last 25 years. (The FCPA is discussed in more detail in chapter 9.) The problem, however, is far more pervasive than the numbers indicate. Consider the following example. Mobil Corporation, the company that later merged with Exxon to form ExxonMobil, is at the center of a major controversy regarding its business practices in Kazakhstan. Mobil won a contract to develop the Tengiz oilfield in an oil-rich region that is believed to contain 6 billion barrels of oil. A deal valued at $11 billion was signed in 1996. James Giffen, an independent U.S. consultant who received a large amount of money associated with the deal, is currently being investigated for violation of the U.S. Foreign Corrupt Practices Act. Giffen has been accused of taking $78 million by way of commissions and fees from various Western oil companies in exchange for contracts and funneling the money to the top levels of government in Kazakhstan. If the charges are proven, ExxonMobil could be fined millions of dollars, forced out of the running for public contracts, and sanctioned. Mobil executive Bryan Williams is also charged in this case as the individual who negotiated the allegedly illicit deal with Mercator, James Giffen's company.

In South Korea, many of the *chaebols* have been accused of encouraging corruption and bribery among government officials at various points in their histories. Similarly, Indian companies are often in the news for having solicited lucrative contracts or licenses through nefarious means. Reliance, one of that country's largest companies, has been accused of building most of its profitable textile and chemical ventures through the implicit connivance of government officials at various levels. This alleged corruption allowed Reliance to manage import tariffs and customs duties in a manner that hurt its competitors but filled its own coffers.[17] In Argentina, kickbacks have become ingrained in the business fabric to the extent that even reputable organizations such as IBM have been accused of offering facilitation payments, a charge that IBM has strongly denied.[18]

MNEs routinely identify corrupt business practices as one of the serious impediments to competing in global markets and especially in emerging economies; table 7.3 shows a ranking of emerging markets on corruption. In summary, the obstacles related to both infrastructure and institutions are quite daunting. However, as many of the world's MNEs are beginning to realize, the tremendous growth potential in emerging markets means that designing strategies to remedy the infrastructural weaknesses could be well worth the effort.

Competing Successfully in Emerging Markets

Emerging-market champions such as Unilever, Nestlé, Coke, Tesco, and Gillette offer several important ingredients for the recipe for success in emerging economies.

Table 7.3.   Ranking of Emerging Markets on Corruption

Country	Corruption Index[a]	Government Favoritism[b]	Business Costs of Corruption[c]
Argentina	70	58	21
Brazil	45	47	52
China	59	34	56
India	71	36	40
Indonesia	96	59	54
Mexico	57	41	45
Poland	45	44	32
South Korea	40	35	43
Turkey	64	46	47
United States	16	17	18

[a]Rankings based on an annual survey published by Transparency International on the incidence of corruption in 102 countries. Higher ranks indicate higher levels of corruption.

[b]Government favoritism rank measures the extent to which the government favors well-connected business groups in key decisions and contracts. Higher ranks indicate higher levels of favoritism. Data are drawn from the annual survey of world competitiveness published by the World Economic Forum (2002).

[c]Business costs of corruption measures the extent to which additional costs are imposed upon an organization due to the incidence of corruption in the particular country. Higher ranks indicate a higher proportion of costs dues to corruption and higher levels of favoritism. Data in above table taken from the annual survey of world competitiveness published by the World Economic Forum (2002).

All of these companies derive a significant proportion of their revenues and profits from emerging markets. Many of them have managed to harness the creative potential of their emerging-market subsidiaries to generate innovations that have then been taken to the global level. In large part their successful experience can be traced to three factors:

1. Targeting a broad market instead of the fortunate few
2. Building distribution systems that reach large segments of the population not easily reachable otherwise
3. Building brands and sustaining image and reputations that deftly blend the local with the global

The sheer size of the market for goods and services in the emerging economies has brought with it an onslaught of multinational corporations seeking to cash in. In China alone, close to 320,000 enterprises have been created with the participation of foreign investors over the last two decades.[19] The track records of these enterprises, however, have been far from stellar. While the business press proclaims victory for a few, many of the companies entering these emerging markets failed and retreated. In many cases of failure, the entries were designed with little consideration of the unique characteristics of the emerging market, its people, and its promise. Those that have survived and prospered have much to offer by way of best practices in emerging contexts.

The Common Myths of Emerging-Market Competition

Given the relative infancy of competition in emerging markets, there are significant gaps in the prevailing wisdom about the competitors, the obstacles to profitability and growth, and the viability of developed-country strategies in such settings. Unfortunately, some of the central assumptions that underlie the design and execution of emerging-market strategies by MNEs are themselves suspect and, hence, the incidence of failure should not come as a surprise.

Myth 1: An Emerging Market Is What a Developed Market Looked Like a Couple of Decades Ago

Many of the world's MNEs seeking to enter emerging economies view them more as incremental opportunities. They believe that these markets are simply behind in terms of development and will take a decade or more to offer the potential that some more developed-country markets offer. Thus, they assume it appropriate to enter with a suite of older products and let the market evolve to the level of sophistication demanded by customers in more developed areas. Emerging markets are consequently seen as ideal sanctuaries for the revival of older product lines and entry costs are minimized because it is assumed that this approach requires very little investment in market development. Mercedes-Benz, for example, entered the Indian market a few years ago with its 190 series, a line that had lost its allure in developed countries a long time ago. The company believed that these models, while unsuitable for developed-country markets, would do well in emerging countries given the lower price point to own an original Mercedes-Benz. The launch was far from successful. These simplistic and often erroneous assumptions precede entry into the industrial sector as well. MNEs routinely ship to emerging markets plants designed to manufacture older lines and handle older technologies. These attempts are defended as appropriate given the potential for loss of competitive knowledge or the inability of the market to assimilate newer technologies.

Emerging markets, by definition, offer tremendous potential for exponential growth. This promise of growth is supported by the rising aspirations of people who are well down the path to becoming sophisticated customers. The novice entrant in such contexts is usually surprised at the level of awareness that already prevails about global brands, products, features, and standards. Given the explosion in information access, this should come as no surprise. Often there is a substantial pent-up demand for goods and services that were not easily available in the country before the entry of the MNE. However, this strong demand may be misinterpreted to mean that the customer is willing to pay even for substantially scaled-down versions of older models or for a "third-world" version of a developed-country product.[20] It is erroneous to assume that the emerging market is in perpetual catch-up mode and that anything the MNE offers is an improvement over prevailing alternatives.

Discontinuous change is a central feature of emerging markets. There are numerous instances where development is far from linear. Technological changes come quickly when the market stirs from its dormant state. Soon the disadvantage of past inaction becomes an advantage. It is this leapfrogging characteristic of emerging markets that offers the best window for an MNE to capitalize. For example, in the key emerging markets of China and India, the availability of digital mobile phones far exceeds the availability of land lines. In many parts of these countries, customers would have to wait several years before they could get a land line, given the poor physical infrastructure. However, these same customers are often able to get a mobile phone in a matter of days since the countries are going to wireless installations without following the typical evolutionary track.[21] Table 7.4 shows the penetration of mobile phone service in emerging markets and in the United States. Similar patterns can be seen in areas such as information technology, where emerging-market consumers are quite knowledgeable and stay current with new developments, thus are more sophisticated buyers than an MNE would expect. This sophistication extends to governments as buyers as well. In large infrastructure projects where the government is the buyer, it is quite common to see the host country insisting on technologies that are reasonably new, if not state-of-the-art.

Myth 2: Emerging-Market Consumers Will Prefer Global Brands over Local Brands

The power of global brands in an emerging market is another dimension that is often overstated. Many new entrants believe that awareness of global brands automatically implies intent to buy. Thus, significant effort is expended in positioning global brands so that suitable premium prices can be extracted. There is likely to be an initial pull to the foreign brands, especially since local customers usually want to experiment with the new offerings. This will be partly a result of sheer curiosity and the prestige that such brands usually connote. However, customers in emerging markets are more prone to frequent brand switching and are unlikely to remain loyal when premiums are high. For example, Indian

Table 7.4.   Mobile Phone Penetration in Emerging Markets and the United States

Country	Cellular Phones in Use, 2002 ('000s)	Cumulative Average Growth Rate, 1995–2002 (%)	% of Digital Phones	Cellular Phones as a % of Total Phones in Use
Argentina	6,500	52.4	n.a.	44.8
Brazil	34,881	60.2	n.a.	47.3
China	206,620	78.1	100	49.1
India	12,687	107.5	100	23.4
Indonesia	11,700	77.5	n.1.	60.5
Mexico	25,928	67.9	n.a.	63.4
Poland	14,000	111.1	n.a.	55.1
South Korea	32,342	53.1	100	58.21
Turkey	23,374	76.6	100	55.3
United States	140,766	22.6	89	42.6

Source: Data in above table taken from International Telecommunication Union, 2003. See http://www.itu.int.

consumers tried 6.2 brands of a single packaged goods category, compared to 2.0 for U.S. consumers.[22] The uphill task of building a brand locally can be quite challenging.

Although emerging-market customers may be aware of the global brand name and the attributes of a product or service, they lack intimate experience with that brand and, hence, are reluctant to pay significant price premiums. Often the global brands encounter stiff competition from other brands that have a longer local history. Local brands might also be better positioned, bolstered by feelings of patriotism or a perception of better value given their local roots. Further, with the onset of global competition, local players typically improve their offerings and may consequently dampen the allure of the foreign brands.[23] For example, when Procter & Gamble entered the China market, there was an initial surge in first-time purchases, but over time sales volume leveled off after local brands began offering a better price-performance proposition. Despite the onslaught of MNEs in China, almost the entire category of white goods (e.g., refrigerators, air conditioners, freezers, washing machines) is dominated by local brands, which hold between 60and 90 percent overall market share.[24] Thus, it is clear that a global brand by itself is an insufficient draw over the medium or long term. Even global brands have to be planted and nurtured locally in order for them to justify the premiums they command. They cannot hope to ride on the coattails of success in developed countries. Companies that have carefully nurtured their global brands are aware of the need to supplement their offerings with local brands. Coca-Cola, for example, derives two-thirds of its sales in Japan from local brands (see the following case study).[25]

Many of the MNEs with leading consumer products and packaged foods have adopted a strategy of deploying a portfolio of brands within the same product suite to more closely align each brand with distinct populations in the emerging market. For instance, Unilever's subsidiary in India has launched several brands that do not form part of its global corporate portfolio. Nestlé sells multiple local brands along with core corporate brands in the same market; for some products, such as the Nescafé brand of instant coffee, Nestlé has the leading seller in its category. For other industry sectors, where the product has to be customized to suit local conditions, a local branding approach is integral to the package. Using local brands offers a context for controlled experimentation without damaging the global brand portfolio that the company might have built in developed markets. For example, HLL offers a range of products in India that Unilever does not sell anywhere else in the world, such as salt and wheat flour. These products leverage the strength of image that HLL, as a company, has established with Indian consumers. Since HLL is known as a leading provider of reliable, high-quality consumer goods, customers are quite indifferent to the specific brand names under which these consumables are marketed. This approach has been a win-win situation for consumers and for the company since Unilever was able to increase revenues without placing its global brands at risk.

Two case studies are provided to illustrate how MNEs have responded to local market demands in emerging markets. The first case deals with Coca-Cola's re-entry into India and the second looks at the beer industry in China.

CASE STUDY: COKE WINS WITH A LOCAL BRAND

Coke re-entered India in the early 1990s, after a long absence from the market. The company left India in the 1970s because of intractable operational constraints imposed by the government then in power. In the 1990s, Pepsi, which had already overtaken Coca-Cola by entering the newly liberalized Indian market, was establishing a strong foothold in the country. The leading cola, however, was a local brand named Thums Up, a beverage that the Indian majority consumed during Coke's absence. This brand had become a powerhouse over the years and was strengthened through astute marketing coupled with a locally responsive product formulation and very good advertising campaigns. Upon its re-entry, Coke initially used a strategy that sought to capitalize on its global brand image. The global campaigns, however, failed to yield results. With the local brands selling well, Coca-Cola had a tough job building market share. Realizing that a global brand was not enough to succeed in the Indian market, Coke acquired Thums Up. Initially the company mothballed the brand and promoted its flagship Coca-

Cola brand. When customers were lukewarm in their response, Coke realized that there could be value in reviving Thums Up. Today, Thums Up accounts for close to 25 percent of the beverage market and has established itself ahead of rival brands such as Pepsi and Coca-Cola. Thums Up has largely been responsible for keeping Coke's hopes alive in India. Coca-Cola has now turned its sights to bottled water with its Kinley brand. However, the competition is quite stiff even in that arena. The main competitor is Bisleri, a brand promoted by the former owners of Thums Up.

CASE STUDY: CHINA'S BEER WARS

China is among the largest beer-producing countries in the world and it promises to become the leader in the industry (on absolute size, not on a per capita basis—the Czech Republic leads the way with an astounding 160 liters per capita in annual consumption). With growth rates averaging 5 percent per year, the country's market seemed very attractive to brewers in Europe and North America, who were facing market saturation in their dominant markets. Foster's of Australia, Anheuser-Busch of the United States, South African Breweries of South Africa, Interbrew of Belgium, Carlsberg of Denmark, and Kirin of Japan were among the biggest players in the beer industry, all of whom were quick to enter the liberalizing China market. Many of them were unprepared for the local nature of competition, however. Given the very high level of fragmentation in the industry (the top three firms account for only 20 percent of the beer output), they found it difficult to develop economies of scale and had to spend significantly to establish their brands locally. Some were unable to take the losses and decided to bail out—Bass, Foster's, and Carlsberg pulled out. One of the reasons for the lack of success is the intense competition from local labels in the rural provinces. Most of these labels had a home region that they dominated and then used to fund expansion into other areas. Their knowledge of the beer-drinking habits in these regions also proved vital to their product formulations and the consequent establishment of customer loyalty. Many of the MNEs thought that they could easily sway the Chinese beer drinkers to try their globally established premium brands. That bet did not pay off. The few remaining global players in China have since turned their attention to acquiring local brands. Anheuser-Busch has recently increased its stake in China's largest brewer, QingDao. South African Breweries, now called SABMiller, offers 20 different local brands in China, which is consistent with its local brand strategy in other emerging markets.

Myth 3: Targeting the Wealthy Few in Emerging Markets
Is a Prudent Entry Mode Choice

A majority of the MNEs that enter emerging markets are driven by fairly sim-plistic computations of market size and local economics. It is customary to use the population base in the given market as a reference point, apply a suitable economic wealth indicator such as income strata, and then extrapolate the num-ber of customers who are likely to buy the goods and services that the company has to offer. This leads to a potential error in estimation because the quality of demand is not factored in: the defined target market is either too large or too small when compared to reality. The definition of the target market should be influenced by other beliefs that the company holds about emerging markets, such as the level of risk, buyer sophistication, and ability to pay.

Often the company finds that its products are priced beyond the reach of the average consumer. However, it takes solace in the assumption that the wealthy 4 to 5 percent of the market would suffice as the ideal target. Invari-ably, in any emerging market there is a small privileged class with incomes com-parable to those in the more developed countries of the world. Therefore, the company believes that if this elite group is the key focus, it can utilize its con-ventional entry strategies that have worked in developed markets. While this may be a defensible approach and a very conservative one, it certainly does not leverage the strengths of the emerging-market context; its focus is woefully in-adequate to make a substantial change to the revenue streams. Many of the new entrants find that the elite group alone is insufficient either to realize the re-quired economies of scale or to warrant the investment in brand building and distribution that a typical market entry calls for. Soon, the top 4 to 5 percent group does not support the infrastructure that the company finds necessary. To exacerbate the situation, local copycats emerge and seek to drive down the pre-mium prices commanded by the MNE. Often, owing to lax intellectual prop-erty control laws, these copycats make a significant dent in the market by focusing on the segments that the MNEs dismiss as nonviable. By the time the MNE decides to target a broader market, it finds entrenched competition and has competed away valuable first-mover advantages.

MNEs seeking to build a tangible and meaningful presence must transcend the limitations of a focus on the wealthy few. The dimensions and the import of this narrow focus can be illustrated by examining the nature of the popula-tion and distribution of incomes in India (see figure 7.1). A multinational com-pany that designs a strategy to target the wealthy few in India is left with an addressable market of about 1 million households. While this market may be

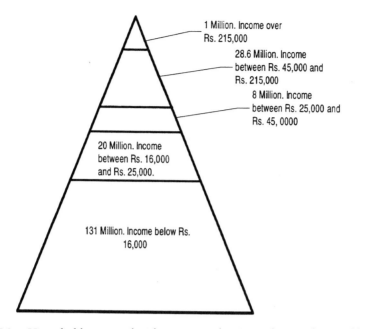

Figure 7.1.   Household income distribution in India. According to the World Bank, the average Indian household had an annual income of $642 (in purchasing parity terms). However, a survey by the National Council of Applied Economic Research shows that there are significant income distribution inequities. Of the roughly 200 million households, about 65% earned Rs. 16,000 or less (equivalent to $333) while a very small proportion (about 0.005%) earned more than Rs. 215,000 (more than $4,480). Despite these inequalities, some believe that India's middle class is about 200–250 million strong. Source: *India Market Demographic Report for 2002* (Delhi, India: National Council of Applied Economic Research).

appropriate in situations where the products or services have a substantial premium price and premium image, it does not leverage the true purchasing power of the masses at the bottom of the pyramid. Since the broader customer audience is far more conscious of the price-performance equation, MNEs can obtain significantly more leverage and revenues if they re-engineer their offerings to penetrate the lower layers of the economic pyramid.

In many cases there may be no choice for the new entrants if they want a meaningful share of the market. Consider the experience of Revlon in China. Revlon entered China with its sights set on the tip of the economic pyramid. It estimated that about 3 percent of the Chinese population would be the extent of its targeted market for its cosmetics. A local competitor, Shanghai Jahwa, offers a lesson in contrast. While Revlon went after the premium market, Shanghai Jahwa developed formulations that could be priced considerably lower than Revlon and within the reach of customers lower down on the pyramid. Shanghai Jahwa was able to display its distribution prowess and local-product-development knowledge to offer a much better valued product than Revlon. Today Shanghai Jahwa has a sales volume of $150 million and ranks only behind Procter & Gamble in cosmetics in China. Although one might argue that Revlon achieved its goal of targeting the premium segment, the company probably lost a significant opportunity to exponentially expand its revenue growth in the country, an opportunity that would be difficult to regain.

The Poor Have No Economic Wealth?

Prahalad and Hammond eloquently argue that, while MNEs may be tempted to cast aside any desire to enter emerging markets given the obstacles of economics and infrastructure, the collective buying power of the poor could indeed make a difference.[26] Building on examples drawn from among the poorest nations, such as Namibia, Bangladesh, and India, they throw new light on some of the common myths of selling to the poorest emerging markets.

For example, many observers believe that that poorer segments of a society do not have enough economic wealth to warrant attention as potential buyers; that the poor spend most of their meager earnings on essentials and have little money to spend on nonessential goods and services; and that emerging markets demand goods that are incredibly cheap, leaving no room for profit. Breaking these myths, Prahalad and Hammond suggest that the aggregate buying power of the poor in many nations is either on a par with people in the developed world or in some cases far exceeds the buying power of the supposedly richer markets. For example, they observe that in Bangladesh, customers for village phones—a mobile telephone unit that is shared by multiple villagers—generate revenues between $90 to $1,000 a month, with some villagers spending around 7 percent of their monthly income on telephone bills, a figure that is much higher than what is spent in developed-country markets.

In contrast to the conventional wisdom, the poor often buy goods and services that could be deemed nonessential. In India, the lowest income segment of consumers accounted for sales of over 3 million bicycles, 5 million wristwatches, 1 million pressure cookers, and 2 million electric fans—some of which are goods that would fall under the general category of nonessential. Further, people in poor countries do buy branded premium products, and many of the savvier MNEs are setting up shop to sell global brands. In clear contrast to their expectations of a higher cost structure, many MNEs are finding that they can realize much higher margins because they can access cheaper labor and save on high rents and other expenses but still command reasonable premiums to render the enterprise profitable. Even luxury-goods manufacturers are beginning to find that the emerging markets are good value propositions. Dom Perignon is sold in Mumbai, India, for Rs 10,000 a bottle; Mercedes-Benz S-Class and E-Class cars are selling extremely well in Thailand, and so are Audi cars in China. There is, however, a fundamental decision that most MNEs are forced to make in such settings: is it better to target the upper crust at handsome premiums or go after the masses where revenues and profits can be much bigger in the aggregate?

CASE STUDY: LOUIS VUITTON—GOING EAST TO CASH IN ON AFFLUENCE

LVMH Group (Moët Hennessy–Louis Vuitton), the world's largest luxury goods maker, has recently established a subsidiary in India.[27] Although the addressable market might appear miniuscule when compared to the progressive markets of Europe and North America, the company believes that it has significant growth potential. LVMH already sells luxury watches such as Tag Heuer, Ebel, Dior, and Zenith in India, and its wines and spirits division sells exclusive wine labels such as Dom Perignon. Its premier showroom in the lobby of the Hotel Oberoi in New Delhi looks much like its other worldwide stores: the showroom carries a full line of LVMH leather goods, including such recent introductions as the painted leather line Takashi Murakami. LVMH believes that it will have less of an uphill climb building its brand in India because the brand is already well known among the well-heeled elite of India's social circles. In addition, the LVMH brand was popular among the Indian royalty during the British era, and the Maharajahs were among the primary customers for custom-made Louis Vuitton products. The government of India has significantly relaxed its policies on investment in the leather sector and LVMH has found it timely to move in. In commemoration of its new India venture, the company launched a line labeled Suhali, named after a wind that sweeps across the Sahara into India. The line uses fine goat leather, a material that has been used for centuries in India. The company has remained true to its global image and pricing approach, and has not cut corners for the Indian market. LVMH has probably learned from the initial misfortunes of Mercedes-Benz, which brought older models to India hoping that they would fit the needs and aspirations of the Indian buyer. (The attempt was a failure and the models were widely panned. Now Mercedes-Benz has gone back to selling its premier E- and S-class models.)

The Product Development Challenge

Given the assumptions about infrastructure costs and the inability of emerging markets to sustain reasonably healthy rates of return, many MNEs offer a different version of their product, which they believe will address the local realities of profitability and the ability of consumers to buy. Often, this involves either recycling older product lines or shrinking the features and functionality of current products. Since the majority population in most emerging markets is quite poor, MNEs targeting the lower layers of the economic pyramid cannot adopt typical high-margin strategies. Gross margins by definition would be small in such targets, but increased sales volume should outweigh any margin disadvantages. An important reality about emerging markets, which many new entrants seem to forget, is that although customer expectations of quality and value may indeed be context-invariant, typical consumers are far more sensitive to the price-performance balance than their counterparts in developed countries.[28] It is possible to leverage large positive swings on the consumption side by making small changes in product design that drive down the price and increase value. But this calls for fundamental shifts in product and packaging, and innovative distribution.

Product development in a global context is often viewed through the narrow lens of accommodated cultural differences or adjustments for differences in language and government regulations. In an emerging market, product development should also embrace price and convenience as equally critical attributes. Consider the experience of Unilever in India. The company's subsidiary HLL was facing stiff competition from a local firm, Nirma, in the laundry detergent market. Nirma was marketing phosphate-free laundry detergent powders in 500-gram sachets instead of the bulkier packs that competitors such as HLL were selling. The packaging was much more convenient for the targeted market—the lower levels of the economic pyramid—and much more cost-effective as well. Poorer consumers could now afford to buy detergent on an as-needed basis rather than buy to store. This value proposition vaulted Nirma to the top in terms of sales volume. HLL was forced to respond quickly, since sales of its brand Surf were affected negatively. Soon, HLL followed suit with similar changes in packaging sold under the Wheel brand. Wheel has proved extremely successful in stemming the tide of market loss, and the parent company has since spun off Wheel as an autonomous company. The lessons learned by Unilever in India are being transplanted in similar markets, such as Brazil and Argentina. For example, when the economic crisis in Argentina forced declines in the sale of consumer goods such as shampoos, soaps, and detergents, Unilever responded with changes in packaging. In many emerging markets as well as developing countries, single-use packs have taken hold and now span a wide variety of products ranging from toothpaste to cooking oil to shampoo.

The following case study of Whirlpool provides a further example of product development for emerging markets.

CASE STUDY: WHIRLPOOL CORPORATION—STRATEGY IN THE GLOBAL WHITE GOODS MARKET

In 1989, Whirlpool Corporation (Whirlpool) embarked on an ambitious global expansion with the objective of becoming the world's market leader in home appliances. Beginning with the purchase of a majority stake in an appliance company owned by Philips, Whirlpool then acquired a majority stake in an Indian firm, established four joint ventures in China, and made significant new investments in its Latin American operations. By 1994, Whirlpool's global strategy appeared to be solidly in place. In a *Harvard Business Review* article called "The Right Way to Go Global," CEO David Whitwam talked about his vision of integrating Whirlpool's geographical businesses so that the company's expertise would not be confined to one location or product. He forecast appliances such as a World WasherMa single machine that could be sold anywhere—and he wanted to standardize the company's manufacturing processes. According to Whitwam, "The only way to gain lasting competitive advantage is to leverage your capabilities around the world, so that the company as a whole is greater than the sum of its parts. Being an international company—selling globally, having global brands or operations in different countries—isn't enough. . . . Today products are being designed to ensure that a wide variety of models can be built on the same basic platform. . . . Varying consumer preferences require us to have regional manufacturing centers. But even though the features . . . vary from market to market, much of the technology and manufacturing processes involved are similar."[29]

By the mid-1990s, however, serious problems had emerged in Whirlpool's international operations. In 1995, Whirlpool's European profit fell by 50 percent and in 1996, the company reported a $13 million loss in Europe. In emerging markets the situation was even worse. Although the Asian region accounted for only 6 percent of corporate sales, Whirlpool lost $70 million in Asia in 1996 and $62 million in 1997. Whirlpool found itself dealing with intense competition and market growth that was slower than expected. In China specifically, the company struggled to understand Chinese distribution and Chinese consumers; Whirlpool products were considered inferior to Japanese products. In Brazil, Whirlpool found itself a victim in 1997, and again in 1998, of spiraling interest rates that killed consumer spending. A new washer introduced in Brazil in 1998 sold poorly because its $300 price was too high for low-income consumers. Although the company invested hundreds of millions of dollars throughout the 1990s to modernize its Brazilian operations, appliance sales plummeted by 25 percent in 1998.

In response to these problems Whirlpool began a global restructuring effort. In September 1997, the company announced that it would cut 10 percent of its global workforce over the next two years and pull out of two joint ventures in China. In Latin America, 3,500 jobs were abolished and significant investments were made to upgrade plants and product lines.

A New Emerging-Market Strategy

Despite problems throughout the 1990s in its emerging-country markets, Whirlpool's research showed that automatic washers were highly desired by low-income consumers and that penetration rates were low: about 25 percent in Brazil, 8 percent in China, and 4.5 percent in India. Whirlpool decided that rather than adapting an existing washer for Brazil and other emerging markets, it had to design a new machine from scratch, described by Whirlpool as "innovating for the masses."[30] Whirlpool spent about $30 million to develop a new washer that could be sold in Brazil, India, and China. The washer was introduced in Brazil and China in 2003 and India in 2004. The target retail price was $150–200, much lower than retail prices in developed-country markets. To save costs, Whirlpool developed a new single-shift motor that was less powerful than motors used in more expensive machines. For Brazil, the washer was designed to stand on four legs because of the Brazilian penchant for washing floors underneath appliances. For China, the machine was designed with a folding lid to save space above the appliance. Also, because low-income customers could be insulted by machines that looked cheap, Whirlpool spent a lot of time on color and design. In Brazil, the washer was white with yellow and blue colors on the control panel. In China, the machines were light blue and gray and in India, the washers will be produced in green, blue, and white. In India, there is a "sari" setting for delicate clothes and in China, a heavy-duty cycle called "grease removal" for clothes stained by bicycles.

Pricing Strategy in Emerging Markets

MNEs often encounter particular challenges when it comes to setting prices in emerging markets. While some choose to adopt a quasi-universal price, making adjustments for currency and exchange variations, others price to the market. The pricing and product-development decisions do indeed work in tandem. The decision on pricing, however, becomes acutely critical when it involves a differentiated product or service. For example, Coca-Cola is widely seen as a differentiated product, and it uses its brand, market position, styling, and other attributes to distinguish itself from other soft drinks. The company has adopted a flexible pricing system whereby it takes into account prevailing local-market conditions, including the market's ability to pay before setting the price. For example, it was widely believed that Roberto Goizueta, who spearheaded the entry of Coca-Cola into China, wanted the local price of Coca-Cola to match that of a cup of tea, the preferred drink of the average Chinese consumer. In contrast, Starbucks, the ubiquitous coffee company, has chosen to adopt a universal pricing approach under which it essentially translates the U.S. dollar price into the local currency. In certain product markets, and especially in emerging markets, the universal pricing approach may not provide maximum benefit for the company. While a universal price can be used if skimming is the objective, it does not help penetrate the lower tiers of the economic pyramid. It is quite possible to adopt a more locally sensitive price structure without jeopardizing the differentiation aims that the company espouses. That is, it may not be an either-or decision for most of the products and services targeted at the emerging markets.

Partnering and Control Issues

Gaining significant insights into local buying behaviors requires constant access to local knowledge. Quite often, new MNE entrants tap into the knowledge base of local partners through joint ventures. While this mode of entry is certainly not limited to companies entering emerging markets, it does take on different colors and complexities in such a context.

Finding well-credentialed local partners is often difficult. Since the pool of qualified partners is normally shallow, the race to establish first-mover advantage is considerably accentuated. In most sectors, the quality of the second- and third-tier firms drops off precipitously, which means that time is of the essence in attracting the best partners. These top-tier firms control premiere brands that are critical to success in markets hobbled by a lack of other viable signals of quality and value. They also have access to well-honed distribution channels that play a vital role in markets plagued by infrastructural weaknesses. Given that firms with these attributes are relatively few, conservative MNEs that play a wait-and-see game to learn from the experiences of the first movers will find themselves without viable partners. The overall risk of a later entry might, in fact, be much higher than that assumed by the first mover. Indeed, moving late may be as bad as not moving at all.

The ownership structure and control issues associated with emerging-market partners are also likely to be unique. Unlike the developed-country context, where firms are well tempered by vibrant capital markets, companies in emerging countries often carry the burden of either direct state ownership or family control. In either case, the objectives of the local partner are likely to be at some variance with the MNE seeking a partner. The visible hand of government often takes precedence over the invisible hand of the market and, hence, a partnership with a state-owned enterprise comes with the usual pressures to increase employment levels, participate in social welfare projects, and pursue other agendas that may not directly relate to shareholder wealth maximization. On the other hand, family-owned partners can deliver crucial connections to the state bureaucracy and open doors that an MNE may not be able to open on its own. However, the family-owned partner's performance metrics may be focused solely on profitability at all cost, rather than growth.

The road to successful joint venturing in emerging markets comes with significant obstacles that are atypical in developed-country contexts. Although the risk of partnering may be relatively higher, the potential payoff of a lasting relationship can considerably ease entry into unfamiliar terrain. Successful partnerships in these settings are predicated upon the ability of managers to:

- Identify key official and unofficial decision makers and involve them early on in the negotiation process.
- Think innovatively about gaining operational control over key strategic dimensions in a manner that is quite distinct from the equity control the company desires. Insistence on majority equity control can sometimes be a stumbling block.
- Identify mutually acceptable performance metrics and guarantees that can be integrated into a review and control process.
- Recognize that an agreement often represents only an initial negotiating position and thus emphasize personal relationships as a key avenue to joint-venture success.

Conclusion

Economic development in the world's many emerging-market countries is likely to be the engine that drives the global economy in the 21st century. For many firms, doing business in emerging markets has been viewed as fraught with risk, uncertainty, and limited potential for profit. We have argued that while risk and uncertainty are inevitable, the potential value-creating opportunities can be significant. Moreover, it is also inevitable that emerging-market companies have aspirations beyond their domestic markets. If developed-country MNEs ignore emerging markets, it is only a matter of time before they find themselves going head-to-head in the United States, Europe, and elsewhere against companies that have expanded beyond their emerging-market home base.

8

Corporate Governance Issues in International Business

Corporate governance refers to "the top management process that manages and mediates value creation for, and value transference among, various corporate claimants (including society at large), in a context that simultaneously ensures accountability towards these claimants."[1] Corporate governance practices and regulations significantly impact the structure of capitalist societies. The broad areas of corporate governance can be seen in table 8.1, which provides a list of the principles of corporate governance prescribed by the Organisation for Economic Co-operation and Development (OECD).

Corporate governance has implications for many aspects of corporate practice and the general business environment, including:[2]

- The roles and responsibilities of boards and top management
- Board committee structure and makeup (audit, compensation, etc.)
- Management compensation and rewards
- The market for corporate control
- The relations among firms, shareholders, and creditors
- Employee and union relationships with firms
- The behavior of the firm under financial distress
- Types of corporate financing and payouts
- Social responsibility

In recent years corporate governance has taken on new importance. In particular, the stock market declines of 2001 and 2002, and the related corporate scandals in the United States and elsewhere, have sharply reignited the debate about shareholder value versus stakeholder value, the appropriate objectives for the corporation, and the roles that management and boards play in creating sustainable and profitable enterprises. In this chapter we examine the nature of

Table 8.1.   OECD Principles of Corporate Governance

The corporate governance framework should:
1. Protect shareholders' rights.
2. Ensure the equitable treatment of all shareholders, including minority and foreign shareholders. All shareholders should have the opportunity to obtain effective redress for violation of their rights.
3. Recognize the rights of stakeholders as established by law and encourage active cooperation between corporations and stakeholders in creating health, jobs, and sustainability of financially sound enterprises.
4. Ensure that timely and accurate disclosure is made on all material matters regarding the corporation, including the financial situation, performance, ownership, and governance of the company.
5. Ensure the strategic guidance of the company, the effective monitoring of management by the board, and the board's accountability to the company and the shareholders.

Source: Organization for Economic Co-operation and Development, *Principles of Corporate Governance* (1999). See http://www.oecd.org.

corporate governance, with an emphasis on issues relevant to the MNE. We begin by examining the nature of corporate governance and asking the question: Why should MNE managers be familiar with the concept of corporate governance?

The Nature of Corporate Governance

Every firm must by governed in a manner that takes into account the interests of various stakeholders and ensures that the firm remain a profitable, going concern. Successful governance practices are a mix of those required by law and those chosen by the firm's board and management, who act as the agents of the shareholders. The legally imposed governance mechanisms are closely linked to, and often altered by, the political process. For example, the recent wave of corporate scandals United States resulted in the Sarbanes-Oxley Act of 2002, which imposed new rules on public companies, such as a requirement to reveal off-balance-sheet arrangements and restrictions on the use of pro forma accounting.

The reaction to the most recent U.S. governance failures mirrors those of previous generations. The U.S. Securities and Exchange Act of 1934 (and the creation of the SEC) and the Glass-Steagall Act of 1932 (which imposed restrictions on bank ownership of corporate stock in the United States so as to limit financial power as well as to protect minority shareholders) came out of the political process in the wake of the 1929 stock market crash and the Great Depression, which resulted in substantial social costs. In the United Kingdom, where governance and corporate conduct are similar to U.S. practices, there have been recent calls for changes in governance practices. In 2003, the U.K. Financial

Reporting Council agreed to a revised Combined Code, which comprises best-practice recommendations for the control and reporting functions of company boards. The overall aim of the code, issued by the U.K. Listing Authority, is to enhance board effectiveness and improve confidence in the capital markets by raising the standards of corporate governance.

At the heart of any corporate governance system is the issue of separation of ownership and control. In the typical modern corporation in the major developed economies, the providers of capital are not the managers of the firm. How do the capital providers ensure that they get their money back after giving it to the firms? As a starting point, contracts can be signed between the capital providers and the managers that specify what the managers can and cannot do. However, complete contracts that can accurately predict future contingencies cannot be written for complex organizations. As a result, managers end up with substantial control rights over how to manage the firm and how to allocate value to investors and other stakeholders. To ensure that managers minimize their self-interested behavior, various governance mechanisms are designed and imposed by legislation. For example, the requirement that financial statements be prepared using generally accepted financial principles is intended to provide comparative financial data and a scorekeeping record. Strict reporting standards exist for firms traded on the world's major stock exchanges. For managers themselves, incentive contracts can be designed that link managerial behavior with compensation (although incentive contracts can create new problems of opportunism and private benefits, as demonstrated by the use of stock options in the 1990s).

The Stakeholder versus Shareholder Debate

In this section we review the debate between stakeholder and shareholder approaches to corporate governance. Notwithstanding what is legally required by the firm, the orientation of top management to one or the other approach can have important consequences for the actual governance practices used in a company. Opposing views on the purpose and accountability of the corporation have been the subject of numerous debates during the past century and a half.[3] These debates have been described in terms such as "contracts versus communities," or "private property versus public," or "the firm as a social entity versus a private profit-seeking enterprise." In recent years this debate has intensified. From a global perspective, the debate is often pitched as the "Anglo-American view versus the European/Japanese view." In reality, all corporate governance systems must be responsive, at some level, to all stakeholders. It is simplistic to say, as critics of different national systems often do, "American corporate governance is too shareholder oriented" or "continental European systems are too stakeholder oriented." Our intent is not to argue that one perspective is better than another. Rather, we highlight some of the underlying philosophical issues on which corporate governance mechanisms are built as the basis for understanding governance from a global perspective.

The stakeholders of a firm include its employees, customers, shareholders, creditors, suppliers, officers, board members, communities, and society at large. The stakeholder approach to corporate governance rejects the idea of maximizing a single objective function and argues that the corporation should be viewed as an entity that has citizenship responsibilities. The stakeholder view professes that the purpose of the corporation is to create and distribute wealth to all the primary stakeholders. In doing so, no stakeholder group should be favored over another. The role of management is not restricted to carrying out shareholder responsibilities; it is also to respond to citizenship responsibilities on behalf of all constituencies. Thus, stakeholder management is a never-ending task of balancing and integrating multiple relationships and multiple objectives.[4] In support of a stakeholder approach, Peter Drucker made the following argument: "Shareholder sovereignty is bound to flounder. It is a fair weather model that works well only in times of prosperity. . . . Top management of the future will need to balance the three dimensions [i.e., objective functions] of the corporation: as an economic organization, as a human organization, and as an increasingly important social organization."[5]

A stakeholder-oriented governance system means that in its decision making, management must take into account the core values of a possibly very diverse group of stakeholders. Management must balance these core values and establish relationships with the various stakeholders. In contrast, a shareholder-maximization approach has a much narrower perspective, perhaps best exemplified by Milton Friedman's classic 1970 statement, "The sole social responsibility of business is to increase profits."[6] A shareholder-oriented governance system views the corporation as a shareholder value-maximizing economic entity and emphasizes various elements: contractual exchanges; the role of law to promote contractual freedom; discipline forced by the invisible hand; a market for corporate control; and competition in product, labor, and capital markets. U.S. corporate governance in the last few decades has shifted to an emphasis on shareholder primacy. A recent study argues that maximizing shareholder value as the objective function will lead to decisions that enhance outcomes for multiple stakeholders. This study makes several supporting arguments:

1. Maximizing shareholder value maximizes the value of the whole firm, and thus the value of the pie to *all* its claimants.

2. Maximizing shareholder value provides the most appropriate incentives for managers to take risks.
3. More than one objective function makes governing difficult, if not impossible.
4. It is easier to make shareholders out of stakeholders, rather than vice versa.
5. All major stakeholders other than shareholders have protection through contracts and the legal system.[7]

In establishing corporate governance practices for a firm, top management must balance what is legally required and what makes sense given the nature of the business, competitor practices, the makeup of the stakeholder set, the corporate values, and so on. This is not an easy task. Regardless of management's orientation, the stakeholder versus shareholder debate is not an either/or issue. Firms must be pro-stakeholder because if they are not, they will lose their access to capital, suppliers, communities, employees, and so on. Nevertheless, managers do have discretion in how value is transferred to the various stakeholders, and it is this value transference that creates enormous controversies, and occasionally disasters, for the various stakeholder groups.

Corporate Governance and the Global Firm

Why does international corporate governance matter for the global firm? And, a related question, why should U.S.-based, or German-based, or Japan-based, MNEs be concerned about corporate governance issues outside their country of domicile? There are multiple reasons why these firms and their managers should care:

1. MNEs have stakeholders in many countries beyond that of their origins. These stakeholders will be in countries where the MNEs do business and perhaps, in the case of shareholders, in countries outside the geographic reach of their business activities. Increasingly, the shareholders of MNEs are scattered around the world. For example, almost 40 percent of Sony's stock is held by investors outside Japan. An estimated 15 percent of institutional and private portfolio capital is invested far from home markets.
2. Many MNEs have their shares listed on stock exchanges in various countries, which means corporate governance decisions must consider different legal and financial jurisdictions. For example, Procter & Gamble's common stock is listed on two U.S. stock exchanges, eight European exchanges, and one Japanese exchange. The situation facing Otto GmbH & Co. in early 2004 is a case of what could happen to firms competing in multiple regulatory environments. Otto GmbH, a privately

held German firm with sales of more than $24 billion, owned 89 percent of Spiegel, a U.S. retailer (including Spiegel Catalog Inc. and Eddie Bauer Inc.). The Spiegel shares not owned by Otto were owned by public shareholders and the firm was listed on the Nasdaq. After the company failed to file required information with the SEC, the SEC in 2003 filed a lawsuit accusing Spiegel of violating securities laws and failing to disclose auditor's doubts about Spiegel's ability as a going concern. Soon after, Spiegel declared bankruptcy, and in 2004 creditors were in negotiation with Otto and the family that controlled the firm. According to the *Wall Street Journal*, "The Spiegel affair promises to become a very expensive lesson in running a public company in the United States and in the pitfalls of operating businesses across borders without a firm grasp of foreign legal and regulatory standards."[8]

3. The differences in how companies are owned and governed in different countries are quite striking. Consider the following questions:

- Why do Italian companies rarely go public?
- Why does Germany have such a small stock market and such large and powerful banks?
- Why is ownership of U.S. and British companies so widely dispersed?
- Why do most of the large firms in countries like Mexico, Greece, and Argentina have dominant controlling shareholders?
- Why is family control of large firms so common in emerging markets and so uncommon in the United States and United Kingdom?
- Why do Japanese companies often have boards as large as 50 members?
- Why are hostile takeovers common in the United States, infrequent in Germany, and virtually unknown in Japan?
- Why do U.S. firms use stock options much more extensively than Japanese and German firms?
- Why, in contrast to those in the United Kingdom and the United States, do European financial reports often fail to provide useful information such as the ownership structure of affiliates, details of CEO contracts, performance-related pay details for executives, the form in which directors' salaries are paid, and the number of shares held by managers in affiliated companies?
- Why are junior managers in Japan usually members of their firm's labor union for the first 10 or more years of their careers?

4. As business continues to globalize, the standards of sound corporate governance will continue to merge to blend elements of best practices from various parts of the world.

5. In light of the recent corporate scandals involving firms like Enron, Tyco, WorldCom, Paramalat, and Vivendi, corporate governance practices of publicly traded firms from all parts of the world are likely to be more closely scrutinized. Until recently, the concept of corporate governance in some countries was rarely discussed publicly. For example, Louis Schweitzer, CEO of French automaker Renault, commented in 2003 that the "job of chairman—a nonexecutive chairman—is new in France. Corporate governance is also a rather new concept in France. I believe the primary responsibility of the chairman of the board is to make sure that there's good corporate governance."[9]

6. The firms with which MNEs compete will operate under a range of corporate governance systems. Since governance systems influence managerial risk-taking and decision making, understanding corporate governance will provide insights into competitors' behavior. For example, a recent study compared the extent and content of company's' communications about corporate social responsibility in France, the Netherlands, the United Kingdom, and the United States.[10] The study found that French and Dutch companies were not as eager as U.S. firms to convey good citizenship images in their corporate communications and suggested that this was because U.S. firms are expected to play a leadership role in the communities in which they operate. French and the Dutch do not have a tradition of encouraging such involvement, implying that they are not confronted with the same community leadership expectations as U.S. firms. For a firm in a competitive environment that includes Dutch and French companies, this insight about community orientation may be valuable in crafting strategic actions.

7. MNEs interested in acquisitions outside their home country will have to understand the corporate governance practices in the target country, since those practices will influence various aspects of the acquisition, such as financing, responsibilities toward lenders and minority shareholders, and interactions with government bodies and labor unions.

8. Better corporate governance by the world's major MNEs may have a positive spinoff impact on emerging-market firms and their national economies, many of which have undeveloped governance systems and stakeholder legal protections. Investors who seek adequate returns and capital protection will invest only in firms that have adequate safeguards in place. As MNEs improve their governance practices and invest in emerging markets, local firms will have to improve their own practices if they are to compete for people and capital. Thus, improved

corporate governance at a local level could result in new capital inflows and foreign direct investment, which in turn generates increased economic activity, more jobs, and so on.

In summary, the corporate governance practices of firms influence their strategies and competitiveness and, therefore, managers involved in international competition should view knowledge of international governance as an essential part of their repertoire of skills.

National Variations in Corporate Governance Systems

In this section we review some corporate governance systems found in different countries. While a detailed examination of corporate governance practices in multiple countries is beyond our scope, we highlight some of the key mechanisms that exist in different countries.

U.S. System

In the United States (and also in Canada, the United Kingdom, and Australia, where corporate governance has evolved along similar lines), there is extensive legal protection for investors, which explains the willingness of small investors to participate in stock markets. The government's main role is to prevent the abuse of corporate power through monopolies or unfair trade practices. Management and corporate accountability incorporate the use of boards that are responsible for ensuring that firms act in a legal and socially responsible manner. In theory, management is accountable to the board, which should have a majority of independent, outside directors, and the board is accountable to the shareholders. In practice, the reliance of U.S. firms on outside directors is fraught with problems: the outside directors have limited time and experience, especially to govern complex, multi-billion-dollar MNEs; interlocking directorships are common; CEOs control information, board selection, and board committees; and the CEO is chairman of the board in 90 percent of publicly traded firms. As events of the past few years have shown, U.S. corporate boards rarely ask tough questions and, as the Enron case shows, are sometimes willing to condone highly questionable behavior.

In the United States, banks have little or no role in the ownership of firms, which is in direct contrast to the situation in Germany, Japan, and many other countries. Increasingly, stakeholder groups are becoming active shareholders. The preponderance of employee stock ownership plans, employee stock option plans, and public pension funds are examples of stock ownership stakeholders. In the 1990s, unions as labor-shareholders (given their role as shareholders-trustees of company pensions) became visible players in the shareholder movement, rivaling traditional institutional shareholders, such as pension and mutual funds. U.S. bankruptcy regulations provide fewer rights to creditors than in Germany and Japan. Finally, although the threat of hostile takeovers is always present in the United States, its effect as a managerial disciplining mechanism is questionable.[11]

Japanese System

The Japanese system of corporate governance incorporates a much broader separation between ownership and managerial control than the U.S. and German systems. In Japan the corporation is a social entity, with survival of the firm and perpetual employment as management's primary goals. Historically, firms have focused much more on market share than on shareholder value. Bankruptcy or mergers were the two worst possible outcomes and hostile takeovers were virtually nonexistent. The words used to describe takeovers in Japan, which include *miurisuru* (to sell one's body) and *nottori* (hijack), imply that takeovers are unacceptable.[12] The system has relied heavily on cross-shareholdings between firms. In the early 1990s, cross-shareholdings constituted 65 to 70 percent of total shares outstanding, which meant that the majority of Japanese shares were not liquid and rarely sold. The practice of cross-shareholding is a manifestation of the close relationships among a company, its affiliates, its suppliers, and its customers. These close relationships can decrease economic efficiency by preventing companies from doing business with the optimal suppliers or customers. In companies where cross-shareholdings result in interlocking directorates, boards are further insulated from effective oversight and the need to maximize long-term shareholder value.[13] Japanese boards often have 20 to 50 directors, usually insiders, reflecting the Japanese concept that board seats are status positions provided to long-term employees and important affiliated executives as rewards for loyalty and long service.

Other characteristics of Japanese corporate governance include limited use of incentives for management compensation; significant share ownership by banks via a system of main banks and relationship banking; and close (some would say cozy) linkages between firms and government bureaucracies. During the 40 years after World War II, the Japanese economy experienced rapid growth and governance was viewed outside Japan as a key explanatory factor for the success of Japanese firms. With the bursting of the Japanese bubble, flaws in the system have been exposed, increasing pressure for changes in governance practices. In particular, the problems associated with entrenched management, a lack of transparency, and an underemphasis on shareholder value have resulted in widespread calls for change from outside Japan.

Although the calls for change within Japan are more muted, some changes have occurred. In 2003 a new commercial code was introduced with the objective of creating a more effective and independent system for monitoring the way companies are run. The new code covers areas such as independent directors, enhanced shareholder rights, and audit committees. Cross-shareholding rates have gradually been falling in recent years, as banks and other shareholders are forced by economic conditions to pursue higher profits and shift capital to more productive investments. Changes in accounting rules have increased the sale of nonperforming cross-shareholdings. Some companies are reducing the size of their boards. For example, in early 2003, under pressure from foreign shareholders, Toyota announced plans to reduce its 58-member board of directors (the largest of any listed company in Japan) by more than half. About 40 of Toyota's 58 directors held the rank of managing director or lower. Similar to the U.S. system, executives will be divided into directors and executive officers. NEC, Toshiba, and Mitsubishi were considering adoption of U.S.-style corporate board governance systems. Companies were also beginning to make more use of stock option programs and other managerial incentive devices.

German System

The German system of corporate governance relies heavily on bank control through equity investment. Banks effectively control 50 to 80 percent of outstanding shares and there are extensive intercorporate and bank shareholdings. There are stronger creditor rights but weaker shareholder rights than in the United States. Until recently, there has been limited participation by small shareholders in the stock market. There are few hostile takeovers, partly because of the existence of large bank shareholders. That said, the hostile takeover of Mannesmann in 2000 by the U.K. firm Vodaphone was quite remarkable for its size and the willingness of the German government to allow it to happen.

German firms use a two-tier system of supervisory and management boards. The supervisory board determines overall corporate policy and appoints the management board, which is responsible for the day-to-day running of the company. The management board answers to the supervisory board. German law provides for *Mitbestimmung* (worker co-determination) in large companies. As a result, an equal number of employee-elected and shareholder-elected representatives are required on the supervisory board (one of the employees must be a senior manager). Boards of German companies suffer from the same interlocking problems found in other countries. German senior managers often serve on the supervisory boards of the companies whose representatives sit on their own supervisory board, creating a system of interlocking directorships and personal relationships. German companies have only recently started using stock options. In 1996 Daimler-Benz was one of the first large German companies to begin an executive stock option scheme (despite the opposition of employee members of the supervisory board). In Germany, pay differentials between top German managers and assembly-line workers are among the lowest in the world.

In 2002 the German government, like its Japanese counterpart, recommended a new Corporate Governance Code. The intent of the code was to deal with five criticisms regularly voiced regarding the governance and legal structure of German companies: (a) a lack of emphasis on shareholder interests; (b) the dual board corporate governance comprising a managing director board and a supervisory board; (c) insufficient transparency (especially compared to the U.S. system); (d) the lack of independent members on the supervisory board; and (e) limited independence of auditors.

Emerging Markets

Even in the countries with the strongest corporate governance systems, such as the United States and Germany, problems exist and there is room for improvement. If the strongest countries, with their decades of experience with capital markets and transparent legal systems, have problem areas, what about emerging markets that are relatively new to the world of international finance and cross-border investment (and in the case of Russia and China, quite new to the basic idea of capitalism)? Consider the following story about the Russian company Yukos that appeared in the *Wall Street Journal* in May 2003:

> Amid the political and economic uncertainty of the 1990s, Yukos's new owners parked their profits in foreign banks rather than reinvest them, and began squeezing minority shareholders out of key subsidiaries in order to gain full control over the company. Those years brought frequent strife. In 1998, workers enraged over months of unpaid wages and 40,000 layoffs, stormed Yukos's Siberian offices, smashing windows and computers. A big joint venture project with Amoco Corp. dissolved into acrimonious accusations by the U.S. company of bad faith on Yukos's part. Yukos's minority shareholders, their stakes rendered virtually worthless by Mr. Khodorkovsky's moves to dilute their shares

in order to solidify control, set off a public outcry that drove Yukos's market value down to $100 million.[14]

While we do not want to paint an entirely pessimistic picture about emerging markets, and we recognize that positive changes are occurring, the Yukos story is far from unusual. The degree and enforceability of investors' and stakeholders' legal protections in many emerging markets are not good. In many emerging markets, investors must cope with a lack of transparency, dubious court rulings, ineffective or nonexistent securities regulations, political meddling, threats of violence, rigged shareholder votes, impenetrable pyramid ownerships, lost or misplaced shareholder records, multiple classes of stock, family members who view the firm as their private fiefdom, powerful banks tied to large shareholders, limited protection for minority shareholders, and a corrupt judiciary system. In other words, the corporate governance systems found in the triad countries are unlikely to be found once an investor enters an emerging market. We offer two case studies to illustrate some of the challenges firms and investors may face when entering emerging markets that are in the process of trying to strengthen corporate governance. One case study deals with a bankruptcy in Thailand and the other with a minority investor in Russia. As a caveat, we emphasize that although the case studies illustrate some corporate governance difficulties, Thailand and Russia (the setting for the two cases) have both attracted a significant amount of foreign direct investment. BP, one of the companies featured in the cases, has become a major investor in Russia after some initial difficulties.

CASE STUDY: THAI PETROCHEMICAL AND THE CORPORATE HOUDINI

When debt financing is used by a firm, creditors expect certain legal rights, such as the right to take action if the borrower defaults. The violation of the rights of lenders is usually easier to verify in courts than the violation of the rights of equity investors. In the absence of legal protection, lenders will be reluctant to make loans. In recent years, many firms in emerging markets borrowed heavily to finance their expansion. As this case illustrates, the absence of a transparent and effective system to protect debt investors can lead to very interesting governance issues.

During the 1990s, Prachai Leophairatana borrowed heavily to transform his family's rice-trading business into an efficient, fully integrated petrochemical complex called Thai Petrochemical Industry Plc. (TPI). The Leophairatana family, through family members, subsidiaries and nominees, owned about 70 percent of TPI. After the Asian financial crisis of 1997, TPI stopped all repayments on its multi-billion-dollar debt. In 2000, after several years of battles between the creditors and management, Thailand's newly established Central Bankruptcy Court declared TPI insolvent, with liabilities of $3.5 billion. TPI was put into the hands of an official receiver. The more than 100 creditors, which included Bangkok Bank, Bank of America, and Citibank, voted to oust the company's founder and chief executive in favor of the Australian company Ferrier Hodgson, thus ending two decades of family management. Effective Planners, a subsidiary of the Australian debt-workout specialist Ferrier Hodgson, was appointed as the debt administrator.

Later in 2000, Effective Planners proposed an $800 million debt-to-equity swap and sale of noncore assets to raise US$200 million for debt repayment. In the proposal, creditors would convert about $756 million in unpaid interest into a 75 percent stake in TPI, and there was no provision for the write-off of principal debt. The deal would be the cornerstone of the restructuring and debt-to-equity swap and would cut Prachai Leophaira-tana's stake from 60 percent to less than 15 percent, ending his control of the company. The proposal had the backing of the biggest creditors. Mr. Prachai rejected Effective Planners's proposal and instead counter-proposed that creditors write off nearly $800 million in accrued interest and raise new capital separately. Anthony Norman, managing director of Effective Planners, rejected the proposal outright.

In December 2000, Central Bankruptcy Court approved the restructuring plan, effectively giving control of the company to creditors. Prachai was removed from the position of CEO. On February 26, 2001, Anthony Norman conveyed to Prachai in writing that he was to stay out of management decisions at TPI. Prachai was told not to sign TPI documents, obtain information from TPI group members, hold private meetings with employees, or use TPI proprietary information, including the name and logo, on his personal Web site. Prachai responded by claiming he was still chief executive by law and that Norman was disrupting company harmony and breaching the law by meddling with his authority. Prachai continued to go to work as usual. Over the next year he brought some 30 court actions against the administrators, making various claims of fraud in a variety of courts.

By early 2002 it was clear that the recovery plan approved by the creditors was too optimistic. The planned repayments at the end of 2001 had not been made. In May 2002 the creditors agreed to a request from Effective Planners to amend the debt-restructuring plan and extend the deadline for selling US$200 million worth of noncore assets until March 31 2003. The approval came despite a protest from Prachai, who lodged a petition with receivership officers in a bid to block the creditors' meeting. In July 2002 Effective Planners said in a statement that it would file a lawsuit against

Prachai and his family, demanding the repayment of 6.4 billion baht in loans extended to Pornchai Enterprise, a property developer; TPI Holding, an investment arm; and TPI EOEG, a manufacturer of basic industrial chemicals. The loans were made by TPI through promissory notes issued between 1994 and 1997. The three companies were claimed to be personally owned by Mr. Prachai and his family, not by TPI.

In 2002, two executives from Effective Planners, including Anthony Norman, were convicted of violating their work permits and forced to leave Thailand. In April 2003, Thailand's Central Bankruptcy Court found in favor of a suit filed by Prachai and removed Effective Planners as TPI's administrator. The court appointed Prachai and court officials as temporary debt administrators until creditors found a new representative after the creditors' representative, Effective Planners, failed to meet a deadline to sell $200 million in noncore assets to repay debt. When a new administrator was announced in early May, Prachai rejected the appointee on the grounds that the proposed team was focused more on protecting creditor rights than on keeping the company afloat.

The battle between TPI and the creditors has become Southeast Asia's most notorious corporate rehabilitation and a key test of Thailand's willingness to uphold new laws to improve corporate transparency. So far, it appears that instead of being an effective venue for creditors to seek redress, the Thailand court system has proved to be a quagmire where Prachai, armed with a battery of lawyers, has bogged down creditors in time-consuming litigation, hampering the restructuring process. According to one analyst, "This was supposed to be a milestone case showing foreign investors that there was effective legal redress for creditors in Thailand. It did the opposite, in effect reinforcing the bargaining position of the big defaulting borrowers."[15] Pushing reluctant corporate defaulters into court-supervised restructuring has also turned out to be difficult. Thailand's bankruptcy court does not use the internationally understood definition of insolvency—an inability to service debt obligations as they fall due. The court defines insolvency as having liabilities greater than total assets, which is tough for creditors to prove. As to Mr. Prachai, he continues to go to work at TPI. Australian newspapers have labeled him the king of prevarication and a corporate Houdini for managing to avoid debt repayment.

CASE STUDY: BP IN RUSSIA

In November 1997, British Petroleum (BP) paid $571 million (£338 million) for a 10 percent stake in Sidanco, Russia's fourth biggest vertically integrated oil company, from Uneximbank, one of Russia's most powerful financial and industrial groups. The deal gave BP 20 percent of voting rights and a seat on Sidanco's board. It also enabled BP to nominate chief operating and financial officers in the company. The intent was that BP and Sidanco would set up a joint venture to develop and operate Russian oil discoveries. The two companies would have an equal vote in how the venture was run. The agreement was witnessed in London by Prime Minister Tony Blair and Russian First Deputy Energy Minister Viktor Ott. John Browne, CEO of BP, described the deal as a "major opportunity for BP in one of the great oil and gas provinces of the world. . . . We believe the time is now right and, more importantly, that we have found in Sidanco a partner with a strong, established position at the heart of Russia's oil industry." Uneximbank President Vladimir Potanin said: "The agreement signed today is of great importance both for Sidanco and the Unexim Group which is the controlling shareholder of Sidanco. For successful development, Sidanco needs a strategic partner with considerable experience and a leading position in the international oil business. BP is this kind of partner."

In February 1998 Russia's Federal Securities Commission annulled a controversial convertible bond issue by Sidanco, a move that investors hailed as a victory for shareholder rights. The commission's decision came in response to complaints from minority investors in Sidanco. Minority shareholders in Sidanco, who had claimed their holdings would be heavily diluted by the convertible issue, praised the decision as a sign that Russia was beginning to grapple with its corporate governance failures.

Later in 1998, problems began to emerge with Sidanco's oil-producing subsidiary Chernogorneft, in which Sidanco held 73 percent control. Although BP thought Chernogorneft was financially stable, oil sold to Sidanco had not been paid for and large tax arrears had accumulated. This helped turn Chernogorneft's management against its parent Sidanco. Also, the Russian financial crisis undermined Uneximbank and sharply reduced Vladimir Potanin's political influence. Alfa, a rival conglomerate, became interested in Sidanco. Meanwhile, BP was drawn increasingly into the daily management of Sidanco. Chernogorneft's debts continued to rise until December, when an obscure local creditor filed a petition that pushed the company into bankruptcy.

Chernogorneft was driven into bankruptcy through the efforts of Tyumen Oil Company (TNK), Alfa's principal oil business. In February 1999 a senior executive from BP was elected chairman of Sidanco and BP was forced to write off $200 million of its investment in Sidanco. In November 1999 Chernogorneft was sold out of bankruptcy for $176 million dollars to TNK. BP's director for external affairs in Russia said: "The entire bankruptcy has been subject to major manipulations. We do not consider it to be valid. In many ways this decision has damaging implications for foreign investors. BP Amoco will be very carefully reviewing its business position in Russia in the light of these events." Simon Kukes, chairman of TNK, said that his company had upheld "international standards of corporate governance and ethical behaviour," and stressed that the purchase had been made in a competitive auction.[16] He offered BP Amoco the chance to enter a strategic alliance with him. Although TNK denied doing anything illegal, it appeared to most outside observers that the company used its political influence and the weaknesses of Russia's laws and judicial system to ensure that a succession of court cases went its way.

In December 1999, TNK and BP announced an agreement under which Sidanco would regain Chernogorneft in return for TNK receiving a 25 percent stake in Sidanco. TNK's principal shareholders, Alfa Group and Access-Renova, would receive 25 percent plus one share in Sidanco. In exchange, TNK's shareholders would return Chernogorneft debt-free. The deal would cost TNK about $200 million, compared with $484 million paid by BP for its 10 percent stake. In 2000, after lengthy negotiations, Alfa's controlling shareholders replaced Unexim group as the dominant shareholder of Sidanco.

After the election of Vladimir Putin as president in spring 2000, the Russian government made some efforts to improve corporate governance; reform the legal, tax, and labor systems; and become more open to the West. In an interesting turn of events, in February 2003 BP announced a major strategic alliance with the same companies with which it had battled for control of Sidanco. Under the terms of the alliance, BP and Alpha group would combine their interests in Russia to create the country's third largest oil and gas business, in which both parties would each have a 50 percent stake. For its 50 percent stake BP would pay Alpha Group $3 billion in cash and three subsequent annual payments of $1.25 billion in BP shares. In describing the deal, BP CEO John Browne said that BP had instituted new governance mechanisms to protect the interests of all parties. He also said that changes in Russia's legal system and an increasing commitment to international rules of trade convinced BP that it was time to deepen its partnership with Alpha. Finally, Browne called the experience with Chernogorneft and Sidanco a key learning experience in Russia.

Corporate Governance in China, India, and Brazil

Here we provide a brief overview of corporate governance in China, India, and Brazil.

China

In China, the rapid pace of privatization and economic growth, along with the country's recent entry into the World Trade Organization (WTO), has increased the need for corporate governance reform. In 1987 companies were allowed to be formed as independent legal entities, and in 1991 China's two official stock exchanges in Shanghai and Shenzhen began operating. By the end of 2000, more than 100 companies were listed on the two stock exchanges, although most were controlled by the state or state enterprises. Since 1993, the Chinese government has made the development of a modern corporate system a focus of its reform of the state-owned sector.

Tam discusses the key features of Chinese corporate governance and pointed out that although China has adopted the stylized features of the Anglo-American model of corporate governance, the emerging reality was a system closer to the Japanese-Germanic approach.[17] For example, China has heavy bank involvement in corporate ownership, no active market for corporate control, and insider-dominated boards. About 65 percent of China's economy was state-owned in 2003. Three governance problems with the state-owned enterprises (SOEs) have been identified.[18] One, the SOEs are not effectively monitored because the bureaucrats, who are supposed to ensure that managers run the firm efficiently, have little incentive for diligently monitoring firm performance. Two, managers have wide discretion and there are few mechanisms to ensure that they act in the firm's or the state's best interests. Managers are often appointed for political or other reasons, rather than their qualifications for the job. Three, SOEs have conflicting and ambiguous goals. In addition to producing goods and services, SOEs have been responsible for providing education, housing, health care, and social security for their workers.

In the finance sector, most Chinese banks are debt-ridden, unprofitable, and heavily protected from competition. Money and capital markets are small and undeveloped with frequent revelations of insider trading, corruption, and other scandals. Given the importance of legal protection in the overall corporate governance environment, the absence of an independent legal system and a transparent and predictable regulatory environment are significant barriers to the development of world-class financial markets. The laws pertaining to corporate governance that do exist are designed to address specific problems and are not embodied in a comprehensive legal system such as in Germany or the United States. According to Tam, China's governance systems are in a state of transition, with many issues still to be resolved, such as full privatization, the role of the government and the Communist party as major corporate stakeholders, the establishment of a truly independent judiciary and a professional framework and mechanism for legal redress, and the fostering of a business culture that is consistent with the demands of globalization.[19]

India

After independence in 1947, India adopted an economic policy of import substitution along with a highly interventionist approach to industrial development. Various regulations created an environment where large conglomerates, or business houses, dominated the economy and institutional barriers stifled the competitive efforts of entrepreneurs and small businesses. Public banks and insurance companies owned large stakes in the business houses.

Serious problems in the Indian economy in the late 1980s created the need for major legal and regulatory reforms. The result was a movement closer to an Anglo-American model of corporate governance. Among the major changes that occurred were: (a) liberalization of Indian capital markets; (b) revision of the Companies Act of 1956; (c) deregulation of the banking industry; (d) elimination of many of the "license-permit raj" regulations; (e) increased private-sector involvement in many industrial sectors; and (f) reduction of barriers to foreign direct investment. Among the more tangible outcomes have been the emergence of a small market for corporate control, greater protections for small shareholders, and an increasing willingness of foreign firms to invest in India. A number of Indian IT companies are now listed on the Nasdaq exchange.

That said, to some observers, the results of India's efforts at corporate governance reform have not been very successful. As evidence of the lack of success, Reed cites the volatility that has been introduced into the Indian economy in terms of growth and employment.[20] Although India was largely spared the Asian financial crisis of 1997, the economy is now much more connected with global economic cycles, which means that India's former isolation can no longer assure steady (but slow) progress. Also, insider trading and corruption remain endemic, and most corporate boards remain largely composed of insider and family members.

Brazil

Like India, Brazil was a closed economy until quite recently. The state was, and still is, heavily involved in most sectors of the economy. Equity markets were underdeveloped and only loosely connected to global financial systems. In the early 1990s, Brazil embarked on a major privatization process that resulted in sell-offs of state-owned companies in sectors such as steel, mining, petrochemical, telecommunications, and energy. A large number of foreign investors entered Brazil as protections were lifted and the economy rapidly expanded.

The dominant form of organization of local Brazilian capital is the family-controlled business group. Much of the Brazilian economy is controlled by large family-owned business groups, such as Unibanco, Itausa, Aracruz, Brahma, and Trikem. Because of a large proportion of nonvoting shares, acquisitions—and especially hostile takeovers—are rare in Brazil. According to Rabelo and Vasconcelos, Brazil does not have an equity culture.[21] Shareholders in the Anglo-American sense of the concept are rare and controlling shareholders do not see minority shareholders as partners. Brazilian corporate ownership is highly concentrated and there is weak legal protection of investors' rights. A study of the Brazilian financial system argued that the state's fiscal problems, with the ensuing enormous need for finance, have seriously compromised the functioning of the domestic financial system and the development of capital markets.[22] Moreover, the domestic stock market plays a minor role as a source of capital for Brazilian firms. Perhaps that explains why many Brazilian firms are issuing American Depository Receipts (ADRs) on the New York Stock Exchange.

As we saw with China and India, corporate governance reform is occurring in Brazil. In 2001 there were three important changes designed to strengthen corporate governance in Brazil's legal framework: amendments in corporate law, introduction of the Novo Mercado equity market with tougher listing requirements, and new regulations for pension fund investments. These changes were enacted to address the perceived problems with the existing governance practices. For example, board committees are largely inactive and ineffective. Most board members are not stockholders and most boards do not have a structured evaluation procedure for board members, the CEO, or the board itself.[23]

Which Governance System Is Best?

There are many differences among the corporate governance systems around the world. As an example, Dore suggests that the following characteristics of Japanese and German governance are clear departures from the shareholder-oriented model found in the United States:[24]

1. Labor market flexibility is tempered by concern for both worker protection and the fostering of organizational loyalties.

2. Organizational loyalties preclude the buying and selling of companies through the stock exchange.
3. Managers have a broader range of responsibilities—to employees and other stakeholders—than a mere obligation to maximize shareholder returns.
4. To ensure citizen solidarity and mutual responsibility, the nation states retain a large public sector for health, education, and other services. A collective social insurance system with a universal equal-rights nature is expected to minimize the need for means-tested safety nets.

While Dore implies that these characteristics provide evidence of the superiority of the Japanese and German systems, not all observers agree. Sundaram and colleagues argue that "contractarian governance structures of countries such as the United States [and the United Kingdom]—which alone appear to provide the necessary context for the pursuit of such strategies [as asset sales, spinoffs, divestitures, mergers, and acquisitions]—will, therefore, determine the shape and structure of corporate capitalism in the years to come."[25] The reality is that there is no clear evidence to suggest that one of the national systems is the best. There is also no evidence that firms in Europe or Japan are more responsible corporate citizens or less prone to stock market bubbles and managerial malfeasance than shareholder-oriented U.S. firms. Schleifer and Vishny conclude that the successful market economies of the United States, Germany, and Japan have some of the best corporate governance systems in the world and the differences between them are small relative to their differences with other countries, including developed countries such as Italy and emerging markets such as Brazil, China, India, and Russia.[26]

There is one important similarity among the corporate governance systems of the major economies: they all have flaws and have generated recent calls for change. Outside the major developed economies there is certainly room for improvement in corporate governance systems. As the next section discusses, adequate legal protection for investors is often nonexistent and minority shareholders have little influence. The situation is not much better for non-share-owning stakeholders. In the developed economies, regulations and laws that protect individuals from product liability, unsafe working conditions, pollution, employee discrimination, and so on are taken for granted. In much of the rest of the world, these regulations do not exist and non-share-owning stakeholders are in a perilous position should they have cause for dispute with corporate entities. In China, for example, occupational safety regulations are virtually nonexistent (as the thousands of annual deaths in unregulated coal mines attests) and independent labor unions are illegal.

In response to the Asian Financial Crisis of 1997–1998, the International Monetary Fund developed a set of "universal principles" (similar to the OECD list in table 8.1) of corporate governance to regulate market behavior in emerging markets. The rationale for reform was that poor governance was one of the causes for the financial crisis. Advocates maintained that reform would strengthen investor confidence, reduce vulnerability to crisis, promote efficiency, reduce corruption, and foster savings and welfare provision. However, the road that emerging-market economies such as China and Russia should take in improving corporate governance is far from clear. Should, for example, corporate governance in China continue to evolve along the Anglo-American method of financial market–derived external controls or toward a more Japanese-oriented system of internal control, in which established patterns of personal relations and ethical systems determine the effectiveness of alternative arrangements. Is there really one best form of corporate governance? Will the standardization of corporate governance practices erode national cultural differences in the name of corporate stability?[27] Although answering these questions is beyond the scope of this chapter, in a world of global communication, investment, and culture and converging product tastes and fashions, it is likely that evolutionary forces will propel governance systems in new directions.

The Role of Institutional Environments, Conglomerates, Family Ownership, and Government Intervention in Corporate Governance

As indicated earlier, the ownership of companies tends to vary significantly from one country to the other. In many countries, and especially where corporate governance is weak, firms typically have controlling owners who are often the founders or their children, with banks often playing a key role as small but influential investors. In many emerging markets, there is no separation of ownership and control and poor legal protection for investors and especially minority shareholders. Moreover, La Porta and colleagues point out that large shareholders often lobby against legal reforms that would enhance shareholder rights because improvement of minority protection would represent a transfer of control away from the controlling shareholders.[28]

In the United States, La Porta and colleagues report that 80 percent of the largest publicly traded firms are widely held (using 20 percent or more control by a controlling shareholder as evidence that the shares are not widely held). The measure as reported for other countries is as follows: Argentina, 0%; Canada, 65%; France, 60%; Germany, 50%; Hong Kong, 10%; Italy, 20%; Japan, 90%; Mexico, 0%; Sweden, 25%; United Kingdom, 100%. Note that if the measure for control is dropped to 10 percent, the Japan number drops to 50 percent, whereas that for the United States remains at 80 percent. For medium-size companies, the percentages dropped to zero for Hong Kong and Italy, 10 percent for Sweden, and 30 percent for Japan. The authors argue that the attractiveness of going public means that both large and small U.S. firms tended to be widely held.

Among firms with controlling owners, the principal owner types were families and the State. Seventy percent of the largest traded firms in Austria, 45 percent in Singapore, and 40 percent in Italy were state controlled. Not surprisingly, firms in countries with good shareholder protection tended to be widely held. Countries with poor protection have more family- and state-controlled firms. Families are often able to exercise control significantly in excess of their cash flow rights because of pyramid structures. The family is typically represented in the firm's top management. In a set of countries, banks are allowed to own majority stakes in firms and invest more than 60 percent of their capital in such firms. This set includes Austria, Finland, France, Germany, Greece, Ireland, Israel, Korea, the Netherlands, New Zealand, Spain, Switzerland, and the United Kingdom.

Legal Systems

The legal rules that protect shareholders and creditors are a key element in comparisons of national corporate governance systems. A detailed study of the legal rules in 49 countries, also by La Porta and colleagues, drew the following conclusions.[29] First, laws differ significantly from one country to another. Second, most countries give investors limited rights and, hence, ownership tends to be quite concentrated. Third, countries with legal rules originating in the common law tradition (including Australia, Canada, India, Thailand, the United States, the United Kingdom) protect investors significantly more than the countries whose laws originate in French civil law (Argentina, Belgium, Brazil, Chile, France, Italy, Mexico, Poland, Spain). Countries with laws originating in German civil law (Austria, Germany, Japan, South Korea, Switzerland, Taiwan) were in the middle, between countries with common law and French civil law. Fourth, law enforcement differed significantly. Law enforcement is strong in German civil law and common law countries and weak in French civil law countries. Fifth, one of the consequences of poor investor protection is ownership concentration.

The Role of Foreign Directors

Increasingly, companies are appointing foreign CEOs and directors. In 2003, about 10 percent of the United Kingdom's 100 largest companies were run by nonnationals compared with less than 2 percent a decade ago. The number of foreign nonexecutives on U.K. company boards (currently about 30 percent) in the top 100 firms was also rising. In the United States, a survey by the Conference Board showed that only after 1995 did U.S. corporations really start to globalize their boards.[30] The percentage of boards that included at least one nonnational member increased from 39 percent in 1995 to 60 percent in 1998. By 1998, 10 percent of all directors of the reporting companies were of a nationality different from the domicile of the company, up from 6 percent only three years earlier. In 2005 Sony appointed Howard Stringer, a U.K. national, as CEO. In doing so, Sony became the first major Japanese firm with a non-Japanese CEO.

Why are companies increasingly looking for foreign directors? The most important reasons are:

- The corporate cultures of global firms are becoming as global as their businesses. The board has to be able to oversee and understand cross-cultural dimensions and handle diverse organizations.
- Global corporations have global citizenship responsibilities and require directors who understand local citizenship issues.
- Cross-border mergers and acquisitions and strategic alliances are becoming common for all leading companies. The board needs to be able to oversee and lead these investments with an understanding of local and global factors.
- Global companies need access to foreign capital. The global makeup of a board helps create and maintain the confidence of foreign investors and helps ensure appropriate investor communication to these groups.

Strategy and Corporate Governance

Earlier in the chapter we argued that MNE managers should be familiar with international corporate governance. Most strategic decisions will be impacted by corporate governance practices. For example, a company contemplating an acquisition will require an understanding of takeover law in the jurisdiction of interest. More important, the company will need to understand how the various stakeholders will respond to the takeover. If layoffs will be necessary to achieve cost synergies, are they possible? Are there labor unions that can block takeovers or make life difficult in the postmerger period? How will related companies and local communities react? What rights do minority shareholders have? How are takeovers communicated to shareholders? What political issues are involved in the proposed acquisition? In the developed-country economies, these questions can be answered more or less unambiguously (although as GE discovered in 2001 in its failed attempt to acquire Honeywell, predicting the outcome of an antitrust ruling is not always easy. In this case, to GE's surprise, the acquisition was rejected by the European Union Competition Commission on the grounds that the deal would have severely reduced competition in the aerospace industry and resulted in higher prices for customers, particularly airlines).

In emerging markets, as the Thailand case shows, there will likely be a high degree of ambiguity and uncertainty regarding specific laws, their interpretation, and the degree to which the laws may or may not be enforced or enforceable. Thus, a solid understanding of the principles of corporate governance will help managers navigate the legal, regulatory, and cultural waters to design and implement appropriate corporate governance practices.

Conclusion

With continued globalization, corporate governance practices around the world will evolve, with increased regional harmonization likely to precede global shifts. For example, in 2003, the EU was working on a new law designed to facilitate cross-border takeovers in the 15-country union and debating changes that could force governments to ban multiple voting rights where shareholders have a majority of the votes even if they own only a minority of shares. In addition, corporate governance will likely continue to be a subject of great interest in both developed and emerging markets. The recent corporate scandals, especially those in the United States, have contributed to much wider scrutiny of corporate governance practices by lawmakers, executives, shareholders, and society at large. For international business managers, corporate governance will, in all probability, take on greater meaning as country practices evolve and more of the world's economic activity is conducted through markets and firms rather than states. When firms rather than states are involved in economic activity, all stakeholders will expect that value creation and transference is fair and that managers are held accountable for their actions. In the absence of an environment that allows fairness and accountability to flourish, firms will be reluctant to invest. Thus, managers involved in international competition should view knowledge of international governance as an essential element of global strategy.

9

Ethics and Global Strategy

Strategy involves the choices a firm makes about where it competes, how it competes, the customers it targets, the nature of its value creation, and its basis for achieving competitive advantage. Strategy also involves another set of choices, or trade-offs, such as where not to compete and which customers not to target. In making strategic decisions about the global marketplace, firms must be prepared to grapple with issues that are absent from or less prevalent in their domestic markets, such as bribery, child labor and workplace safety issues, human rights violations, intellectual property theft, product liability and customer safety questions, and questionable environmental practices.[1]

In this chapter we explore the issues surrounding global strategy and the ethical dimensions of competing across borders. In doing so, we acknowledge that much of the chapter will raise questions rather than provide answers. Given the broad range of potential situations that firms can encounter in international markets, a normative approach identifying specific business practices that qualify as ethically proper cannot, in our view, capture the reality of global competition. Thus, it is not our intent to prescribe what we think global managers should do in international markets. Rather, we seek to inform readers about ethical issues and how they might be identified, analyzed, and linked to global strategy decisions.

Why Does Ethics Matter in the Global Arena?

When we speak of ethics and global strategy we are referring to the interactions and business conduct between MNEs and their various stakeholders around the world. This conduct is based on a combination of legal, societal, and cultural norms as to how business should be done. In the chapter on corporate governance we discussed the debate between stakeholder and shareholder approaches. Regardless of one's orientation as to the appropriate corporate objective, even Milton Friedman would agree that business must be conducted while conforming to the basic rules of society, which are embodied in law and in ethical custom. The problem and challenge for MNEs is to define what is meant by "basic rules of society." There will always be gray areas not defined by laws or regulations, or where laws differ from country to country, or where laws and practices diverge. In some countries, there may be a complete absence of laws in areas such as pollution and environmental protection. In chapter 7 we discussed some of the challengers of politics and corruption that are faced by MNEs doing business in emerging markets.

Because of these gray areas, MNEs face ethical considerations that vary from one market and geographic region to another. A list of ethical issues that may confront MNEs is shown in table 9.1. The list is far from exhaustive and is connected to a wide range of strategic and managerial decisions. Some of these issues have become highly public in the past few years, such as the safety and compensation practices of manufacturing plants in emerging markets that supply MNEs. Ethical considerations also tend to be connected to the political mood of the day. For example, the decision to move a company's headquarters outside the United States for tax reasons has become politically charged

Table 9.1. Typical Questions of Ethics Confronting Multinational Enterprises (MNEs)

1. Should a firm do business in a country in which the government may be violating human rights?
2. Should a firm market a product in a country or region that lacks adequate consumer protection, product liability laws, and certain penalties for unlawful behaviors?
3. If a firm makes a product that has potentially harmful side effects when used improperly, should that firm market its product in a country where a high level of illiteracy is likely to mean that some customers will be unable to follow directions for safe product usage?
4. Should a firm have a responsibility for end-user behavior that may not be legal?
5. Should a firm use bribery in a country where corruption is widespread?
6. Should a firm pay facilitation fees to ensure that goods clear customs in a timely manner?
7. Should a firm follow local laws in areas such as employee safety and environmental protections?
8. How should female employees be treated in countries where the rights of women are not equal to those of men?
9. Should MNEs use tax avoidance strategies, such as moving the head office to a lower tax regime in order to reduce taxes?
10. Should an MNE do business with a firm that engaged in actions that would be illegal in the home country of the MNE but are legal in another jurisdiction?

while in the past that decision may have gone largely unnoticed. Other ethical considerations are more subtle, but not necessarily less strategic. In China, gift giving can play a key role in solidifying trust and understanding with potential customers, suppliers, government officials, and so on. Many MNEs forbid gift giving in their home market—what happens when they go to China? Is gift giving in China morally acceptable because it is part of Chinese culture and morally unacceptable in the United States because it is not part of the U.S. culture?

While there will always be disagreements about the meaning of what is morally and ethically appropriate, in most societies the boundary between ethical and unethical business practices is reasonably clear. Obviously, illegal actions are not morally acceptable. When the boundary is not clear, or the law has not yet been established, or when firms go against what is publicly acceptable, governments may have to step in. For example, growing public awareness and concern for controlling water pollution in the United States led to enactment of the Clean Water Act in 1972. The act established the basic structure for regulating discharges of pollutants into U.S. waters. As a result of the act, lakes, rivers, and other bodies of water are much cleaner than they were 30 years ago, and few people would argue that it is ethically acceptable for a company to deliberately discharge harmful pollutants into a body of water.

When a firm crosses an international border, there is a need to develop new understanding of ethical norms. In the previous paragraph we said that there is clarity within societies. When a firm crosses a border, it must learn about the new market or society. As a starting point, it should be easy to say that firms should avoid illegal activities when doing business in new markets. Unfortunately, the legal environment in countries such as China is murky at best, and what is legal or illegal is often far from clear. Moreover, laws in many countries are not transparent and seem to be almost a moving target. When shifting from the rule of law to the more ambiguous notion of ethical custom, it is easy to see why international managers often struggle to make the "right" decision. What may be legal and culturally acceptable in the home country may be illegal and culturally unacceptable in the new market. In a country like India, the rule of law may be clearer than in China because of the British legal heritage. However, India's different religions, languages, geographies, and cultural traditions impose many challenges to determining what is culturally acceptable. What is a norm in one part of the country may be a major violation of acceptable behavior in another region. Moreover, the ancient India exists in tandem with a modern government and regulatory environment characterized by red tape and bureaucracy.

As an example of an emerging global ethical issue, consider the pharmaceutical industry and the increasingly common practice of doing clinical trials outside the United States and other developed countries.[2] In poorer countries, such as Russia, it is easier to find patients willing to take part in clinical trials, as well as doctors willing to supervise those trials. However, in the event that the trial is successful, and the drug is approved for sale, patients in the countries where the trials were conducted probably cannot afford that drug if it is sold at a real market price. Thus, the issue confronting the pharmaceutical companies is whether or not companies have an obligation to make drugs available to patients in poor countries who have taken part in clinical trials. With the exception of AIDS drugs, there is no industry consensus on this issue, especially when drugs are not lifesaving. And, like most ethical issues, there are plenty of arguments on both sides of the debate.

Whose Values and Whose Ethical Standards?

The question of whose morals and whose ethical standards rule confronts MNEs as soon as they cross a border. For example, the issue of environmental laws and regulations is highly controversial. In the debate about the merits of free trade, those against free trade often argue that firms take advantage of lax environmental standards in emerging markets (in other words, firms export their pollution and garbage to less developed nations). Most MNEs will publicly promise to obey all applicable laws and regulations in the countries in which they operate. However, what if the environmental regulation is weak or nonexistent? In this case, MNEs need to make decisions about which environmental laws to uphold: those of the home country, those of the country in which a subsidiary is located, or those of a third country? If the environmental laws of one country are not very stringent, it could be cheaper for the subsidiary to produce in that country. But, is it ethically acceptable to knowingly operate a manufacturing facility in an emerging market that creates more pollution than a similar plant in, say, the United States or Germany? As an example, consider the American firm Newmont Mining Company, the world's largest gold producer. Newmont operates several mines in Indonesia, and on August 31, 2004, an Indonesian government panel announced that Newmont had illegally disposed of waste containing arsenic and mercury in the ocean near a mine site and had failed to get the required operating permits from the Ministry of Environment.[3] Newmont denied the charges and said that it operated in full compliance with Indonesian standards. At that site, Newmont was using a waste disposal method called submarine tailing, which involved piping treated mine waste into the ocean. This method of waste disposal, which is lower in cost than land-based waste storage, is banned in the United States. Assuming Newmont was acting, or at least believed it was acting, in compliance with Indonesian environmental standards, is it ethical for the company to use a waste disposal system that is illegal in the United States?

As another example, the ship-breaking industry has become international in scope and has generated great controversy in recent years because of arguments that environmental problems are being outsourced (and safety issues are being ignored). The average life span of a ship is 25 to 30 years, after which the ship is "broken" to recover the scrap steel. Scrap ships usually contain a large amount of hazardous materials. The U.S. Navy found itself embroiled in controversy in 2003 when it announced that most of a $17.8 million military contract would be awarded to a British ship scrapyard. The contract called for scrapping 13 ships. Environmentalists complained about taking old ships full of hazardous materials across the Atlantic and through the English Channel. American companies complained that they were not given a fair chance to compete for the contract. Soon after the United States awarded the contract, the British government was accused of planning to export old Royal Navy vessels to be broken in countries with more lenient environmental standard than Britain. Meanwhile, countries such as Pakistan and Bangladesh have become world leaders in ship breaking. Pakistani and Bangladeshi firms break the world's largest ships in countries with few environmental rules and regulations guiding this industry. Health, safety, and environmental conditions are generally very poor, and deaths on the job are not uncommon. In 2000, 40 workers were killed in two explosions aboard ships being scrapped in Bangladeshi ship-breaking yards.

Very few shipyards in OECD countries are still in the ship-breaking business because they cannot compete with Asian firms. One of the reasons for the low costs of using Asian firms is their little regard for environmental remediation and less stringent worker safety conditions. For the owner of a ship that must be scrapped, how should these environmental and safety issues be factored into a decision about awarding such a contract? More generally, when ethical standards in one country are different from the norms of behavior in the home market, global firms face three basic choices:[4]

1. The firm can avoid doing business in that particular country.
2. The firm can enter the country, maintain its home market standards, and risk being at a competitive disadvantage to firms that follow the prevailing norms.
3. The firm can change its standards and play the game the way the locals do, following an argument such as "What is corruption to one person may be the norm for the other."

Relativism, Objectivism, and Pluralism

So does an MNE have a moral and ethical responsibility to ensure a safe, fair, environmentally sustainable, and legal working environment in emerging markets when local laws are silent or less stringent than other countries? Addressing this question can lead one into a philosophical debate involving relativism, objectivism, and pluralism. Ethical relativism holds that morality is relative to the norms of one's culture. That is, whether an action is right or wrong depends on the moral and cultural norms of the society in which it is practiced. Ethical objectivism suggests that there is a single universal standard of ethical truth against which all behaviors can be measured. That is, what is ethical behavior in one society should also be followed in another society. Ethical pluralism is, in a sense, somewhere between relativism and objectivism. The core claim of ethical pluralism is that there may be multiple correct answers to ethical questions of right and wrong. The obvious question is, what is the basis for finding the correct answers and how is this much different from relativism?

In an attempt to deal with the vexing issue of international business ethics, Thomas Donaldson and Thomas Dunfee developed a pluralistic framework and applied it to global ethics.[5] The framework, called *integrative social contracts theory*, is based on the argument that firms must understand the transcultural value implications of their actions. The framework incorporates the concept of norms of behavior against which an MNE's actions can be plotted. Hypernorms are principles that exist in all cultures, such as fundamental human rights. Consistent norms are more culturally specific but likely consistent with most cultures. Moral free space involves norms that are inconsistent with at least some legitimate norms found in other economic cultures. Illegitimate norms are those that are clearly inconsistent with hypernorms.

Although the Donaldson and Dunfee framework does not completely eliminate the question of whose values to follow, it does suggest that firms must never resort to "When in Rome do as the Romans do" behavior, nor should they insist that "We have one set of ethical values that we employ wherever we do business." For those actions that do not clearly fall within the hypernorm category, managers have to be creative. Donaldson and Dunfee do not pretend that a firm can behave exactly the same wherever it does business. Cultures are different, which means that those making ethical decisions must respect the right of other cultures to shape their own societal values. MNE managers will often experience moral tensions and dilemmas; this should be viewed as the natural way of global business and not something that must be avoided. For example, in Singapore the concept of maternity leave exists but is not well developed, and many businesspeople (men and women) are openly dismissive of the idea that women should have guaranteed job security after taking time off to have a baby. In Sweden, a country with one of the most generous maternity-leave policies in the world, women can get up to 96 weeks of leave at 80 percent of their salary. Should a Swedish company operating in Singapore offer the same maternity-leave benefits as in Sweden? This issue would appear to fall within both the consistent norm and moral free space areas. While short maternity leave in Singapore is generally considered reasonable, the Swedish model would be seen as excessive and unfair to employers.

Global Strategy Issues and Ethics

As we have discussed, the actions and decisions of many firms have ethical dimensions. From a global strategy perspective, a particularly important decision deals with the product markets and geographic regions in which a firm competes, or seeks to compete. From an international ethics perspective, the question of "Where should a company do business?" has various subquestions, such as "Should a firm do business in a country in which the government may be violating human rights or should a firm market a product in a country or region that lacks adequate consumer protection, product liability laws, and certain penalties for unlawful behaviors?"

For the oil and gas and the mining industries, the reality is that much of the world's natural resources are in countries with some of the most unsavory political regimes. One of these unsavory regimes runs Myanmar (formerly Burma). In the 1990s, a consortium of firms including the American firm Unocal, Total of France, and the Petroleum Authority of Thailand signed a contract with the Myanmar government to extract and transport natural gas using a pipeline from the Yadana Field located 43 miles off Myanmar's coast. This contract created a firestorm of controversy. Myanmar democracy movement leader Aung San Suu Kyi called for economic sanctions against Myanmar, arguing that foreign investment creates jobs for some people but also makes an already wealthy elite wealthier, which harms the democratic process by increasing the desire of the military rulers to hang on to power. For a broader perspective, consider whether firms should invest in countries ruled by corrupt dictators. Thomas Donaldson said the following on the subject of investing in dictatorships, and Myanmar specifically, "Basically, we will tolerate a fair amount of unethical behavior from a person, firm or nation with whom we just have business dealings, but when matters reach the point of a dramatic threshold, most people say you just don't do business with that type of person. I don't think China reaches that point, but if any country might qualify as passing the threshold, it would be Burma."[6]

CASE STUDY: MOBIL AND ACEH, INDONESIA

Indonesia is one of the world's largest producers of natural gas, ranking sixth in total gas produced and 13th in proven reserves. The country's gas reserves are concentrated in several areas, including the Arun field in Aceh province. Located on the northwestern end of the island of Sumatra, the Special Territory of Aceh is home to a population of roughly 4.5 million, with more than 95 percent Acehnese and the remainder mainly Javanese. The territory covers an area of 55,392 square kilometers and the capital is the city of Banda Aceh.

For the past few decades, Aceh has seen battles between the Indonesian army and guerrilla rebels advocating independence. The intensity of the guerrilla campaign escalated significantly in 1988, when the government declared Aceh a military operation zone, giving the military a free hand to crack down on separatists. The military occupation was prompted by clashes between the Acehnese and Javanese settlers that threatened the security of gas operations. Throughout the 1990s there were thousands of soldiers in Aceh. Several military posts were established—one, near a gas field that was allegedly used for interrogating local people, and a second near a liquefied natural gas plant called P.T. Arun on a site formerly used as housing for construction workers and P.T. Arun employees.

To appease the Aceh population, the Indonesian government poured funds into Aceh for development projects. However, the gesture only fueled resentment because little of the money trickled down to local Acehnese. A combination of levies, taxes, and royalties ensured that the central government in Jakarta acquired almost all the revenue from Aceh oil, gas, timber, and minerals. Indeed, the issue of financial transfers from the provinces and territories to Jakarta was so sensitive that the government did not reveal how much was collected. Observers speculated that less than 10 percent of the oil and gas revenue generated in the 1990s from Aceh remained in the territory. After the 2004 tsunami, many questions were raised about the lack of urgency in distributing much-needed aid to the devastated Aceh region.

Mobil and P.T. Arun

Indonesia's oil and gas industries were controlled by P.N. Pertamina (Pertamina), a state-owned organization. Pertamina, a bloated and inefficient bureaucracy, was formed in 1968 when the government combined two state-owned companies to form a single organization that controlled all oil and gas exploration, production, processing, marketing, and distribution activities in Indonesia. In Indonesia, 90 percent of the oil and gas production operations were operated by foreign companies under production-sharing contracts that allowed the foreign companies a profit after tax and cost recovery of 15 to 35 percent on oil and 30 to 40 percent on gas. Pertamina had production-sharing contracts with various large oil companies, including Mobil (now part of ExxonMobil), Total, Unocal, and Vicol.

In 1998 there were a series of allegations about military atrocities involving the P.T. Arun liquefied natural gas plant. Pertamina held a 55 percent stake in P.T. Arun, Mobil owned 35 percent, and a Japanese consortium owned 10 percent. Mobil had been doing business in Indonesia for decades. The initial contract between Mobil and the Indonesian government that would lead to the construction of the P.T. Arun plant was signed in 1965. This contract gave Mobil exploration access to the rich oil and gas fields in the Lhokseumawe area in north Aceh province. The discovery of natural gas in 1971 resulted in the development of one of the world's richest onshore reserves of gas, estimated at 40 billion cubic meters. This gas field, named Arun, quickly became Indonesia's largest producing gas field and the most important source of revenue for the Indonesian government. By the late 1980s, Aceh oil and gas reserves provided an estimated 11 percent of Indonesia's total exports. The P.T. Arun plant processed the gas for export. The plant in north Aceh was one of the largest LNG processing facilities in the world.

Through various production-sharing contracts, Mobil was a major producer of gas from the Arun field. Mobil's investment in P.T. Arun was made through its wholly owned subsidiary in Indonesia. The joint venture agreement for P.T. Arun specified that Pertamina would be responsible for operational management of the plant. Mobil's official role was mainly in a technical advisory capacity. The general manager was appointed by Pertamina. Several Mobil expatriates were working and living in Aceh.

According to various human rights and environmental groups, the gas fields had been a heavy burden on Acehnese communities that depended on agriculture and fish farming. The list of alleged abuses included land seizures with minimum compensation; explosions that destroyed farmland and villagers' homes; numerous oil and industrial spills into the rivers, sea, and bay; erosion of villagers' riverside gardens; and extreme noise pollution.

In 1998, Indonesian human rights organizations and government officials identified 12 mass graves in Aceh. One grave was located on Pertamina-

owned land less than three miles from a Mobil gas-drilling site. Other sus-
pected graves were in close proximity to Mobil sites. Indonesian human
rights groups alleged that Mobil provided logistical support to the Indonesian army, including lending earth-moving equipment to dig the mass graves.
The human rights groups demanded that Mobil and P.T. Arun apologize,
pay compensation, and rehabilitate the victims of human rights abuses carried out by the military. They also urged Amnesty International and Human
Rights Watch to investigate Mobil's finances, especially its funding for
military operations.

Both Mobil and Pertamina executives denied allegations that they knew
of any human rights abuses in the Aceh area. In November 1998, Mobil's
president met with the U.S. ambassador to Indonesia in Jakarta and denied
knowledge of any misuse of Mobil equipment or facilities. A Pertamina
public relations executive echoed that response, saying, "Incidents connected
to human rights violations were beyond Pertamina's and Mobil's authority
and knowledge." Mobil acknowledged that it loaned the army excavators
and supplied troops with food and fuel on occasion for three decades. But,
the company insisted, Mobil managers had no record that the army was
using this help for anything but peaceful purposes. A Mobil spokesman said:
"Mobil was told that any equipment used was for projects beneficial to the
community, such as building roads. If facilities and equipment were used
for other reasons I don't believe we can be held responsible."[7]

As well, Mobil said that all equipment and land was owned by Pertamina
or leased from outside contractors. The Indonesian army helped to exca-
vate the graves and said that it regretted any suffering, but denied that the
deaths were caused by the army. Complicating matters was a December
1999 report in which one of the rebel leaders claimed that P.T. Arun had
been willingly giving contributions to the movement.

Various individuals argued that Pertamina and Mobil had to have known
what was going on. A former P.T. Arun manager maintained that everybody
in Aceh knew that massacres were taking place. A former P.T. Arun employee
said that rumors of massacres and other atrocities near the plant were frequently
discussed in the workplace. A contractor said he told local Mobil managers
that he had found human body parts close to Mobil sites, which he claimed
was reported to a Mobil heavy-equipment supervisor. The discovery was made
on land owned by Pertamina and acquired for Mobil to develop, subsequently
named Skull Hill by local villagers. According to villagers, the stench of rot-
ting flesh from Skull Hill could be smelled half a mile away.

The public spotlight on Mobil emboldened some local communities to
take action. One Aceh attorney, who intended to sue Mobil on behalf of

victims, said, "The crimes occurred over a long period of time. Mobil cannot utter the words, 'We didn't know.'"[8]

Implications from the Mobil and Aceh Case

This case study provides a detailed look at Mobil's (now part of ExxonMobil) experience in Aceh, the oil- and gas-rich Indonesian province. In the late 1990s, Mobil found itself accused of providing support to the Indonesian army in its efforts to suppress the Aceh independence movement. Mobil strongly denied the allegations. Over the next few years the situation remained tense, and in 2001 ExxonMobil suspended operations in Aceh for four months because of security concerns.[9] Would ExxonMobil be better off by leaving Aceh altogether? The problem with this perspective is where to draw the line, especially in the natural resources exploration business. More generally, how do you decide which countries are acceptable in which to do business? Coming up with a decision rule will not be easy. There are rankings of countries in terms of democratic and economic freedoms as well as numerous rankings based on different measures of risk. The problem for oil and gas companies is that the majority of oil producing countries do quite poorly on measures of freedom, corruption, business climate, and so on. If ExxonMobil were to leave Aceh, should it also stop doing business in Angola, the Middle East, Chad, and other countries?

If ExxonMobil remains in Aceh, should it make any changes in its operation? The company was in a difficult position in the late 1990s. There were numerous allegations against the company that could hurt its reputation elsewhere, regardless of the validity of the allegations. In the near term, the security situation was escalating out of control and Aceh was in danger of having a full-fledged guerrilla war. Although the P.T. Arun plant had not been targeted, if it was kept running it could be burned or blown up, with huge losses of life. Employees could be targeted for kidnapping or murder (this actually happened in 2002). On the other hand, the plant was an important employer in the area and even the separatists would have to acknowledge this. As well, targeting an American-run plant would probably not help the secession movement and its international reputation.

Another question was, should ExxonMobil try to change the situation in Aceh? ExxonMobil's critics have said that the company must have known about the activities taking place outside the plant. How could the firm not know? Why, according to critics, was nothing done? Continuing this line of argument, if the government does not care for the interests of its own people, an MNE must take on the delinquent government's role by considering the interests of the citizens who are affected by the MNE's actions. This suggests that ExxonMobil could have supported Aceh's efforts to reduce the flow of gas revenues out of the province and even mediated between the separatists and the Indonesian government. The opposing perspective is the one advocated by Milton Friedman: engage in open and free competition without deception or fraud, and stay within the rules of the game. The problem is that the rules in Aceh have changed with the downfall of Suharto, Indonesia's former leader, and the new rules are not clear. Should ExxonMobil try to create new rules between MNEs and the Indonesian government? Or should the firm respect the rules as they are understood and stay out of the political arena?

In an attempt to clarify MNEs' responsibilities to their host nations, Richard DeGeorge suggested moral guidelines for MNEs, such as "Multinationals should do no intentional direct harm."[10] (See table 9.2 for a list of the guidelines.) It is unlikely that too many people would oppose these guidelines in principle. However, they raise practical questions about how a firm could measure and account for harm, development, cooperation, and other suggested outcomes. How would you answer these questions in looking at ExxonMobil's record and experience in Indonesia? For example, Has ExxonMobil produced more harm than good for the host country? The answer to the last question is probably yes: Arun has provided much of the revenue flow for the Indonesian government. But narrow the question down to Aceh province: Is Aceh better off because of ExxonMobil's investment? This question is more difficult to answer.

Table 9.2.   Richard DeGeorge's Seven Moral Guidelines for Multinational Enterprises (MNEs) Competing in Emerging Markets

- Multinationals should do no intentional direct harm.
- Multinationals should produce more good than bad for the host country.
- Multinationals should contribute by their activity to the host country's development.
- Multinationals should respect the human rights of their employees.
- To the extent that local culture does not violate ethical norms, multinationals should respect the local culture and work with and not against it.
- Multinationals should pay their fair share of taxes.
- Multinationals should cooperate with the local government in developing and enforcing just background institutions (i.e., laws, government regulations, consumer groups, labor unions).

Source: Richard DeGeorge, *Competing with Integrity in International Business* (New York: Oxford University Press, 1993).

MNEs and Intellectual Property

We offer a second case study to illustrate a different type of MNE strategy choice. Should a firm be responsible for end-user behavior? The case that follows deals with the manufacturing of CD replicators, a legitimate product for producing music CDs. Some of the replicators allegedly end up in the hands of music counterfeiters.

CASE STUDY: CD PIRACY

Should the manufacturer of a product be held accountable for its end use? Consider the case of CD replicators, which are used to reproduce CDs from master copies. Twenty years ago, producing CDs required large, clean rooms that sealed out dust and other substances that could damage disk quality. The equipment was very expensive, required great technical expertise to operate, and cost about $30 million. In 1987, a German company developed technology that greatly simplified CD manufacturing. This technology resulted in glass-enclosed units that were much smaller than the clean rooms and could be used as self-contained assembly lines. The machines were easy to use and transport, and most important, were priced at about $2.5 million.

Many replicators were sold in Hong Kong and rumored to then be shipped to China to be used for the production of pirate CDs. CD piracy in China began to flourish in the early 1990s, when other Asian countries took steps to curb the piracy within their borders. In particular, when the government of Taiwan shut down pirate CD plants, Chinese CD piracy took off. Despite the efforts of the Chinese government to crack down on piracy by closing CD plants and destroying illegal CDs, piracy continued to flourish. It was estimated that about 90 percent of the CDs purchased in China were counterfeit.[11] Many of the illegal factories reportedly were joint ventures with Taiwanese businesses, which helped finance the purchase of the equipment used to produce the counterfeit CDs.

Until the development of small replicators, China-based pirate CD manufacturers struggled to deal with the environment and in particular, the high humidity prevalent in South China.. The new replication equipment overcame this problem and could be operated virtually anywhere. One report suggested that with a reliable and portable power supply, pirates could produce CDs from the back of container trucks in the near future, perpetually and untraceably roving the countryside like truck-mounted cold war Soviet missiles.[12]

Many of the pirate CDs produced in China were shipped around the world through Hong Kong. Given the huge volume of goods that passed through Hong Kong, there was little customs inspectors could do to stem the flow of illegal goods. In China, pirate CDs were estimated to account for about 90 percent of the local CD market.

For the MNE company producing replicators and other equipment that could then be used to make counterfeit CDs, DVDs, computer software, and other products, is there an obligation to understand how the product is used by the customer? One perspective is that the producer of the product has no responsibility to ensure that the end user engages in legal activities. This perspective might be expressed in the following manner by a hypothetical executive involved in the production of equipment for CD factories:

> If CDs are being made illegally with equipment produced by my firm, it is up to the various countries to enforce their laws. In a free market, we should be able to sell to any customer who wants the product and has the money to pay for it. If I refuse sales because I am concerned about possible illegal use of the equipment, I can assure you there are other CD equipment firms who would gladly take the orders. I have to keep my costs down and improve my technology. I cannot afford to cut my sales back. If I do, I might as well shut my business down. How am I supposed to explain that to my employees? I have worked hard to build this business and support my community. My replication equipment is the best in the industry. Why should I stop selling to certain customers just because of rumors that my customers are not using the equipment properly?

A very different perspective is that firms should not sell products when there is a known probability that the equipment could be used. For this to happen, firms must be quite familiar with their customers' activities and processes and make an assessment as to the likelihood that the product will be used for legal purposes. The firm must also decide the probability threshold beyond which a sale will not be made.

The ethical consideration involves the manufacturer's responsibility for determining how the product is used. As the hypothetical executive says in the case, should a firm be held accountable for what may or may not be happening after the product is sold? In a global world where products may be sold and used in multiple countries, few firms will have the resources to police the sale of their products On the other hand, several opposing points could be raised in support of replicator firms being responsible: firms have a moral responsibility to protect the use of intellectual property; doing nothing harms the music recording artists; if manufacturers do not take unilateral action, the pirating organizations will never get the message; and if there is reasonable knowledge that replicators are linked to illegal activity, the manufacturers are morally wrong if they stand idly by and pretend they have no culpability. As with the question of where to do business, this issue is complex and multifaceted.

As knowledge-based competition increasing becomes the norm, issues involving intellectual property will grow more interesting and more challenging, especially in emerging markets with weak or nonexistent intellectual property laws. Consider the case of Abro Industries (Abro), a small U.S. company that sells glue, spray paint, and epoxy products mainly in emerging markets. A *Wall Street Journal* article reported that a Chinese company called Hunan Magic had gone far beyond trademark piracy and was attempting to steal Abro's identity.[13] According to the article, Hunan Magic was showing its products at trade shows in China using packaging and labels identical to those developed by Abro. The company was selling more than 40 Abro products in exact replicas of Abro's packaging. Hunan Magic's CEO had Abro's logo on his business card and claimed that his company was the real Abro. Hunan Magic's catalog included products that were identical to Abro's and investigators found products labeled Abro and "Made in the U.S.A." in a factory owned by the CEO's wife. Even when presented with what looks like an open-and-shut case of flagrant piracy, Chinese authorities were reluctant to take legal action and fined the company token amounts. As a result, Abro's CEO was forced to hire lawyers and spend a significant amount of money and time trying to resolve the problem.

Ethical Guidelines, Laws, and International Accords

In managing ethical issues, MNEs must deal with different laws in the countries in which they compete. They must also deal with competitors that come from different countries and legal jurisdictions. An area that continues to challenge MNEs is bribery and corruption. Corruption, as we indicated in chapter 7, is defined by *Transparency International* as "the abuse of entrusted power for private gain." Corruption is pervasive in many countries. Most MNEs will, at some point, encounter government officials seeking bribes. It is estimated that in Russia, for example, government officials receive an estimated $37 billion in bribes each year, according to one of Moscow's leading think tanks.[14] Moreover, corruption is a worldwide phenomenon and can be found in both developed and developing economies.

The challenge for MNEs is how to stay within the law and successfully compete in a global environment. U.S. companies, unlike many of their international competitors, must deal with the Foreign Corrupt Practices Act (FCPA). The FCPA was passed in 1977 and prohibits bribery of a foreign official or a foreign political-party official in order to obtain or keep business. The statute also prohibits paying money to an intermediary, knowing that some or all of the amount will be given to foreign government officials. To violate the FCPA, the person making or authorizing the payment must have a corrupt intent, and the payment must be intended to induce the recipient to misuse his official position. The FCPA includes an exception to the antibribery prohibition for payments to facilitate or expedite performance of a "routine governmental action." For the latter, the statute lists examples such as obtaining permits, licenses, or other official documents; processing governmental papers, such as visas and work orders; providing police protection, mail pick-up and delivery; providing phone service, power and water supply, loading and unloading cargo, or protecting perishable products; and scheduling inspections associated with contract performance or transit of goods across country.

The criminal penalties for violations of the FCPA can be severe. For business entities, the criminal fines may be as much as twice the gain or loss caused by the corrupt payments, which could be millions of dollars. For an individual, penalties may be as much as five years in prison plus payment of a fine. Individuals' fines may not be paid by employers. When the FCPA was passed, it was expected that the result would be significantly higher standards for U.S. firms, especially relative to their international competitors. The actual results of the FCPA are more ambiguous. While every U.S. company would acknowledge that bribery is unethical, a study by Wesley Cragg and William Woof conclude that the FCPA has had limited impact on the standards of conduct of American companies in international markets with respect to the bribery of foreign public officials.[15] According to *Transparency International*'s Bribe Payers Index of 2002, the reputation of the United States was not much different from that of a number of countries that do not have the same type of laws about bribery. There have been only a small number of prosecutions associated with the FCPA, and American companies compete successfully in countries notorious for having highly corrupt regimes. That said, Cragg and Woof indicate that the FCPA has ambitious goals and has encouraged a number of U.S. companies to implement antibribery policies. In addition, it is possible that the FCPA has allowed some American firms to set higher ethical standards, which helps create an advantage relative to international competitors (although empirical evidence to confirm this would be a difficult task).

In 1997, the industrialized world agreed to an OECD convention modeled on the FCPA. As an example of more recent anticorruption efforts, in 2004 the heads 19 international construction firms agreed to embrace a policy of zero tolerance toward business bribery and to enforce it with internal compliance systems. The executives signed the anticorruption pledge during the World Economic Forum in Davos, Switzerland. The list of signatory companies included U.S.-based Fluor, Sweden's Skanska, Canada's SNC-Lavalin Group. Liechtenstein-based Hilti AG, Obayashi Corporation of Japan, and firms from South Africa, Switzerland, Italy, Lebanon, Malaysia, Greece, Argentina, the United Kingdom, Kuwait, and Mexico.

Formal Corporate Ethics Programs

Given the wide array of ethical challenges created by globalization, the MNE's use of formal and informal structures in its management of ethical issues is an important consideration. A formal corporate ethics programs will usually include some or all of the following elements:[16]

- Formal ethics codes that articulate a firm's expectations about ethics
- Ethics committees charged with developing ethics policies, evaluating company or employee actions, and/or investigating and adjudicating possible violations
- Ethics communication systems to provide a means for employees to report abuses or obtain guidance
- Ethics officers or ombudspersons charged with coordinating policies, providing ethics education, or investigating allegations
- Ethics training programs aimed at helping employees to recognize and respond to ethical issues
- Disciplinary processes to address unethical behavior

In an interesting study, Sharon Watson and Gary Weaver examined how internationalization influenced the role of ethics in MNEs. They found a positive relationship between the internationalization of a firm and its top executives' visible concern for ethical issues. From this finding, the authors concluded that internationalization appears to heighten executives' concern to see that ethically proper behavior occurs. They also found that both formal and informal controls play a role in managing ethical issues. A study some years ago looked at the prevalence of formal ethics codes in different countries and found that European companies were less likely to use ethics codes than were U.S. firms.[17]

S. Prakash Sethi, an expert on corporate social responsibility, argued that individual company codes of conduct, while not totally ineffective, have suffered from a lack of effective validation of performance.[18] He identified several problems with corporate codes of conduct: they lack specific content, managers and employees often do not understand the codes or take them seriously, and the codes do not provide a framework for external communication. He also rejected arguments for industry-wide codes of conduct, suggesting that a go-it-alone strategy offers the most potential advantage for a firm. Sethi recommends that companies create codes of conduct and then allow the company codes to be externally and independently verified. He also argues that MNEs tend to adopt a "public affairs" strategy based on accusing their foes (usually a local or international NGO) of having incorrect data about the company and issuing incomplete and self-serving information. He makes the case that such strategies invariably fail and further damage corporate reputations.[19]

For a code of conduct to meet the expectations of the various involved parties, Sethi identified four elements that must be present. The code must:

1. Be economically viable for the MNE
2. Address substantive issues that are of importance to the various MNE stakeholders
3. Engage important stakeholders in the formation and implementation
4. Have specific measurable performance standards

In his concluding comments, Sethi suggests that firms have an obligation to become involved in social change, stating "The large corporation, and especially the multinational corporation, must become an active agent for social change. . . . As a dominant institution in society, the corporation must assume its rightful place and contribute to shaping the public agenda instead of simply reacting to policy changes advocated by others."[20] While this argument would surely stimulate a lively debate, there is no question that with continued globalization, MNEs will increase their share of world economic output, putting the largest MNEs in a unique position to impact people's lives.

Conclusion

We stated at the beginning of this chapter that our intent was not to offer prescriptive advice and solutions. The problem with advice on global ethics, as Donaldson and Dunfee argue, is that it often appears either too oriented toward the MNE or hopelessly impractical.[21] Thus, rather than offering advice we will conclude by saying:

- All major strategic decisions have social, political, and ethical consequences.
- The corporation is not just an economic actor and all managers operating in the international arena will have to make decisions that involve more than just economic analysis.
- Although Milton Friedman says "stay within the rules of the game," it is not always clear what the rules are or who sets the rules or when the rules change.
- Just as innovation and creativity are the foundation of strategic choices with respect to product, markets, and customers, innovation and creativity will inevitably be necessary to manage global ethical challenges.

In evaluating the ethical dimensions of strategic decision, managers have access to various tools and data. For example, the data and rankings about corruption produced by Transparency International provide useful information for market entry decisions. Ultimately, however, the ethical stance taken by a company will depend on the decisions made by its managers. In some cases, no matter what the company does, it will be accused of ethical lapses. When Enron successfully negotiated the first power purchase agreement by a foreign company in India, the immediate reaction from the opposition government and the public was that Enron must have bribed someone. Without bribes, how could Enron have possibly negotiated a successful deal? Enron denied the allegations vigorously and proceeded with the Dabhol project. India, unfortunately, has a corruption problem and there is a tendency there to assume that whenever a company wins a contract involving the government, corruption has to be part of the equation. Enron subsequently experienced many problems in India and eventually the project was shut down.[22] However, despite extensive investigations and court cases, the allegation of bribery against Enron was never proven. That said, Enron's failure to manage the perception associated with its ethical stance certainly contributed to its subsequent difficulties with the government, the media, and other stakeholders in India.

In conclusion, we reiterate that our goal was to inform readers about ethical issues and how they might be identified, analyzed, and linked to global strategy decisions. As globalization continues, more and more managers will find that international ethical dimensions must be incorporated in their decision-making processes.

Strategy and Globalization: A Final Note

Continued globalization is inevitable. While there surely will be some bumps along the road, further integration among people, countries, governments, cultures, and organizations is going to happen, and just about every industry is going to be impacted. Some industries will see the change in more substantial ways than others, but overall no industry will remain untouched. As we discussed in chapter 1, globalizing industries bring together far-flung buyers and sellers in a network of local, regional, and global players. From the sushi industry to the diamond industry, new players are shaking up incumbent firms and expanding the presence of already well-established industries. One of the authors of this book recently purchased a diamond ring for his daughter. The ring was purchased in Singapore from a Singapore-owned retail chain that has a significant local-cost advantage in the moderately priced diamond jewelry market. The ring was manufactured in China in a factory owned by the retailer. The diamond was from South Africa and was cut in Belgium. The Singapore retailer claimed that it was able to undercut its local jewelry competitors through its economies of scale in low-cost manufacturing and bulk diamond purchasing. Not long ago, this type of approach with diamonds would have been difficult because of a fragmented and secretive diamond industry. But as the diamond industry globalizes, it takes on characteristics similar to those of other industries, such as firms searching for low-cost manufacturing and fierce competition across industry value-chain activities.

New competitors will emerge that will challenge the incumbents of today, and these competitors may come from some unlikely sources. Until a few years ago in the home furnishings industry, conventional wisdom was that the cost of shipping and the fragmented nature of the industry meant that manufacturing and retailing close to the customer would remain the norm. Instead, the furniture manufacturing sector has very rapidly moved to China and other low-cost countries, leading to substantially lower prices in developed-market retail stores and, unfortunately for the communities affected, a significant loss of manufacturing jobs. Consider another example. The United States, Japan, and Western Europe dominate the automobile industry today. However, the largest markets in terms of volume growth are in India and China. Will world-class car companies emerge from India and China? A decade ago such a proposition would have been laughable. However, three decades ago few industry observers would have believed that Korean cars would, within a short time, become legitimate competitors to Japanese and American products. By 2004 Hyundai had become a company with a strong reputation for quality products. In the United States, the *J.D. Power and Associates 2004 Initial Quality Study*, the highly influential survey of automobile consumers, Hyundai tied for second in the corporate rankings. In doing so, Hyundai's score exceeded the industry average and that of most brands sold in the highly competitive U.S. market.

Other industries will surely see newcomers that are unexpected, surprising, and highly capable of challenging the so-called industry leaders. As this happens, industries with historically strong, fully integrated domestic value chains will evolve rapidly to global integration. The bicycle industry is a case in point. Fifty years ago, the United States had a large and vibrant bicycle-frame manufacturing industry across all market segments. After World War II, Taiwan was heavily dependent on Japanese imported bicycles. Gradually, a fledging local industry developed in Taiwan, and by 1969, Taiwanese bicycle manufacturers had begun exporting. In the early 1970s, they began exporting to the United States and by the 1990s, Taiwan had become one of the world's most important sources of bicycles and bicycle parts, with Taiwanese bicycles like Giant becoming real global brands. Bicycle exports to the United States reached a peak of more than 4 million units in 1998.[1] How did this happen? In the 1990s, Taiwanese firms were forced to look for lower cost production in countries like China and Vietnam. Simultaneously, the Taiwanese industry began upgrading its technology and increasing its commitment to innovation. Meanwhile, the United States bicycle-manufacturing sector largely disappeared. Some U.S. bicycle companies continue to prosper, such as Cannondale, Specialized, and Trek. These companies focus on the most valuable knowledge-intensive parts of the value chain, such as design, marketing, branding, and distribution.

Many of the new industry challengers will come from emerging markets, which is why we devoted a full chapter to this topic. To compete in emerging markets and succeed in competing against emerging-market companies, U.S. companies need new thinking on defining and implementing strategy. For example, Whirlpool's successful washer strategy in emerging markets, which we discussed in chapter 7, came after the company tried and failed with a single machine that could be sold anywhere. By designing a new machine from scratch and adapting it to the specific demands of local markets, Whirlpool was able to make inroads into countries such as Brazil and India. This type of innovative global thinking will become the norm in many industries for leading companies.

Innovative thinking will have to come from MNEs, the engine that drives the global economy. The archetypal global firm of the future may look something like Semiconductor Manufacturing International Corporation (SMIC). SMIC is registered in the Cayman Islands and the CEO is Taiwanese. SMIC headquarters is in Shanghai and the majority of its investment capital comes from the United States. The largest shareholder is Chinese and the company is listed on both the Hong Kong and the New York Stock Exchanges.[2] SMIC's customers include companies like Texas Instruments, Infineon, and Toshiba. Within companies like SMIC, there will be a huge need for globally savvy managers who can operate in an increasingly complex world. MNEs will need to invent new organizational processes to handle the greater complexity and size, and they will need to evolve beyond the dominant organizational structures that exist today. Just as the first MNEs in the 20th century had to create new ways to deal with integration and local responsiveness, so will the MNEs of the 21st century. Finding global managers will be a key to success in global markets. Firms that do not globalize and do not seek managers capable of creating strategy in a global environment will become tomorrow's losers. As evidence that globalization is on the minds of many firms, the *Wall Street Journal* recently reported that executives with global experience are among the most in demand—in particular, those with global manufacturing and global logistics experience.[3] We also believe that the global managers of the future will have to be much more knowledgeable about areas such as corporate governance, the ethical dimensions of international business, and knowledge management.

In summary, strategy making in a global environment poses many challenges, from deciding how to organize for global competition to choosing the optimal geographic locations for performing value-chain activities. In this book we have identified a series of issues, scenarios, and decision areas associated with global strategy choices. In doing so, we have tried to present a future-oriented perspective, one that provides insights for both the student of management and the practitioner of global strategy.

Notes

INTRODUCTION

1. "A World of Work," *The Economist*, November 13, 2004, pp. 3–20.

CHAPTER 1

1. Rebecca Buckman, "H-P Outsourcing: Beyond China," *The Wall Street Journal*, February 23, 2004, p. A14.

2. Lisa Bannon and Carlta Vitzthum, "Small World: One-Toy-Fits-All: How Industry Learned to Love the Global Kid," *The Wall Street Journal*, April 29, 2003, p. A1.

3. Anthony Giddens, *Runaway World: How Globalisation Is Reshaping Our Lives* (London: Profile Books, 1999).

4. Vijay Govindarajan and Anil K. Gupta, *The Quest for Global Dominance: Transforming Global Presence into Global Competitive Advantage* (San Francisco: Jossey-Bass, 2001), p. 4.

5. Pankaj Ghemawat, "Semiglobalization and International Business Strategy," *Journal of International Business Studies* 34 (2003): 138–152.

6. Alan M. Rugman and Alain Verbeke, "A Perspective on Regional and Global Strategies of Multinational Enterprises," *Journal of International Business Studies* 35 (2004): 3–18.

7. Rosabeth Moss Kanter and Thomas D. Dretler, "Global Strategy and Its Impact on Local Operations," *Academy of Management Executive* 12 (November 1998): 60–68.

8. Tarun Khanna, "Local Institutions and Global Strategy," Harvard Business School Note #9-702-475 (2002).

9. Moss Kanter and Dretler, "Global Strategy and Its Impact on Local Operations."

10. Nicholas Stein, "The De Beers Story: A New Cut on an Old Monopoly," *Fortune* 143 (February 19, 2001): 186–199.

11. Dan Bilefsky, "Indians Unseat Antwerp's Jews as the Biggest Diamond Traders: Lower-Cost Production in Bombay, Gujarat Has Facilitated the Change," *The Wall Street Journal*, May 27, 2003, p. B1.

12. Mathew Hart, *Diamond: A Journey to the Heart of an Obsession* (New York: Walker, 2001).

13. Theodore C. Bestor, "How Sushi Went Global," *Foreign Policy* (November–December 2000): 54–63.

14. Jon E. Hilsenrath, "Junk Bond: How U.S. Trash Helps Fuel China's Economy," *The Wall Street Journal*, April 9, 2003, p. A1.

15. Govindarajan and Gupta, *The Quest for Global Dominance*.

16. Andrew C. Inkpen, "The Characteristics and Performance of Japanese-North American Joint Ventures in North America," *Advances in International Comparative Management* 9 (1994): 83–110.

17. Michael E. Porter, "Clusters and the New Economics of Competition," *Harvard Business Review* 76 (November–December 1998): 77–90.

18. Pankaj Ghemawat, "Distance Still Matters: The Hard Reality of Global Expansion," *Harvard Business Review* 79 (September 2001): 137–147.

19. "Special Report International Law Firms," *The Economist*, February 28, 2001, pp. 65–67.

20. Medard Gabel and Henry Bruner, *Global, Inc.: An Atlas of the Multinational Corporation* (New York: New Press, 2003).

21. Yasheng Huang and Tarun Khanna, "Can India Overtake China?" *Foreign Policy* (July–August 2003): 74–81.

22. Victoria Emerson, "An Interview with Carlos Ghosn, President of Nissan Motors, Ltd. and Industry Leader of the Year (Automotive News, 2000)," *Journal of World Business* 36 (2001): 7.

CHAPTER 2

1. Christopher A. Bartlett and Sumantra Ghoshal, *Managing across Borders: The Transnational Solution* (Boston: Harvard Business School Press, 1989); C. K. Prahalad and Yves Doz, *The Multinational Mission: Balancing Local Demands and Global Vision* (New York: Free Press, 1987); Gary Hamel and C. K. Prahalad, "Do You Really Have a Global Strategy?" *Harvard Business Review* 63 (July–August 1985): 139–148.

2. George Yip offers a framework that synthesizes some of the common drivers of global strategies into firm-specific and industry-specific factors. See George Yip, "Global Strategy—in a World of Nations," *Sloan Management Review* 31 (Fall 1989): 29–41.

3. Michael E. Porter, *The Competitive Advantage of Nations* (New York: Free Press, 1990).

4. Martin Kenney, Ed., *Understanding Silicon Valley: The Anatomy of an Entrepreneurial Region* (Stanford, CA: Stanford University Press, 2000).

5. AnnaLee Saxenian, "The Origins and Dynamics of Production Networks in Silicon Valley," *Research Policy* 20 (1991): 423–437.

6. Porter, *The Competitive Advantage of Nations*.

7. Michael E. Porter, "Competing across Locations: Enhancing Competitive Advantage through Global Strategy," in *On Competition*, ed. Michael E. Porter (Cambridge, MA: Harvard Business School Press, 1998), pp. 309–350.

8. Based on Veronica Gould Stoddart, "A Valentine Salute to Chocolate," *USA Today*, February 13, 2004.

9. For a discussion of the impact of globalization and the impact of changes to WTO agreements in the textile industry, see "Special Report: The Textile Industry," *The Economist*, November 13, 2004, pp. 75–77.

10. Theodore Levitt, "The Globalization of Markets," *Harvard Business Review* 61 (May–June 1983): 92–102.

11. Ibid.

12. "Time Marches On: The Worldwide Watch Industry," 2004, Thunderbird Case #A07-04-0003.

13. Myron Magnet, "Timex Takes the Torture Test," *Fortune* 107 (June 27, 1983): 112–120.

14. "Seiko Finds Now Is Time to Expand," *New York Times*, February 26, 1968, p. 53.

15. Andrew Rosenbaum, "Switzerland's Watch Industry: Changing with the Times," *Hemispheres* (June 1994): 39.

16. Claudia Deutsch, "Watchmakers Are Ringing the Old Back In, as a Varied Industry Revives and Thrives," *New York Times*, December 5, 1991, p. 1, special section.

17. This case study draws on Bartlett and Ghoshal, *Managing across Borders: The Transnational Solution*.

18. Michael E. Porter, "Changing Patterns of International Competition," *California Management Review* 28 (Winter 1986): 9–40.

19. Steve Hamm, "Borders Are So 20th Century," *Business Week*, September 22, 2003, pp. 68–69.

20. Ibid.

21. Ibid.

22. Ibid.

23. See http://divisions.aomonline.org/im/about/newsletters/aom_dec04.pdf.

24. Marieke de Mooij, *Consumer Behavior and Culture: Consequences for Global Marketing and Advertising* (Thousand Oaks, CA: Sage, 2003).

CHAPTER 3

1. For a summary of various MNE organizational structures see D. Eleanor Westney and Srilata Zaheer, "The Multinational Enterprise as an Organization," in *The Oxford Handbook of International Business*, ed. Alan M. Rugman and Thomas L. Brewer (Oxford: Oxford University Press, 2001), pp. 349–379.

2. These questions are explored in detail in Vijay Govindarajan and Anil K. Gupta, *The Quest for Global Dominance: Transforming Global Presence into Global Competitive Advantage* (San Francisco: Jossey-Bass, 2001).

3. "Sesame Workshop and International Growth," 2001, Thunderbird Case #A07-02-0004.

4. Tom Mudd, "Nestlé Plays to Global Audience," *Industry Week.Com*, August 13, 2001.

5. Julian Birkenshaw, "Strategy and Management in MNE Subsidiaries," in *The Oxford Handbook of International Business*, ed. Alan M. Rugman and Thomas L. Brewer (Oxford: Oxford University Press, 2001), pp. 380–401.

6. "Warner-Lambert Company," 1996, Thunderbird Case #A07-97-0006.

7. Quote from original research by the authors.

8. Christopher A. Bartlett and Sumantra Ghoshal, *Managing across Borders: The Transnational Solution* (Boston: Harvard Business School Press, 1989).

9. Ibid.

10. Birkenshaw, "Strategy and Management in MNE Subsidiaries."

11. Sumantra Ghoshal and Christopher A. Bartlett, *The Individualized Corporation* (London: Harper Business, 1997).

12. Walter Kuemmerle, "Building Effective R&D Capabilities Abroad," *Harvard Business Review* 75 (March–April 1997): 61–70.

13. "Honeywell Inc. and Global Research & Development," 1998, Thunderbird Case #A07-98-0017.

14. Following the merger of Honeywell and Allied Signal in 1999, Honeywell's size and product portfolio substantially expanded. Honeywell also moved its headquarters to Morristown, New Jersey.

15. Quote from original research by the authors.

16. Quote from original research by the authors.

17. Mitchell Pacelle, Martin Fackler, and Andrew Morse, "For Citigroup, Scandal in Japan Shows Dangers of Global Sprawl," *The Wall Street Journal*, December 22, 2004, pp. A1, A10.

18. Ibid.

19. Christopher Bartlett, "MNCS: Get Off the Reorganization Merry-Go-Round," *Harvard Business Review* 61 (March–April 1983): 138–146.

20. Deborah Ball, "Despite Revamp, Unwieldy Unilever Falls Behind Rivals," *The Wall Street Journal*, January 3, 2005, pp. A1, A5.

21. Gunnar Hedlund, "The Hypermodern MNC: A Heterarchy?" *Human Resource Management* 25 (1986): 9–35.

CHAPTER 4

1. Patricia O'Connell, Ed., "The Man Who Steered Renault to Japan," *Business Week* [online], January 13, 2003. See http://www.businessweek.com/bwdaily/dnflash/jan2003/nf20030113-_1789.htm.

2. Steven C. Currall and Andrew C. Inkpen, "A Multilevel Approach to Trust in Joint Ventures," *Journal of International Business Studies* 33 (2002): 479–495.

3. Wilfried Vanhonacker, "Entering China: An Unconventional Approach," *Harvard Business Review* 75 (March–April 1997): 130–140.

4. Andrew C. Inkpen, "Creating Knowledge through Collaboration," *California Management Review* 39 (September 1996): 123–140.

5. Steven E. Prokesch, "Unleashing the Power of Learning: An Interview with British Petroleum's John Browne," *Harvard Business Review* 75 (September–October 1997): 146–168.

6. T. K. Das and Bing-Sheng Teng, "Managing Risks in Strategic Alliances," *Academy of Management Executives* 13 (1999): 50–62.

7. Robert B. Reich and Eric D. Mankin, "Joint Ventures with Japan Give Away Our Future," *Harvard Business Review* 64 (March–April 1986): 78–86.

8. Gary Hamel, Yves L. Doz, and C. K. Prahalad, "Collaborate with Your Competitors—and Win," *Harvard Business Review* 67 (January–February 1989): 133–139.

9. "Matra-Ericsson Telecommunications," 1999, Thunderbird Case #A07-99-0011.

10. Rajesh Kumar and Kofi O. Nti, "Differential Learning and Interaction in Alliance Dynamics: A Process and Outcome Discrepancy Model," *Organization Science* 9 (1998): 356–367.

11. Hamel, Doz, and Prahalad, "Collaborate with Your Competitors—and Win."

12. There are some similarities between the organizational fit issues in alliances and the integration issues in mergers and acquisitions. The key difference is that with an acquisition, the target firm is "killed" in the sense that it ceases to be independent. With alliances, the partners remain independent outside the alliance, which means that the integration that occurs in an alliance is confined to the specific collaborative activity.

13. Prokesch, "Unleashing the Power of Learning: An Interview with British Petroleum's John Browne."

14. Louis Kraar, "China's Car Guy," *Fortune* 140 (October 11, 1999): 238–246.

15. J. Peter Killing, "How to Make a Global Joint Venture Work," *Harvard Business Review* 60 (May–June 1982): 120–127.

16. Yves L. Doz and Gary Hamel, *Alliance Advantage: The Art of Creating Value through Partnering* (Boston: Harvard Business School Press, 1998).

17. Yves L. Doz, "The Evolution of Cooperation in Strategic Alliances: Initial Conditions or Learning Processes?" *Strategic Management Journal* 17 (Summer [special issue] 1996): 55–84.

18. Victoria Emerson, "An Interview with Carlos Ghosn, President of Nissan Motors, Ltd. and Industry Leader of the Year (Automotive News, 2000)," *Journal of World Business* 36 (2001): 3–10.

19. Vijay Pothukuchi, Fariborz Damanpour, Jaepil Choi, Chao C. Chen, and Seung Ho Park, "National and Organizational Culture Differences and International Joint Venture Performance," *Journal of International Business Studies* 33 (2002): 243.

20. Randall S. Schuler, Susan E. Jackson, and Yadong Luo, *Managing Human Resources in Cross-Border Alliances* (London: Routledge, 2003).

21. For a discussion of the difficulties of measuring alliance performance, see Erin Anderson, "Two Firms, One Frontier: On Assessing Joint Venture Performance," *Sloan Management Review* 18 (Winter 1990): 19–30.

CHAPTER 5

1. Gary Hamel, "Strategy as Revolution," *Harvard Business Review* 74 (July–August 1996): 69–82.

2. Steven E. Prokesch, "Unleashing the Power of Learning: An Interview with British Petroleum's John Browne," *Harvard Business Review* 75 (September–October 1997): 146–168.

3. David J. Teece, "Strategies for Managing Knowledge Assets: The Role of Firm Structure and Industrial Context," *Long Range Planning* 33 (2000): 35–54.

4. Christopher A. Bartlett and Sumantra Ghoshal, *Managing across Borders: The Transnational Solution* (Boston: Harvard Business School Press, 1989); and Bruce Kogut and Udo Zander, "Knowledge of the Firm, Combinative Capabilities, and the Replication of Technology," *Organization Science* 3 (1992): 383–397.

5. Yves L. Doz, Jose Santos, and Peter Williamson, *Global to Metanational: How Companies Win in the Knowledge Economy* (Cambridge, MA: Harvard Business School Press, 2001).

6. Gunnar Hedlund and Ikujiro Nonaka, "Models of Knowledge Management in the West and Japan," in *Implementing Strategic Processes: Change, Learning, and Cooperation*, ed. Peter Lorange, Bala Chakravarthy, Johna Roos, and Andrew Van de Ven (Oxford: Blackwell, 1993), pp. 117–144.

7. Sydney G. Winter, "Knowledge and Competence as Strategic Assets," in *The Competitive Challenge*, ed. David Teece (Cambridge, MA: Ballinger Publishing, 1987), pp. 159–184.

8. Ikujiro Nonaka, Hirotaka Takeuchi, and Hiro Takeuchi, *The Knowledge-Creating Company: How Japanese Companies Create the Dynamics of Innovation* (New York: Oxford University Press, 1995).

9. Verna Allee, *The Knowledge Evolution: Expanding Organizational Intelligence* (Boston: Butterworth-Heinemann, 1997).

10. Thomas H. Davenport, David W. De Long, and Michael C. Beers, "Successful Knowledge Management Projects," *Sloan Management Review* 39, no. 2 (1998): 43–57.

11. Paul A. Carlile, "Transferring, Translating, and Transforming: An Integrative Framework for Managing Knowledge across Boundaries," *Organization Science* 15 (2004): 555–568.

12. Peter J. Buckley and Martin J. Carter, "A Formal Analysis of Knowledge Combination in Multinational Enterprises," *Journal of International Business Studies* 35 (2004): 371–384.

13. Gabriel Szulanski, "Exploring Internal Stickiness: Impediments to the Transfer of Best Practice within the Firm," *Strategic Management Journal* 17 (special issue 1996): 27–43.

14. Linda Argote and Paul Ingram, "Knowledge Transfer: A Basis for Competitive Advantage in Firms," *Organizational Behavior and Human Decision Processes* 82 (2000): 150–169.

15. Eric D. Darr and Eric R. Kurtzberg, "An Investigation of Partner Similarity Dimensions on Knowledge Transfer," *Organizational Behavior and Human Decision Processes* 82 (2000): 28–44.

16. *CSSIP Prospectus*, 1999, p. 10.

17. Mui Hoong Chua, "Suzhou Park Ready to Take Off, Says SM Lee," *Straits Times*, September 13, 1996, p. 35.

18. Stephen E. Weiss, "Explaining Outcomes of Negotiation: Toward a Grounded

Model for Negotiations between Organizations," in *Research on Negotiations in Organizations*, Vol. 6., ed. R. J. Lewicki, R. J. Bies, and B. H. Sheppard (Greenwich, CT: JAI Press, 1997), pp. 247–233.

19. Maryann Keller, *Rude Awakening: The Rise, Fall, and Struggle for Recovery at General Motors* (New York: William Morrow, 1989), p. 88.

20. Bussey J. Tharp, "NUMMI Auto Venture Is Termed Success: GM, Toyota, UAW Are Nearing Their Goals," *The Wall Street Journal*, May 20, 1986, p. A1.

21. Paul S. Adler and Robert E. Cole, "Designed for Learning: A Tale of Two Auto Plants," *Sloan Management Review* 34 (Spring 1993): 85–94.

22. Phillip A. W. Käser and Raymond E. Miles, "Understanding Knowledge Activists' Successes and Failures," *Long Range Planning* 35 (2002): 9–28.

23. Ibid.

24. Kevin Desouza and Roberto Evaristo, "Global Knowledge Management Strategies," *European Management Journal* 21, no. 1 (2003): 62–67.

25. Kazuhiro Asakawa and Mark Lehrer, "Managing Local Knowledge Assets Globally: The Role of Regional Innovation Relays," *Journal of World Business* 38 (2003): 31–42.

26. Joesph L. Badaracco, *The Knowledge Link* (Boston: Harvard Business School Press, 1991), p. 98.

27. Andrew C. Inkpen, "Creating Knowledge through Collaboration," *California Management Review* 39, no. 1 (1996), pp. 123–140.

28. Yves L. Doz, José Santos, and Peter Williamson, *Global to Metanational: How Companies Win in the Knowledge Economy* (Boston: Harvard Business School Press, 2001).

CHAPTER 6

1. Pete Engardio, Aaron Bernstein, and Manjeet Kripalani, "The New Global Job Shift," *Business Week*, February 3, 2003, pp. 50–58.

2. Philip Evans and Thomas S. Wurster, *Blown to Bits: How the New Economics of Information Transforms Strategy* (Boston: Harvard Business School Press, 1999).

3. "A World of Work," *The Economist*, November 13, 2004, pp. 3–20.

4. Khozem Merchant, "GE Champions Indian's World Class Services," *Financial Times*, June 3, 2003, p. 11.

5. John Ribeiro, "The Back Office Moves to India," *InfoWorld* 23 (October 21, 2000): 26–28.

6. Stefan Thomke, "Siemens A. G.: Global Development Strategy (A)," 2002, Harvard Business School Case #BS 9-602-061.

7. Diana Farrell, "Beyond Offshoring: Assess Your Company's Global Potential," *Harvard Business Review* 82 (December 2004): 82–88.

CHAPTER 7

1. C. K. Prahalad and Kenneth Lieberthal, "The End of Corporate Imperialism," *Harvard Business Review* 76 (July–August 1998): 69–79.

2. Eric Bellman, "Easing India's Export Jam: New Delhi, Seeking to Boost Trade, Tries Special Economic Zones," *The Wall Street Journal*, November 30, 2004, p. A16.

3. See Russell R. Miller, *Selling to Newly Emerging Markets* (Westport, CT: Quorum Books, 1998).

4. See http://www.unilever.com/environmentsociety/community/ economicdevelopment/Creating_rural_entrepreneurs_in_India.asp; Namrata Singh, "10% of HLL's Rural Sales from Project Shakti," *Financial Express*, November 25, 2003; see also http://www.financialexpress.com; K. T. Jagannathan, "HLL's Project Shakti Gains Momentum," *The Hindu*, May 15, 2003, http://www.hinduonnet.com.

5. Rafael La Porta, Florencio Lopez-de-Silanes, Andrei Shleifer, and Robert W. Vishny, "Legal Determinants of External Finance," *Journal of Finance* 52 (1997): 1131–1150.

6. I. M. Pandey, *Venture Capital: The Indian Experience* (New Delhi, India: Prentice Hall, 1999).

7. Stipon Nestor and John K. Thompson, *Corporate Governance Patterns in OECD Economies; Is Convergence under Way?* (Paris: OECD, 2001).

8. Tarun Khanna and Krishna Palepu, "Why Focused Strategies May Be Wrong for Emerging Markets," *Harvard Business Review* 75 (July–August 1997): 41–51.

9. See, for example, Kannan Ramaswamy, M. Li, and R. Veliyath, "Variations in Ownership Behavior and Propensity to Diversify: A Study of the Indian Corporate Context," *Strategic Management Journal* 23 (2002): 345–358.

10. Larry Fauver, Joel F. Houston, and Andy Naranjo, "Capital Market Development, Integration, Legal Systems, and the Value of Corporate Diversification: A Cross-Country Analysis," working paper, University of Florida, 2002.

11. Tarun Khanna and Jan Rivkin, "Estimating the Performance Effects of Business Groups in Emerging Markets," *Strategic Management Journal* 22 (2001): 45–74.

12. See http://www.transparency.org.

13. Simeon Djankov, Rafael La Porta, Florencio Lopez-de-Silanes, and Andrei Shleifer, "The Regulation of Entry," *Quarterly Journal of Economics* 117 (February 2002): 1–37.

14. Pankaj Ghemawat, "Repositioning Ranbaxy," 1996, Harvard Business School Case #9-796-18.

15. Miller, *Selling to Newly Emerging Markets*.

16. Thomas Catán and Joshua Chaffin, "Bribery Has Long Been Used to Land International Contracts," *Financial Times*, May 8, 2003, p. 19.

17. Hamish McDonald, *The Polyester Prince: The Rise of Dhirubhai Ambani* (London: Allen-Unwin, 1999).

18. Miller, *Selling to Newly Emerging Markets*.

19. Yadong Luo, *Multinational Corporations in China* (Copenhagen: Copenhagen Business School Press, 2000).

20. See David J. Arnold and John A. Quelch, "New Strategies in Emerging Markets," *Sloan Management Review* 40 (Fall 1998): 7–20.

21. See, for example, Edward Tse, "The Right Way to Achieve Profitable

Growth in the Chinese Consumer Market," *Strategy + Business* (Second Quarter 1998): 10–21.

22. Prahalad and Lieberthal, "The End of Corporate Imperialism."

23. See Niraj Dawar and Tony Frost, "Competing with Giants: Survival Strategies for Local Companies in Emerging Markets," *Harvard Business Review* 77 (March–April 1999): 119–129.

24. Tse, "The Right Way to Achieve Profitable Growth in the Chinese Consumer Market."

25. John Quelch, "As Global Brands Retrench, a New Force Is Gathering in the East," *Independent*, May 4, 2003, p. 8.

26. C. K. Prahalad and Allan Hammond, "Serving the World's Poor, Profitably," *Harvard Business Review* 80 (September 2002): 48–55.

27. Edwina Ings-Chambers, "A Brand New Passage to India," *Financial Times*, May 10, 2003, p. W7.

28. Prahalad and Lieberthal, "The End of Corporate Imperialism."

29. Regina Fazio Maruca, "The Right Way to Go Global: An Interview with Whirlpool CEO David Whitwam," *Harvard Business Review* 72 (March–April 1994): 134–145.

30. Miriam Jordan and Jonathan Karp, "Machines for the Masses: Whirlpool Aims Cheap Washer at Brazil, India, and China," *The Wall Street Journal*, December 9, 2003, pp. A19, A20.

CHAPTER 8

Valuable insights from Anant Sundaram are gratefully acknowledged for this chapter.

1. Michael H. Bradley, Cindy A. Schipani, Anant K. Sundaram, and James P. Walsh, "The Purposes and Accountability of the Corporation in Contemporary Society: Corporate Governance at a Crossroads," *Law and Contemporary* 62, no. 3 (1999): 9–86.

2. Note that this definition is much broader than the narrower financial definition of governance as "the ways in which suppliers of finance to corporations assure themselves of getting a return on their investment" as presented by Andrei Shleifer and Robert W. Vishny, "A Survey of Corporate Governance," *The Journal of Finance* 52 (1997): 737–783.

3. Bradley, Schipani, Sundaram, and Walsh, "The Purposes and Accountability of the Corporation in Contemporary Society."

4. R. Edward Freeman and John McVea, "A Stakeholder Approach to Strategic Management," in *The Blackwell Handbook of Strategic Management*, ed. Michael Hitt, Edward Freeman, and Jeffrey Harrison (Oxford: Blackwell, 2001), pp. 189–207.

5. Peter Drucker, "The Next Society: A Survey of the Near Future," *The Economist* (November 3, 2001): 17–18.

6. Milton Friedman, "The Social Responsibility of Business Is to Increase Its Profits," *New York Times Magazine* 33 (September 13, 1970): 122–126.

7. Anant K. Sundaram and Andrew C. Inkpen, "The Corporate Objective Revisited," *Organization Science* 15 (2004): 350–363.

8. Mitchell Pacelle and Mathew Karnitschnig, "Catalog of Woes: Spiegel's European Owner Gets a Hard Lesson in U.S. Business," *The Wall Street Journal*, March 2, 2004, pp. A1, A6.

9. Patricia O'Connell, Ed., "The Man Who Steered Renault to Japan," *Business Week* [online], January 13, 2003. See http://www.businessweek.com/bwdaily/dnflash/jan2003/nf20030113-_1789.htm.

10. Isabelle Maignan and David A. Ralston, "Corporate Social Responsibility in Europe and the U.S.: Insights from Businesses' Self-Presentations," *Journal of International Business Studies* 33 (2002): 497–514.

11. James P. Walsh and Rita Kosnik, "Corporate Raiders and Their Disciplinary Role in the Market for Corporate Control," *Academy of Management Journal* 36 (1993): 671–700.

12. Bradley, Schipani, Sundaram, and Walsh, "The Purposes and Accountability of the Corporation in Contemporary Society."

13. "International Corporate Governance," in *CalPERS' Corporate Governance* [online]. See http://www.calpers-governance.org/principles/international/.

14. Jeanne Whalen, "Pumping Up—New Force in Energy Markets: Russian Oil Tycoon's Ambitions—Yukos Chief Khodorkovsky, after Big Merger, Eyes a Move beyond Siberia—a Bid to Clean Up His Image," *The Wall Street Journal*, May 16, 2003, p. A1.

15. Amy Kazmin, "The Defaulters' Delight: Litigation: A Huge Thai Bankruptcy Case Has Failed to Herald a New Start for Foreign Creditors," *Financial Times*, April 16, 2003, p.16.

16. Andrew Jack, "BP Amoco to Review Its Russian Interests," *Financial Times*, November 27, 1999, p. 15.

17. On Kit Tam, "Ethical Issues in the Evolution of Corporate Governance in China," *Journal of Business Ethics* 37 (2002): 303–320.

18. Pamela Mar and Michael N. Young, "Corporate Governance in Transition Economies: A Case Study of Two Chinese Airlines," *Journal of World Business* 36, no. 3 (Fall 2001): 280–302.

19. Tam, "Ethical Issues in the Evolution of Corporate Governance in China."

20. Ananya Mukherjee-Reed, "Corporate Governance Reforms in India," *Journal of Business Ethics* 37 (2002): 249–268.

21. Flávio M. Rabelo and Flávio C. Vasconcelos, "Corporate Governance in Brazil," *Journal of Business Ethics* 37 (2002): 321–335.

22. C. A. Rocca, M. E. Silva, and A. G. Carvalho, "Sistema Financeiro e a Retomada do Crescimento Econômico," *Relatório de Pesquisa*, FIPE–USP (1998).

23. Ricardo P. C. Leal and Claudia L. T. De Oliveira, "An Evaluation of Board Practices in Brazil," *Corporate Governance* 2, no. 3 (2002): 21–25.

24. Ronald Dore, "Corporate Governance and Firm Organization: Nexuses and Frontiers," paper presented at Bocconi University, December 5–7, 2002.

25. Anant K. Sundaram, Michael Bradley, Cindy A. Schipani, and James P. Walsh, "Comparative Corporate Governance and Global Corporate Strategy," in *Thunderbird on Global Business Strategy*, ed. Robert Grosse (New York: Wiley, 2000), pp. 110–150.

26. Shliefer and Vishny, "A Survey of Corporate Governance."

27. Susanne Soederberg, "The Promotion of 'Anglo-American' Corporate Governance in the South: Who Benefits from the New International Standard?" *Third World Quarterly* 24 (2003): 7–27.

28. Rafael La Porta, Florencio Lopez-de-Silanes, and Andrei Shleifer, "Corporate Ownership around the World," *Journal of Finance* 54 (1999): 471–517.

29. Rafael La Porta, Florencio Lopez-de-Silanes, Andrei Shleifer, and Robert W. Vishny, "Law and Finance," *The Journal of Political Economy* 106 (1998): 1113–1155.

30. Sigrid Esser, "Globalizing the Board of Directors," *Corporate Board* 22 (January–February 2001): 1–5.

CHAPTER 9

1. Nader Asgary and Mark C. Mitschow, "Toward a Model for International Business Ethics," *Journal of Business Ethics* 36, no. 3 (2002): 239–246.

2. Gina Kolata, "Companies Facing Ethical Issue as Drugs Are Tested Overseas," *New York Times*, March 5, 2004 (Section A), p. 1.

3. Jane Perlez and Evelyn Rusli, "Spurred by Illness, Indonesians Lash Out at U.S. Mining Giant," *New York Times*, September 8, 2004. See http://www.nytimes.com.

4. Allen Morrison, "Integrity and Global Leadership," *Journal of Business Ethics* 31 (May 2001): 65–76.

5. Thomas Donaldson and Thomas W. Dunfee, "When Ethics Travel: The Promise and Peril of Global Business Ethics," *California Management Review* 41 (Summer 1999): 45–63.

6. Gregory Millman, "Troubling Projects," *Infrastructure Finance* (February–March 1996):17–19.

7. Michael Shari, Pete Engardio, and Sheri Prasso, "What Did Mobil Know?" *Business Week*, December 28, 1998, pp. 68–75.

8. Ibid., p. 72.

9. The situation in 2004 in Aceh was not much better. Martial law was imposed in the province in 2003 as armed clashes between government troops and Aceh separatist movement rebels continued, resulting in thousands of Aceh residents having to leave their homes to live in refugee camps. The Indonesian government deployed a battalion of marines to protect operations and employees of four companies in Aceh, including ExxonMobil and Arun.

10. Richard DeGeorge, *Competing with Integrity in International Business* (New York: Oxford University Press, 1993).

11. Mark Landler, "Piracy Is Rampant Globally; The Music Industry's Biggest Hurdle May Be Cultural, with Swapping Files Viewed as Routine—Not Illegal," *The International Herald Tribune*, September 29, 2003, p. 8.

12. B. Atwood and G. Burpee, "War on Piracy Continues in China," *Billboard*, July 20, 1996.

13. Neil King, "Stuck on You: A Tiny Glue Seller Claims Identity Theft," *The Wall Street Journal*, November 22, 2004, pp. A1, A7.

14. Paul J. Herz and Robert K. Larson, "Keeping Bribery at Bay," *The Internal Auditor* 61 (February 2004): 60–67.

15. Wesley Cragg and William Woof, "The U.S. Foreign Corrupt Practices Act: A Study of Its Effectiveness," *Business and Society Review* 107 (Spring 2002): 98–143.

16. Gary R. Weaver, Linda Klebe Trevino, and Philip L. Cochran, "Corporate Ethics Programs as Control Systems: Influences of Executive Commitment and Environmental Factors," *Academy of Management Journal* 42 (1999): 41–57.

17. Catherine C. Langlois and Bodo B. Schlegelmich, "Do Corporate Codes of Ethics Reflect National Character? Evidence from Europe and the United States," *Journal of International Business Studies* 21 (1990): 519–539.

18. S. Prakash Sethi, *Setting Global Standards: Guidelines for Creating Codes of Conduct in Multinational Corporations* (New York: Wiley, 2003).

19. David Lowry, "A Review of Setting Global Standards: Guidelines for Creating Codes of Conduct in Multinational Corporations," *Business and Society Review* 109 (March 2004): 107–113.

20. Sethi, *Setting Global Standards*, p. 288.

21. Donaldson and Dunfee, "When Ethics Travel."

22. The Dabhol power plant project had two phases with a total capital cost of about $2.5 billion. Phase 1 was completed in 1999. Phase 2 was about 90 percent complete in 2001 when the project experienced various difficulties. In mid-2001, Enron decided to shut down phase 1 and halt construction on phase 2. Not long after, Enron declared bankruptcy. The result has been years of litigation, negotiations, and discussions among the Indian government, banks, contractors, Enron, OPIC and other interested parties. In late 2004, the situation remained unresolved: the completed phase 1 plant was not operating and construction of phase 2 was still not finished. There was speculation that it would be 2006 before the plant could be restarted.

STRATEGY AND GLOBALIZATION: A FINAL NOTE

1. See http://www.biketaiwan.com.

2. "My Fab Is Bigger than Yours," in A Survey of Taiwan, *The Economist*, January 15, 2005, p. 10.

3. Erin White, "Executives with Global Experience Are among the Most In-Demand," *The Wall Street Journal*, January 25, 2005, p. B6.

Additional Reading

CHAPTER 1

Bhagwati, Jagdish N. *In Defense of Globalization*. New York: Oxford University Press, 2004.

Buckley, Peter J., and Mark Casson. *The Future of the Multinational Enterprise*. London: Macmillan, 1976.

Hamel, Gary, and C. K. Prahalad. "Do You Really Have a Global Strategy?" *Harvard Business Review* 63 (July–August 1985): 139–148.

Hansen, Karen Tranberg. *Salaula: The World of Secondhand Clothing and Zambia*. Chicago: University of Chicago Press, 2000.

Micklethwait, John, and Adrian Wooldridge. *A Future Perfect: The Challenge and Hidden Promise of Globalization*. New York: Crown Business, 2000.

Taylor, William. "Logic of Global Business: An Interview with ABB's Percy Barnevik." *Harvard Business Review* 69 (March–April1991): 89–105.

Wolf, Martin. *Why Globalization Works*. New Haven, CT: Yale University Press, 2004.

CHAPTER 2

Ghoshal, Sumantra. "Global Strategy: An Organizing Framework." *Strategic Management Journal* 8 (1987): 425–440.

Hofstede, Geert, and Jan Hofstede. *Cultures and Organizations: Software of the Mind*. New York: McGraw-Hill, 2005.

Murtha, Thomas, Stefanie Ann Lenway, and Jeffrey A. Hart. *Managing New Industry Creation: Global Knowledge Formation and Entrepreneurship in High Technology*. Palo Alto, CA: Stanford University Press, 2001.

Rugman, Alan M., and Thomas L. Brewer (Eds.). *The Oxford Handbook of International Business*. Oxford: Oxford University Press, 2001.

Tallman, Stephen B., and George S. Yip. "Strategy and the Multinational Enterprise." In *The Oxford Handbook of International Business*, ed. Alan M. Rugman and Thomas L. Brewer. Oxford: Oxford University Press, 2001, pp. 317–348.

CHAPTER 3

Bartlett, Christopher A., and Sumantra Ghoshal. "The Multinational Company as a Differentiated Network." *Academy of Management Review* 15 (1994): 603–625.

Ghoshal, Sumantra, and D. Eleanor Westney (Eds.). *Organization Theory and the Multinational Corporation.* New York: St. Martin's Press, 1994.

Kogut, Bruce. "Designing Global Strategies: Profiting from Operational Flexibility." *Sloan Management Review* 27 (Fall 1985): 27–38.

Roberts, John. *The Modern Firm: Organisational Design for Performance and Growth.* Oxford: Oxford University Press, 2004.

CHAPTER 4

Bamford, James, David Ernst, and David G. Fubini. "Launching a World Class Joint Venture." *Harvard Business Review* 82 (February 2004): 90–100.

Beamish, Paul W. "The Design and Management of International Joint Ventures." In *International Management: Text and Cases*, 5th edition, ed. Paul W. Beamish, Allen J. Morrison, Andrew C. Inkpen, and Philip M. Rosenzweig. Burr Ridge, IL: Irwin/McGraw-Hill, 2003, pp. 120–139.

Bleeke, Joel, and David Ernst. *Collaborating to Compete: Using Strategic Alliances and Acquisitions in the Global Marketplace.* New York: Wiley, 1993.

Gomes-Casseres, Benjamin. *The Alliance Revolution: The New Shape of Business Rivalry.* Cambridge, MA: Harvard University Press, 1996.

Inkpen, Andrew C., and Paul W. Beamish. "Knowledge, Bargaining Power and International Joint Venture Stability." *Academy of Management Review* 22 (1997): 177–202.

Spekman, Robert, and Lynn Isabella. *Alliance Competence: Maximizing the Value of Your Partnerships.* Boston: Harvard Business School Press, 2000.

Yoshino, Michael Y., and U. Srinivasa Rangan. *Strategic Alliances: An Entrepreneurial Approach to Globalization.* Boston: Harvard Business School Press, 1995.

CHAPTER 5

Birkinshaw, Julian, and Tony Sheehan. "Managing the Knowledge Life Cycle." *Sloan Management Review* 44, no. 1 (Fall 2002): 75–83.

Gupta, Anil K., and Vijay Govindarajan. "Knowledge Flows and the Structure of Control within Multinational Corporations." *The Academy of Management Review* 16 (1991): 768–792.

Murtha, Thomas P., Stefanie A. Lenway, and Jeffrey A. Hart. *Managing New Industry Creation: Global Knowledge Formation and Entrepreneurship in High Technology.* Palo Alto, CA: Stanford University Press, 2001.

Pfeffer, Jeffrey, and Robert I. Sutton. *The Knowing-Doing Gap: How Smart Companies Turn Knowledge into Action.* Boston: Harvard Business School Press, 2000.

Quinn, James Brian. *The Intelligent Enterprise.* New York: Free Press, 1992.

Spender, J. C. "Making Knowledge the Basis of a Dynamic Theory of the Firm." *Strategic Management Journal* 17 (special issue 1996): 27–43.

Teece, David J. "Capturing Value from *Knowledge* Assets: The New Economy, Markets for Know-How, and Intangible Assets." *California Management Review* 40 (Spring 1998): 55–79.

Von Krogh, George, Kazuo Ichijo, and Ikujiro Nonaka. *Enabling Knowledge Creation: How to Unlock the Mystery of Tacit Knowledge and Release the Power of Innovation.* New York: Oxford University Press, 2000.

CHAPTER 6

Davies, Paul. *What's This India Business? Offshore Outsourcing and the Global Services Revolution.* London: Nicholas Brealey, 2004.

Greaver, Michael F. *Strategic Outsourcing: A Structured Approach to Outsourcing Decisions and Initiatives.* New York: AMACOM, 1999.

Kobayashi-Hillary, Mark. *Outsourcing to India: The Offshore Advantage.* New York: Springer-Verlag, 2004.

Linder, Jane C. *Outsourcing for Radical Change: A Bold Approach to Enterprise Transformation.* New York: AMACOM, 2004.

Robinson, Maracia, and Ravi Kalakota. *Offshore Outsourcing: Business Models, ROI and Best Practices.* Alpharetta, GA: Mivar Press, 2004.

CHAPTER 7

Clissold, Tim. *Mr. China.* London: Constable & Robinson, 2004.

Kiggundu, Moses N. *Managing Globalization in Developing Countries and Transition Economies.* Westport, CT: Praeger, 2002.

Luo, Yadong. *Multinational Enterprises in Emerging Markets.* Copenhagen: Copenhagen Business School Press, 2002.

Prahalad, C. K. *The Fortune at the Bottom of the Pyramid.* Upper Saddle River, NJ: Wharton School Publishing, 2004.

Studwell, Joe. *The China Dream: The Quest for the Last Great Untapped Market on Earth.* New York: Grove Press, 2003.

CHAPTER 8

Blair, Margaret M. *Ownership and Control: Rethinking Corporate Governance for the Twenty-First Century.* Washington, DC: Brookings Institution, 1995.

Charkham, Jonathan P. *Keeping Good Company: A Study of Corporate Governance in Five Countries.* Reprint. Oxford: Oxford University Press, 1999.

Clarkson, Max B. E. "A Stakeholder Framework for Analyzing and Evaluating Corporate Social Performance." *Academy of Management Review* 20 (1995): 92–117.

Dore, Ronald P. *Stock Market Capitalism: Welfare Capitalism: Japan and Germany Versus the Anglo-Saxon.* Oxford: Oxford University Press, 2000.

Freeman, R. Edward. *Strategic Management: A Stakeholder Approach*. Boston: Pitman, 1984.

Hoshi, Takeo, and Hugh T. Patrick (Eds.). *Crisis and Change in the Japanese Financial System*. New York: Springer, 2000.

Jensen, Michael C. *A Theory of the Firm: Governance, Residual Claims, and Organizational Forms*. Cambridge, MA: Harvard University Press, 2002.

Kester, W. Carl. *Japanese Takeovers: The Global Contest for Corporate Control*. Boston: Harvard Business School Press, 1990.

Koke, Jens. *Corporate Governance in Germany*. New York: Springer, 2002.

Reed, Darryl. "Corporate Governance Reforms in Developing Countries." *Journal of Business Ethics* 37, no. 3 (2002): 223–247.

Roe, Mark J. *Political Determinants of Corporate Governance: Political Context, Corporate Impact*. New York: Oxford University Press, 2002.

CHAPTER 9

Boddewyn, Jean J., and Thomas L. Brewer. "International-Business Political Behavior: New Theoretical Directions." *Academy of Management Review* 19 (1994): 119–143.

Desai, Ashay B., and Terri Rittenburg. "Global Ethics: An Integrative Framework for MNEs." *Journal of Business Ethics* 16, no. 8 (1997): 791–800.

Donaldson, Thomas. *The Ethics of International Business*. New York: Oxford University Press, 1989.

González, Ana Marta. "Ethics in Global Business and in a Plural Society." *Journal of Business Ethics* 44, no. 1 (2003): 23–36.

Haley, Usha C. V. *Multinational Corporations in Political Environments*. River Edge, NJ: World Scientific, 2001.

McMurtry, John. "Why the Protestors Are Against Corporate Globalization." *Journal of Business Ethics* 40, no. 3 (2002): 201–205.

Rivoli, Pietra. "Labor Standards in the Global Economy: Issues for Investors." *Journal of Business Ethics* 43, no. 3 (2003): 223–232.

Singer, Peter. *One World: The Ethics of Globalization*. New Haven, CT: Yale University Press, 2002.

Index